The Politics of the US Supreme Court

By the same author:

Public Opinion Polls and British Politics
(Routledge & Kegan Paul, 1970)

The Politics of the US Supreme Court

by
RICHARD HODDER-WILLIAMS
University of Bristol

19

London
GEORGE ALLEN & UNWIN
Boston   Sydney

First published in 1980

GEORGE ALLEN & UNWIN LTD
40 Museum Street, London WC1A 1LU

© Richard Hodder-Williams, 1980

British Library Cataloguing in Publication Data

Hodder-Williams, Richard
    The politics of the US Supreme Court.
    1. United States. Supreme Court
    I. Title
    347'.73'26   KF8748   79-41275

    ISBN 0-04-328010-2
    ISBN 0-04-328011-0 Pbk

Typeset in 10 on 11 point Times by Red Lion Setters, London
and printed in Great Britain
by A. Wheaton & Co. Ltd., Exeter

Contents

For Matthew

without whom the writing of this book would
have been much easier and quicker

Preface

To launch another book about the United States Supreme Court on to an academic market already saturated with worthy publications clearly requires some explanation. There were three factors, however, which persuaded me to add my contribution to what already existed. In the first place, virtually all the literature on the Supreme Court has been written by Americans, largely for a North American readership. It is interesting to note that by 1979 no single full-scale article on the Court had been published by a British scholar resident in the United Kingdom in an academic journal devoted consciously to the study of politics. Consequently, the literature available to British students of American politics has been almost universally American. This is a pity, because an introduction to the Supreme Court is needed which does not assume a familiarity with the American judicial system and its intimate connection with the political process. With the belated realisation in Britain that judges have discretionary authority which grants them in effect a certain degree of political power (Griffith, 1977) and the beginnings of a discussion on the advantages and dis-advantages of a Bill of Rights, it is particularly apposite to look in some detail at how the United States Supreme Court operates and functions within the whole political system. The first purpose of this book is thus to pander to non-Americans in presenting the unique institution of the Supreme Court consciously for those who have not grown up in the American political system.

Secondly, although there are many excellent monographs on individual aspects of the Supreme Court to which graduates and teachers alike can, and should, refer, there seems to me at any rate to be none that satisfactorily synthesises and examines in a manageable form the Court's historical role in the United States' developing Constitution, its decision-making processes, and its relationship with the other two branches of government and the American people. There is an obvious danger in attempting such a synthesis; for it must inevitably oversimplify in places and omit material which some may think important or fascinating. Each of the chapters in this book will seem to experts in the particular topic to be deficient in terms both of analysis and of range of illustrations. But undergraduates and general readers are constantly pressed for time, and it is for them that the synthesis here is primarily intended. Naturally, therefore, it is based almost entirely on secondary sources and only Chapter 3 can really claim to be grounded on any original research.

Thirdly, most of the literature on the Supreme Court has left my students almost as bored as confused. Perhaps this derives from the very legalistic, and therefore unfamiliar, approach of much of the writing; or, perhaps, too much of the available material on the Court evidences an astonishing aversion to the human events and individual personalities involved in the case-names which necessarily abound in any study of the Supreme Court. I have found that attempts to dig behind the titles to the adversaries and to the Justices themselves pay handsome dividends. In many ways Anthony Lewis's story about *Gideon* v. *Wainwright* (1963), which asserted a constitutional right to a lawyer in state courts for all those accused of a felony, remains the best introduction (Lewis, 1964). The third purpose of this book, then, is to put a human face on this most fascinating aspect of American politics, where specific crises and individual Justices have played such major parts.

The six chapters, I hope, follow a logical development. The first is intended to be no more than a scene-setter, to illustrate both the relationship of the Supreme Court to the political system as a whole and also the types of problems faced by the Justices in the course of their duties. The following three chapters describe the interrelations of the legislative, executive and judicial branches of government, the process of decision-making within the Court and the problems of enforcement, respectively. The fifth chapter provides three case studies to illustrate the consequences of Supreme Court action. The final chapter can then address itself to the perennial normative problem of justifying a powerful, but unaccountable, institution within an overtly democratic political culture.

The focus of this book is unashamedly political. It concentrates on the political role played by the Court, its relations with the political realities of the nation and the politics within the Court itself. Yet it should not be forgotten that the Supreme Court is primarily a judicial institution, a court of law, and thus subject to the rules and norms of judicial behaviour. The fascination of the Court, as we shall see, is that behind the framework of an adversary system of justice with courts adjudicating on conflicting claims lies a political body as well. Throughout this book, therefore, it should be remembered that there is more to a full study of the Supreme Court than just the political aspects, but no complete study can possibly ignore them.

All that remains to be done now is to acknowledge the assistance of various institutions and individuals. A grant in 1973 from the United States Information Service, as it then was, enabled me to visit Washington and talk to several of the Justices, their law clerks and other officials of the Supreme Court; small grants from Bristol University and from the American Politics Group of the Political Studies Association of the United Kingdom assisted in visits to libraries in Oxford and London; the Bristol University Publications fund provided an advance to cover the costs of typing; Martin Crouch read the whole manuscript with his usual skill at spotting ugly phrases, embarrassing lacunae and ill-organised presentation; Anne Merriman typed the manuscript with remarkable speed from my handwritten manuscript and fiercely kept me to the deadlines; and Michael Holdsworth ensured that my ideas and ambitions did ultimately get translated into substance.

Richard Hodder-Williams

Winford, 1979

The Politics of the US Supreme Court

1

Some Perspectives
on The Supreme Court

On 24 July 1974 the Supreme Court handed down its unanimous decision in the case of *United States* v. *Nixon* and found itself, not for the first time, in the headlines of the world press. The decision asserted that the tapes of the conversations in the White House during Richard Nixon's presidency were not so private and privileged that they could be denied to the Grand Jury then considering criminal charges against some of the President's subordinates. As a consequence, the full involvement of the President in covering up the 1972 burglary of the Democratic Party's headquarters in the Watergate complex was made known and within a short space of time the President had resigned office. Without this decision of the Supreme Court, it is doubtful whether Nixon's complicity in the Watergate affair would have been so publicly and clearly revealed and the United States might have had to suffer the protracted and embarrassing process of impeaching its President. This sole example in United States history of a presidential resignation can thus be laid largely at the Supreme Court's door. Such is the potential significance of the institution.

The publicity and manifest importance of a decision like *United States* v. *Nixon* is extremely rare. Nevertheless, during each year the Supreme Court decides more than 150 cases, the consequences of which can affect a large number of people very profoundly, sometimes removing privileges, sometimes extending rights, sometimes limiting arbitrary official behaviour. The highest in the land and the humblest may both be the subjects of Supreme Court decisions; the President, his executive branch assistants, Congress, state governments, all from time to time may be affected. During the 1977 Term (a Court's Term runs from October to October), the Court decided in a much-publicised case that Allan Bakke had been improperly denied entry to the Medical School of the University of California at Davis, since the criteria used for selection discriminated against him because of his race (*Regents of the University of California* v. *Bakke*). The public interest in this 'reverse discrimination' case had tended to draw attention away from other cases of major significance decided during the year. The Court also found that the Ohio law permitting the death penalty in certain crimes was too narrowly drawn to pass constitutional muster (*Lockett* v. *Ohio*; *Bell* v. *Ohio*); it upheld a lower judge's order requiring particular changes in the operations of Arkansas prisons since the conditions there were so bad that they violated the constitutional ban on cruel and unusual punishment (*Hutto* v. *Finney*); it invalidated an Alaskan law reserving jobs on the Trans-Alaska pipeline for Alaska residents (*Hicklin* v. *Orbeck*); it also invalidated a New Jersey law which banned the importation of garbage from Pennsylvania and New York into its own garbage tips (*Philadelphia* v. *New Jersey*); it found yet again that testimony taken from a witness, or a witness's house, without permitting the witness a lawyer or issuing a search warrant cannot be used in an ensuing trial (*Mincey* v. *Arizona*); it held that Congress acted unconstitutionally when it authorised inspectors for the Occupational Safety and Health Administration to inspect, without search warrants, business premises for violation of health and safety standards (*Marshall* v. *Barlow's Inc.*); it sharply curtailed the immunity which top-level civil servants had enjoyed from lawsuits resulting from injuries they caused in the course of their official duties (*Butz* v. *Economou*); it supported environmentalists acting on behalf of the three-inch snail darter, a tiny fish safeguarded by the 1973 Endangered Species Act, and in effect instructed the Tennessee Valley Authority to stop construction on a \$120 million dam (*Tennessee Valley Authority* v. *Hill*).

The examples could be multiplied even for the 1977 Term. These decisions, many of which could in the United Kingdom only be made by Parliament, illustrate the enormous political importance of the Supreme Court. It is, in a very real sense, the third branch of government. But, unlike the other branches of government, it keeps very much to itself and provides the one major exception to the Washington rule that no information can remain secret for long. Leaks from the Court are rare indeed.

The Supreme Court building stands across the park-like space on Capitol Hill opposite the Capitol itself. It was completed in 1935 at the cost, then, of \$10 million. It is a vast, monumental structure, as marbled and classical as any Roman temple. It is, indeed, a 'grand affair ... almost bombastically pretentious', as Harlan Fiske Stone wrote a few days after he had visited it for the first time, perhaps 'wholly inappropriate for a quiet group of old boys such as the Supreme Court' (Mason, 1956, pp. 405-6, fn.). Louis Brandeis more than shared Stone's initial reaction and he refused to move his place of work from his own home and continued to regret leaving the cramped, but homely, quarters of the Old Senate Chamber in the Capitol Building where the Court's formal sessions had long been held (Keeffe, 1973, p. 183). By the 1920s congressional expansion and Howard Taft's great designs for enhancing the status of the Supreme Court combined to create the impetus for a new building, 'a building of dignity and importance', as the architect Cass Gilbert was to put it, 'suitable for its use as a permanent home of the Supreme Court of the United States' (Federal Bar Association, 1965, p. 114). Marble came from Vermont, Georgia and Alabama from within the United States, and from Spain and Italy in Europe, each particular type being carefully chosen for its special qualities and colour. The end-product, nearly square, is more than 100 yards long and presents a prodigious monument to the austere virtues, and vices, of marble. It has been described, rather unkindly, as 'a classical icebox decorated by an insane upholsterer' (Alsop and Catledge, 1938, p. 135), but, classical icebox or not, it amply provides for the needs of the Court.

Within this imposing structure are the Justices' chambers, normally three sizeable rooms with bathroom, offices for the permanent officials of the Court, dining rooms for the Justices and the public, a printing press, a woodwork and repair shop, a gymnasium, a library, the grand Courtroom itself, staircases of unusual distinction (which elevators have largely made redundant), and endless corridors of marble chastely decorated with portraits and mementoes of past Justices. As if to emphasise its separation from the less aetherial qualities of Washington politics, the Court employs its own police force.

This is the physical environment in which the Court acts. But, although the building symbolises the distance that the sanctity of 'the law' should be from the rough and tumble of the political process elsewhere in Washington, its actions are, and always have been, political, for the type of conflict which it is called upon to resolve often requires it to adjudicate between divergent claims and the consequences of its decisions affect the distribution of power, status and rights on which partisan politics flourish. As a former Supreme Court Justice, Robert Jackson, wrote late in his life: 'Any decision which confirms, allocates or shifts power as between different branches of the Federal Government or between it and a constituent state is . . . political, no matter whether the decision be reached by a legislature or a judicial process' (Jackson, 1955, p. 55). This does not of itself make the Supreme Court unique; courts throughout the world are called upon to decide between competing claims and to interpret statutes passed by legislatures. A great deal of the energies expended by the

Justices are directed to resolving disputes which would be familiar to members of the highest courts of other countries. In the last few decades the federal government, either through laws of its own or through the powers delegated to various administrative agencies, has extended the range of its activities enormously and consequently increased the amount of litigation arising from actions of the federal government. The number of cases being filed in the federal district courts, the lowest level of courts in the federal system, has risen from 68,235 in 1940 to 145,227 in 1972, two-thirds of which arose under federal statutes or regulations. Much of this initial litigation is appealed to the next tier of federal courts, the courts of appeal, so that their load has increased also, in fact at an even faster rate, expanding in the decade before 1972 from 4,823 to 14,535. Slightly less than a quarter of these were appealed to the Supreme Court. The subject matter of the Court's docket is therefore concerned to a considerable degree with disputes over the applicability of congressional legislation and interpretation of federal statutes. In these cases, the Supreme Court must interpret federal legislation just as British courts interpret legislation in the United Kingdom and, as in the United Kingdom, the legislature may amend legislation if it finds fault with the Court's interpretation.

What sets the Supreme Court of the United States apart from most other supreme courts is its additional power to consider a law passed by Congress or one of the states or an action performed by the President or some other governmental official and declare it in violation of the Constitution and therefore null and void. This power is called judicial review. In 1952, for instance, when President Truman nationalised the steel mills on the grounds that their closure through strike action was detrimental to America's national interest at the height of the Korean War, the Supreme Court found that such action went beyond the limits of presidential authority and was therefore unconstitutional (*Youngstown Sheet & Tube Co.* v. *Sawyer*); in 1970, after Congress had passed a law lowering to 18 the age at which citizens of the United States would be eligible to vote in federal and state elections, the Court found that setting qualifications for state elections exceeded the power granted to Congress under the Constitution (*Oregon* v. *Mitchell*); in 1965, the Court decided that a Connecticut statute forbidding the dissemination of information about birth control or of materials and medicines to prevent conception deprived citizens of several rights protected by the Constitution and was therefore invalid (*Griswold* v. *Connecticut*). Such examples of the Court's overruling the decisions and judgements of elected representatives are numerous. The fact that its members are responsible to no electorate and accountable to no one but their God and their conscience makes the power of judicial review, and its concomitant the principle of judicial supremacy, truly remarkable.

The power of judicial review is not new. From at least 1803, when one section of the 1789 Judicature Act was found to be unconstitutional, the Court has continually exercised this power, sometimes, it must be said, more cavalierly than at others, and mostly at the expense of state laws and state independence, so that there is now what amounts to a constitutional convention that the ultimate arbiter of constitutionality is the Supreme Court. This convention took many years to establish, and even now there are politicians and public figures in the United States who will challenge the convention. For it was not the Constitution itself nor the words of the Founding Fathers at the Convention which granted this extensive power to the Court, although nothing that was written in that revered document nor anything that was said at the Convention suggests that the Founding Fathers positively disapproved of such a grant of power. Time and history, justified by common sense and the eloquent subtleties of the great Chief Justice John Marshall at the beginning of the nineteenth century, established the Court's authority to oversee the constitutionality of governmental actions. And it is this power, this ability at times to deny to elected legislatures and executive officers the full fruits of their electoral victories, which inevitably draws the Court into partisan politics. It cannot in reality avoid being drawn into such disputes. For, when one group of citizens in the United States claims one thing—for example, that the compulsory reading of the Bible before the beginning of the school day contravenes the First Amendment's prohibition against any 'law respecting an establishment of religion'—and another group of citizens denies this claim, ultimately only the Supreme Court can mediate. What it decides becomes the law of the land; or, more precisely, what a majority of its membership decides becomes the law of the land, because the Court is often divided and a simple majority is all that is required to decide a case.

Time, history and usage have not worked in an arbitrary fashion. There are excellent reasons for the Court's being drawn into the political forum. First and foremost, the United States of America has a written Constitution, which is the supreme law of the land. Those Americans who rebelled against the alien rule of British governors subordinate to the British monarch were very conscious that the powers which the governors wielded were constitutionally unfettered. Furthermore, some had read their Locke and Montesquieu and many more of them had left Europe precisely to escape the theoretically illimitable authority of church or prince, monarch or lord. For them, liberty was essentially a negative concept; it was the freedom to be unconstrained by governmental edict as far as possible. Consequently it was of paramount importance to establish precisely what a government could do and what it was to be prevented from doing. Limited government was, to them, good government and the Constitution was intended to establish those limitations. Suspicious of power which depended for its virtuous exercise purely on the virtue of men—and the Founding Fathers, for all their high idealism and eloquence, were acutely aware of the frailty of men—the delegates who met in Philadelphia in 1787 were united on two things, if no more: that the ideal government was a limited government and that limited government required a written Constitution to State those limitations.

However, to realise such lofty ideals was not easy and the language with which the limitations were to be spelled out is far from precise. This is not surprising, for there were gathered in Philadelphia men of widely different backgrounds and interests, men of stature and confidence, eloquent men and stubborn men, and men for whom a union of thirteen states might mean the diminution of their own power and authority. A convention composed of such men does not speak with one voice; the American Constitution does not speak with one voice. It was in any case an uneasy compromise between the philosophical belief in popular government and the practical fear of popularly elected politicians. The addition of the first ten Amendments, the so-called Bill of Rights, in 1791 spelled out the worry of many that governments might act arbitrarily and majorities oppress minorities. But it also created an inbuilt source of conflict between the rights of the individual and the powers of an elected government without establishing any clear rules for settling such disputes. It was the Supreme Court which stepped into the void and adjudicated between the rival claims, just as it took it upon itself to pronounce authoritatively on those parts of the Constitution whose meaning and application were disputed. Given the democratic rhetoric of American political philosophy, such adjudications could not be seen to be the partisan preferences of men but had to be grounded in the Constitution and, as it were, discovered by legal experts. Limited government demanded a political system characterised, as many proud Americans have put it, by a government of laws, not men.

Arbitrariness, extreme exponents of this view would claim, has no part in the American constitutional system, because the law establishes certainties and supreme among these laws is the Constitution. If Congress gets carried away by the political emotion of the day and passes a law which conflicts with the Constitution, that law will be null and void and only a Constitutional Amendment could rehabilitate it. In Britain, by comparison, the sovereignty of Parliament—that is, the undisputed will of a number of *men*—knows no limitations; rights may be abridged, citizenship emasculated, *ex post facto* laws passed and constituency boundaries partisanly regulated, if a majority of that Parliament so wishes. It would not be unfair to say that the British Constitution is what Parliament allows it to be; in the United States of America, on the other hand, it has been argued that governments at all levels are limited by the clear expression of the law.

This is a dangerous oversimplification. For one thing, there is the simple historical fact that rights have been abridged, citizenship emasculated, constituency boundaries partisanly regulated, and arbitrary governmental actions sanctioned without the Supreme Court's always denying the constitutionality of the actions. More to the present point, the whole idea that the Constitution creates definitive and certain boundaries to governmental actions, and that its true meaning can be 'discovered', is plainly not supported by the facts. The myth may survive and the importance of this survival must not be underestimated; indeed, it is part of the Supreme Court's function to see that the myth continues. But it also has to deal with reality, with concrete disagreements demanding a single response, and its guidelines here are by no means crystal clear. The fact that the Constitution is a compromise has led inevitably to a certain vagueness in those areas where agreement was hardest to reach and the fact that it was drawn up in 1787 inevitably resulted in its being less than ideally suited to the vast, heterogeneous, urbanised, technologically advanced nation that is now the United States of America. Was the Constitution, as Chief Justice John Marshall insisted in 1819, 'intended to endure for ages to come and consequently to be adapted to the various crises of human affairs', or did it, as his successor Roger Taney asserted nearly forty years later, 'speak not only in the same words but in the same meaning' for all time? The answer, not unnaturally, depended on what meaning each contestant considered the Constitution to enshrine. In 1937 President Roosevelt maintained in one of his fireside chats to the nation that the Constitution was an easy document to understand; but it was in his interests to think so at the time.

Discovering what the Constitution 'means' is a central part of the Supreme Court's work and it is not straightforward, except in very exceptional cases. A state law categorically denying blacks or Roman Catholics the right to vote, or a federal law establishing titles of nobility, are clearly unconstitutional. In such cases, Justice Owen Roberts's explanation of the simplicity of the judicial function may be applicable. 'The judicial branch of the Government has only one duty,' he wrote, '—to lay the article of the Constitution which is invoked beside the statute which is challenged and to decide whether the latter squares with the former' (*United States* v. *Butler*, 1936). Unfortunately, the conflicts reaching the Supreme Court can rarely, if ever, be so easily dealt with. For one thing, the Constitution does not

speak plainly. Phrases like 'the general welfare' or 'interstate
commerce' or 'due process of law' are far from specific; even some
clauses which appear at first glance to be straightforward contain
ambiguities. The First Amendment, for instance, states that 'Congress
shall make no law . . . abridging the freedom of speech or of the
press . . . ' and Justice Black was fond of emphasising that 'no law
means *no* law'. But there were definitional problems which the
defence of free speech, however passionate, could not easily sur-
mount. Complications arose out of what was to be included as speech
or the press, so that the regulation of obscenity, itself a supremely
subjective word, in films or in books presented a genuine difficulty in
constitutional interpretation. There were also problems of conflict
between Congress's conception of the nation's 'general welfare', for
which the Constitution had assigned it responsibility, and freedom of
speech and press, not to mention liberty and property. In addition, the
First Amendment seemed to be binding only upon Congress and not
upon the states, while the Fourteenth Amendment forbade the states
to abridge the privileges or immunities of citizens of the United States.
Did that part of the Bill of Rights restraining Congress's authority to
limit the individual's liberty provide privileges and immunities of
citizenship? This question cannot be answered by Owen Roberts's
simple test of squaring the Constitution with the statute; it can only be
resolved by personal judgement, not impersonal calculation.

Consider the Fourteenth Amendment a little further. Different
phrases have dominated the Court's attention in different periods; the
precise definition of a citizen's privilege and immunities, the incorporation of the company into the concept of a person, and the
delineation of practices to be considered as an exercise of liberty or a
concomitant of property have all been matters of central importance
to the rights of American citizens and to the functioning of the
American economic system. More permanent, however, has been the
argument over 'due process of law' and the 'equal protection of the
law'. Such phrases did not appear in the Constitution as the result of
some imaginative initiative on the part of delegates at Philadelphia,
for they brought with them a long history in British law and a meaning which practising lawyers then understood in a technical sense.
'Due process of law', for example, was generally held to imply some
clear and regular set of procedures by which complaints were to be
arbitrated. It invoked no picture of what those procedures should be.
Similarly, the 'equal protection of the law' was normally thought to
ensure merely that no man was beyond the reach of law, not that the
laws should protect the rights of rich and poor equally. In later years
the phrases came to be interpreted less formally and with a greater
concern for the substance of the procedures and the particular laws

being challenged and this development derived not from some sudden historical discovery of the intentions of those who formulated and ratified the Amendment (which remain unclear and sometimes contradictory), but from the subjective evaluation of succeeding Justices. This development, for which history provides much less defence than common sense, has still not given these phrases any greater precision than they enjoyed 100 years ago; nor, indeed, will they gain any more precision at the hands of future Justices.

A simple illustration will show how crucial the interpretation of these clauses can be. In 1942 the Court maintained that a man called Betts, who was too poor to hire a lawyer, had not been denied due process of law by the state of Maryland's refusal to provide him with one. The subjective nature of the justification of the Court's decision can be gleaned from the words in which the opinion was written. It admitted that due process was 'a concept less rigid and more fluid than those envisaged in other specific and particular provisions of the Bill of Rights', but it still held that the facts in Betts's case were not so 'offensive to the common and fundamental idea of fairness' as to amount to a denial of due process (*Betts* v. *Brady*, 1942). In 1962 the Court considered a very similar case and came up with a different answer. Hugo Black observed that governments and wealthy litigants always hired lawyers so that they had become, in effect, necessities not luxuries in the adversary system of trials in America. 'The right of one charged with crime to counsel,' he wrote in the Court's opinion, 'may not be deemed fundamental and essential to fair trials in some countries, but it is in ours' (*Gideon* v. *Wainwright*, 1963). So a new constitutional principle was articulated, that there is a right to a lawyer in criminal proceedings. The innovation began with the pencilled plea of Clarence Earl Gideon in a Florida penitentiary claiming just this right and it reached fulfilment as the nine Justices of the Supreme Court reinterpreted the implications of the phrase 'due process of law'. Gideon was thereupon retried by the state of Florida in the same courtroom, before the same judge, with the same witnesses, but with a lawyer appointed by the court at Gideon's insistence. He was acquitted (Lewis, 1964).

In the United States, the fifty states decide their own constitutions, make laws binding upon their residents and visitors, raise taxes and spend the revenue as they think fit. Educational policy, building regulations, the granting of business licences, the vast range of criminal law from murder and bigamy to speeding and petty larceny, all this is essentially the preserve of the state governments. But over the years Congress, aided and abetted by the Supreme Court's everwidening interpretation of phrases like 'interstate commerce' and 'the general welfare' (for both of which Congress is constitutionally responsible), has legislated more and more on matters of day-to-day concern. Such legislation frequently conflicts with state laws and it is the Court's duty both to decide on the constitutionality of the federal law and to arbitrate between the two rival claims to political authority. Often Justices disagree on this; for some, congressional legislation and the Bill of Rights lead inexorably to universal standards of practice throughout the country and minimise the variations between states and communities; for others, the federal system implies diversity and the right of localities to organise their affairs in their own, possibly unique, fashion, provided the great absolutes of the Constitution are not abridged.

The pull between universality and diversity inherent in a federal system and the problem of definition are nicely illustrated in the Supreme Court's grappling with the problem of obscenity. Many states and local authorities enjoy the power to ban obscene material. The first problem here concerns the scope of the First Amendment's injunction against laws abridging the freedom of speech or of the press, for some would argue that this implicitly safeguards any form of communication, whether spoken on film or written in books. For these absolutists, no question of obscenity arises. The majority of Justices, however, have held that there is a definitional problem here. Some would deny their suitability to be censors and acknowledge the subjectivity of such a position by allowing elected governments the right to define what is obscene. This can be done, not merely by asserting that Justices are not the proper judges of pornography, but by emphasising the federal and diverse nature of America and making a virtue out of its differences. Most Justices tend to hover uncomfortably between the abdication of power implicit both in the federalist's position and in the absolutist's. The test to be used, according to Justice Brennan, was to determine 'whether to the average person, applying contemporary community standards, the dominant theme of the material, taken as a whole, appeals to prurient interests . . . [and is] utterly without redeeming social importance' (*Roth* v. *United States*, 1957). While this left unsaid who was to define contemporary community standards, it acknowledged the possibility of diversity without finding a definition of the indefinable. As Potter Stewart once wrote, and frequently reiterated, he could not define hard-core pornography—'but I know it when I see it' (*Jacobellis* v. *Ohio*, 1964).

The ambiguities of the Constitution unquestionably provide Justices to some extent with the opportunity to write into the document their notions of what the distribution of power should be between federal government and state government or between governments in general and the individual. The first Justice Harlan once observed to a group of law students: 'If we don't like an act of

Congress, we don't have much trouble to find grounds for declaring it unconstitutional.' And the great Chief Justice Charles Evans Hughes once commented that 'We live under a Constitution, but the Constitution is what the Judges say it is' (quoted in Schwartz, 1957, pp. 4, 11). Nevertheless, there is a great danger in laying too much stress on the subjective nature of judicial decision-making and in emphasising the boundless authority of the Supreme Court. Harlan and Hughes were both correct, but both were misleading. For the Supreme Court, for all the political consequences of its actions and for all the subjective philosophies underlying the interpretation of vague clauses, is nevertheless a court of law. It is bound by accepted procedures, by accepted conventions, by an interest in establishing a coherent and lasting system of law, and by an awareness of its status and importance as the court of last resort and the fountain of certain law. Public attention tends to be focused on the discontinuities, rather than on the reaffirmation or partial redefinition of existing precedents. Although the Court differs from British courts in its readiness to overturn precedents, it normally does so only with care. The three-year gap between affirming local governments' right to make the children of Jehovah's Witnesses salute the national flag and prohibiting that requirement is the exception, not the rule. The creative innovation for which the Warren Court of 1953-69 was famous, despite the historic decision of *Brown* v. *Board of Education of Topeka* (1954) which deemed segregated state schools unconstitutional, came as much from incremental redefinition as from the overturning of past precedents. Yet even then the Court could not, of itself, desegregate the southern schools; it needed congressional action and executive will to do so.

It is in the field of discrimination against blacks that the intricacies and ambiguities of constitutional interpretation, as well as political motivation and consequences, are well illustrated. The Fourteenth Amendment does not state uncompromisingly that discrimination is unconstitutional, yet the Court, employing this Amendment, has done a great deal to outlaw discrimination. In the course of its efforts, it has antagonised many for writing its policy preferences into law, it has perturbed others by its less than strictly logical development of thought, and it has satisfied yet others precisely because it has not felt fettered by the absolute imperatives of judicial consistency to reach praiseworthy conclusions in line with the spirit, if not the word, of the Constitution.

The history of dismantling the barriers of racial segregation in public places throughout the southern states is a long one. From 1896, when the Supreme Court decided that 'separate but equal' facilities did not deny blacks their equal protection of the laws (*Plessy* v.

Ferguson, 1896), until the 1950s, it had been generally understood that the Fourteenth Amendment did not require the states or their agents to provide facilities, whether educational, recreational, or transportational, open to people of all races. In the 1950s, however, the Court increasingly came to view inequality as the inevitable consequence of separation in intellectual matters and decided, in one of the most-quoted cases in America's history, that 'separate educational facilities were inherently unequal' and thus contravened the Equal Protection Clause (*Brown* v. *Board of Education of Topeka*, 1954). In the years following, the Court pronounced on a series of issues in which segregation had been authorised by states' legislation; there were no arguments before the courts, no opinions, merely pronouncements that in the light of *Brown* v. *Board of Education* state-supported segregation was unconstitutional. Leaving aside for the moment the propriety of this judicial path, the fact remained that by 1960 state actions which discriminated against blacks were unconstitutional.

But this did not yet touch one of the most obvious areas in which segregationary practices flourished. Throughout the southern states, cinemas, eating-places, hotels and other privately owned businesses catering to the public remained firmly segregated. In November 1962, a number of cases were argued before the Supreme Court in which this issue of discrimination in privately owned property was raised. At first sight, it is difficult to see how the Court, despite its personal wish to outlaw practices of which its members strongly disapproved, could find in favour of the young blacks convicted of trespass because of their 'sit-ins' at counters where service for whites only was the house rule. The problem was to discover whether the state had become involved, in the Court's words, 'to some significant extent', in the discriminatory practice and in one instance this was not too difficult. One of Greenville City's ordinances explicitly required separation of the races in restaurants; Greenville City was an agency of the state in the sense that authority had been delegated to it by the state government; the store manager had no choice but to segregate his patrons, and this segregation was not, therefore, an act of private choice but effectively a state act and therefore in violation of the Fourteenth Amendment (*Peterson* v. *Greenville*, 1963). The other cases were less straightforward; indeed, in one the Court had to argue that public pronouncements of executive officers in New Orleans demanding the cessation of 'sit-ins' and threatening police action against those involved in them were, in effect, state support for racial discrimination and therefore violated the equal protection clause of the Fourteenth Amendment (*Lombard* v. *Louisiana*, 1963).

The conclusion which the Court reached may be wholly admirable, but the process by which it was reached was open to challenge. Apart from the continuing debate over the precise meaning of equal protection, whether this is procedural or substantive, and the lack of clarity surrounding definitions of liberty and property, there is clearly also a conflict between a man's liberty to use his property and a man's right to be treated equally. Nor was there any principle by which to decide the relative inviolability, if any, of private rights, to choose one's guests, or neighbours, or customers. The sanctity of private property, the cornerstone of much of the United States' economic and social values in 1960 hardly less than in 1789, is seriously undermined if recourse to state law enforcement officers in order to preserve the liberty to control the use of property is thereby defined as state action and therefore subject to the Fourteenth Amendment. Furthermore, extending the concept of state action to activities receiving the public and publicised approval of government officials would open a whole Pandora's box of litigation on the standing of public pronouncements. These cases naturally antagonised large segments of vocal American opinion, and not only in the south, and lent fuel to those who were arguing that the Court's decisions did not reflect the true meaning of the Constitution but rather the personal predilections of the Justices. Nobody knows what the few who drew up and the many who ratified the post-Civil-War Amendments really intended to be covered by their vague phraseology; there were enough people in 1963, however, both friends and opponents of the Supreme Court, who were perturbed by its interpretations of these clauses. During 1964, the Court struggled with a case in which their elastic concept of state action fitted even more uncomfortably; they seemed in the end to be arguing that any discriminating practice, even by a private owner of private property, could be state action by the simple expedient of arguing that a private citizen's so-called rights could only be realised if the state intervened on his behalf by arresting individuals for trespass (*Bell* v. *Maryland*, 1964). Such a reading of the Fourteenth Amendment, even the Court's friends agreed, was really going too far, desirable though the end result may have been.

Ten days later, Congress passed the Civil Rights Act of 1964 and Lyndon Johnson's presidential signature granted blacks the legal right, among other things, of being served in privately owned establishments catering to the public. It is instructive to note that Congress was forced to employ its constitutional power 'to regulate commerce . . . among the several States' in order to achieve the desegregation of lunch counters. That such an apparently tortuous route was necessary is due to the Constitution and its meagre grant of powers to Congress, but its success depended upon a long line of Supreme Court decisions which had steadily expanded the meaning of 'commerce' and the range of permissible regulation. Title II of the 1964 Civil

Rights Act is largely devoted to defining the kind of places of public accommodation within the reach of Congressional control whose operations are deemed to affect commerce within the Act's meaning. In effect, any public place which may either serve individuals travelling between states or sell products which have moved between states is deemed to be within the purview of the Act. Almost immediately, litigation was instigated claiming that the Act, for all its sophisticated attempts to squeeze small hotels and private restaurants under the control of congressional legislation, was an improper exercise of the powers of Congress, violated the Fifth Amendment, and also subjected the owners of such businesses to involuntary servitude in contravention of the Thirteenth Amendment. Before the end of the year, the Court had heard argument on two cases so appealed and rendered their judgement.

Justice Tom Clark wrote the Court's opinion. He drew considerably on the legislative record, a voluminous testimony, as he put it, to show that discrimination by hotels and motels impeded the interstate travel of blacks. Having reaffirmed that travel, being so indissolubly concerned with commerce, was part of interstate commerce and that Congress had used an appropriate remedy to deal with a problem within its constitutional jurisdiction, Clark found that Title II of the Civil Rights Act was clearly constitutional in so far as it affected hotels dealing with transient guests (*Heart of Atlanta Motel* v. *Katzenbach*, 1964). Clark now turned to a slightly more problematical case where interstate travellers were not concerned. Ollie's Barbecue was a family-owned restaurant in downtown Birmingham, Alabama, some distance from an interstate highway or the railway and bus stations. The district court in Birmingham had found that Ollie McClung's discriminating practices could continue because Congress had exceeded its constitutional powers in the Civil Rights Act, for there was no showing that the purchase of meat from outside Alabama for the exclusive use of white customers affected interstate commerce. Tom Clark disagreed. Citing once again the testimony of congressional hearings, he asserted that there was ample evidence that segregated eating-houses sold less interstate goods than they might have done if desegregated and that this generalised practice obstructed interstate travel, if only psychologically, as it also deterred business. Since this was so, Congress had a right under the 'interstate commerce' clause to rectify the situation and Title II of the 1964 Civil Rights Act was an appropriate way of doing it. Since no one denied that Ollie McClung spent $69,683 on food from outside Alabama, he was subject to the provisions of the Act, which was itself a proper exercise of Congress's constitutional powers (*Katzenbach* v. *McClung*, 1964).

There may be something intrinsically bizarre in a constitutional system which requires it to be established that a downtown hamburger emporium uses beef imported from another state before the right of blacks to be served in cafés is confirmed. Yet it also emphasises two other things. It is a reminder that each case that comes before the Court, however significant it may ultimately prove to be, concerns named individuals, often very humble people, whose own lives have been directly affected. The decisions revolve around particular questions: did Linda Brown's exclusion from the whites-only school in Topeka, Kansas, inevitably mean that her educational opportunities were so attenuated that she had been denied the equal protection of the law? Was Clarence Earl Gideon, the petty criminal in a Florida penitentiary, denied the equal protection of the law because he was not provided with a lawyer by the state? Great principles may emanate from these decisions, but the context of such litigation is normally surprisingly commonplace.

In the second place, behind the formal title of *Katzenbach* v. *McClung* lies not only the complaint of Ollie McClung and the vindication of an important part of the 1964 Civil Rights Act, but also the appreciation and argument of the nine men who constitute the Supreme Court of the United States. As far as the litigants are concerned, it is the decision pure and simple which is of interest. But many a particular case incorporates within it a general proposition applicable to the whole range of similar disputes, so the precise grounds on which the decision is based are crucial. The opinion of the Court establishes the principles on which the case was decided; sometimes the principles can be very narrow ones and apply only to one specific instance, but they can also be of considerable generality. Linda Brown won her case, not because the Court decided narrowly that her particular school failed to provide facilities equal to the separate white schools, but because it decided broadly that all racially separated educational systems inevitably deprived the black pupils of the equal protection of the law. Consequently, *Brown* v. *Board of Education* became binding not merely on those individual instances where schools were shown to be separate but unequal but in all dual systems of education.

The Justices do not always agree on the appropriate decision; nor do they always agree on the correct line of argument to be used in coming to an agreed decision. They disagree over the interpretation of statutes, over the relative importance of clauses in the Constitution, over the basic issues involved in a controversy brought to them for mediation, and over the extent to which the philosophy of the separation of powers requires them to give comparatively free rein to elected governments. Less than a quarter of the decisions in recent years have been unanimous. This is not surprising, since the major purpose of the Court and the procedures by which disputes reach it for ultimate decision are designed to cope with problems for which there is no obvious solution and over which there is a genuine division of opinion. The nine men on the Court are not magicians able to conjure order out of confusion, or harmony out of deep divisions. De Tocqueville observed nearly 150 years ago that 'scarcely any political question arises in the United States that is not resolved, sooner or later, into a judicial question'. This is still true; even Watergate needed the Supreme Court's intervention. Whether the Constitution itself or the practicalities of the federal system or some peculiar aspect of the American political culture is to take the blame, the fact remains that disagreements, on great and small matters, are again and again taken to the judiciary for resolution. Much of this litigation would reach the courts in the United Kingdom; the present Race Relations Act and litigation over personal injuries in work and leisure-time spawn litigation which courts must adjudicate. But the extent to which governments are entitled to limit individual freedom, the procedures which police officers are obliged to follow, the methods of financing state education, to take but three major problems which confronted the Supreme Court in 1973, are all issues which in the United Kingdom would be resolved by elected politicians but which, in the United States, must be decided by the Justices of the Supreme Court. There are no simple solutions; if there were, the Supreme Court would not have become involved. Thus, it matters greatly to the American people who exactly occupies the nine seats on the Court, for it is their conception of the Constitution and their application of it to concrete disputes argued before them which will establish for the time being what is, and what is not, the law.

In certain circumstances, the law depends in a very real sense on a single man. Perhaps the most famous case concerned Justice Owen Roberts who, in the autumn of 1936, provided one of the five votes in a decision which found that a New York law establishing a minimum wage contravened the employer's rights under the Fourteenth Amendment to use his liberty and property as he thought fit (*Morehead* v. *New York ex rel Tipaldo*, 1936). In March 1937, however, Roberts had joined the losing four in the New York case to uphold an almost identical Washington state law establishing a minimum wage (*West Coast Hotel* v. *Parrish*, 1937). The fate of minimum wage laws, and possibly Roosevelt's New Deal itself, thus depended upon a single pivotal figure. Roberts's 'switch in time', which was supposed to have 'saved the nine', came before Roosevelt's Court-packing plan was announced, although the decision and accompanying opinion was not handed down until afterwards (Frankfurter,

1955-6). Since many cases are decided by five votes to four and Justices may remain on the Court for many years, it is hardly surprising that each new appointment to the Court is the subject of intense interest and concern.

This concern is clearly related to the ideologies of possible nominees. But it would be oversimple to think of the Supreme Court's being ranged along a liberal/conservative continuum, for the issues before the Court are by no means always of the kind amenable to simple ideological responses. Some cases are; but others (and this is increasingly the case) pose problems of such complexity and conflicting principles that they defy simple ideological solutions. Furthermore, it is erroneous in any case to imagine that deciding is nothing more than a personal choice of preferred values. Justices, of course, often have a clear and coherent set of priorities which can simplify some judging. The so-called liberals tend to argue that the Bill of Rights is applicable almost in its entirety to the states, that free speech and suspects' rights can be infringed in only rare instances and that national power is extensive in its reach; the so-called conservatives, on the other hand, are more selective about incorporating the Bill of Rights into the Fourteenth Amendment, believe that federalism permits disparities among the states on how to deal with redistricting, criminal procedure, obscenity and educational provisions and argue that, at the margin, the national welfare is better served by backing the law enforcement officers than the suspected criminal. Such tendencies, however, are only starting points from which to judge on the details of a concrete dispute.

People interested in politics are conscious that nominees' views cluster regularly around a few central values. Yet liberals and conservatives have varied over time in their judgement of what principles the Court *ought* to espouse. The truth of the matter is that estimation is often related directly to an individual's support for the substance of the Court's decisions and these, as has been noted, are often intensely political. To be political is to be controversial, for politics is the very process by which mutually incompatible demands are attempted to be mediated. The Supreme Court's decisions, authoritatively allocating values as they unquestionably do, inevitably give rise to both support and opposition. In the 1930s it was the liberal American who complained of the Court's conservatism; in the 1940s, as Roosevelt's revamped New Deal met with a much-altered Court's approval, it was the turn of conservatives to claim the Constitution's death; in the 1950s, following Harry Truman's appointment of four of his closest personal friends, liberals were again complaining about the shortcomings of the Court (Gordon, 1958); in the 1960s, the pendulum had swung again and conservatives inveighed against the activity and partiality of the Warren Court; in the 1970s, both conservatives and liberals have had things to cheer and things to bemoan. The Supreme Court may be a judicial body, but its judgements have political overtones and they are judged politically.

. One can thus study the Supreme Court from a number of perspectives. Constitutional philosophers can trace the developments in the meaning of particular clauses and phrases; constitutional historians can indicate how these developments have altered the distribution of power as between the central government and the state governments or between governmental agencies and the individual; students of politics can illustrate the ebb and flow of reciprocal relationships as the Court influences American society and is then itself influenced by pressures from that society. Each of these interests has a macro dimension, for the Court's actions flow from a long pedigree of earlier conflicts and resolutions and affect many people often for generations to come; but there is also a micro dimension which focuses on the particular case, the particular Justices and the particular political environment in which the Court operates. The sum of these individual decisions, some of greater consequence and notoriety than others, creates the overall impact of the Supreme Court. Thus any study of the Court should move easily between the particular and the general, between Ollie McClung's beef and the scope of interstate commerce, between the political calculations surrounding a specific appointment and presidential powers of nomination, between the agonies of Linda Brown and the enunciation of a principle of racial equality in schooling, between the misdemeanours of Clarence Gideon and the right to counsel. The fascination of the Supreme Court lies precisely in this synthesis, where important general principles emerge from the actions of nine known and named individuals deciding a concrete dispute between specific parties.

2

The Supreme Court and the Separation of Powers

One of the basic principles of the American system of government is said to be the separation of powers. This implies that the three branches of government, legislature, executive and judiciary, each exercises its authority within a distinct area and is independent of the others. Such a complete separation exists nowhere. In the United States, often held up as a prime example of the separation of powers, constitutional provisions as well as developed practices indicate a considerable interrelationship between the theoretically separate branches of government. It is still proper to argue that Congress is largely independent of the President, that the President is largely free of congressional control over a wide range of matters, and that the judiciary can exercise considerable authority with which neither Congress nor President can interfere. But the use of words like 'largely' and 'considerable' emphasises the degree to which legislature, executive and judiciary are in fact dependent upon each other.

As far as the Supreme Court is concerned, the Constitution makes the dependence very clear. Its membership, for example, is nominated by the President and confirmed by the Senate; its numbers are regulated by statute and much of its jurisdiction derives from congressional legislation. Against this are certain provisions which insulate it from the pressures of the elective branches, such as its original jurisdiction or the right against any diminution of its members' salaries. The Justices hold their offices 'during good behaviour', whatever that means, but they can, like other officers of the United States, be removed from office on impeachment and conviction. Although attempts to impeach Justices have been made, Earl Warren and William Douglas being the latest targets, nobody has reached the trial stage since Samuel Chase did in 1805. The constitutional convention has developed, therefore, that Justices retire only as a result of an act of God or an act of will.

The choice of a new member of the Court is one of the President's most significant acts. The man he nominates, if confirmed by the Senate, is likely to outstay his sponsor on the national scene for many years. Hugo Black and William Douglas, for example, were appointed by Roosevelt and witnessed the presidencies of Truman, Eisenhower, Kennedy, Johnson and Nixon, Douglas ultimately retiring while Ford was President. The average length of time served by a Justice leaving the Court is fourteen years. The impact of each appointment is related not only to the length of time he serves, but to the balance of the Court which he joins. The Court has nearly always been divided on the great issues which come to it for adjudication, so that each new member may be in a position to alter the balance somewhat. In 1968, for instance, the Court's membership could be ranged on a liberal-conservative spectrum roughly in this order: Douglas, Brennan, Warren, Marshall, Fortas, Black, Stewart, White, Harlan. The pivotal Justices were thus Marshall, Fortas and Black. In 1969 Warren was replaced by Burger; in 1970 Fortas was replaced by Blackmun. Both these Nixon appointees were judicial conservatives, tending towards the position held by Harlan. The pivotal Justices at this juncture were Black, Stewart and White. When Black and Harlan retired from the Court in 1971, Nixon's successful appointments were Powell and Rehnquist, again jurists of a conservative hue. By 1972, therefore, the balance of the Court had altered markedly; the liberal trio of Douglas, Brennan and Marshall, who had been consistently in the majority in the four years preceding Warren's retirement from the Chief Justiceship, now needed the support of two from Stewart, White and the Nixon nominees to muster a majority. Although the Court rarely divides quite as neatly and consistently as this suggests, the point remains valid; a single appointment has the potential to alter the balance of the Supreme Court's output and thus the distribution of powers and rights within the United States while a series of appointments almost certainly does.

Congress, too, plays a crucial role. For one thing, the President does not have a completely free hand in filling Supreme Court vacancies. His nomination must find favour with the Senate and this is by no means a foregone conclusion. In the nineteenth century, indeed, when Senators often considered themselves the President's equal, one in three nominations failed to win senatorial approval. Presidents have been significantly more successful in the twentieth century but the events of 1968 and 1970, when Lyndon Johnson's nominee for the Chief Justiceship and two nominees of Richard Nixon's for Associate Justiceships did not receive consent, reaffirmed the Senate's right and power to oversee these important appointments. Potentially of even greater significance is Congress's legislative power. It can alter, and has altered, the number of Justices sitting on the Supreme Court either to create additional vacancies through which a newly victorious political movement could alter the balance of the Court or, by revising the number, to deny unpopular Presidents the fruits of their victory. Furthermore, Congress controls most of the matters over which the Court has appellate jurisdiction and thus could, if it so willed, prevent a number of contentious issues ever reaching the Court for final judgement. This immense potential has been used sparingly, but it has not by any means fallen into disuse.

While it is a commonplace to point out the formal interconnections between the three branches of government and to note how the Supreme Court's exercise of judicial review itself sets limits on presidential and congressional behaviour, it is not often noted how the Supreme Court is directly involved in the legislative and executive processes. Congressional statutes have delegated to the Court and various well-funded bodies subject to the Court's ultimate authority a great deal of the organisation and policing of the processes of federal justice in the United States. Furthermore, some members of the Court have not felt averse to lobbying quite actively in Congress for alterations to planned legislation or for the introduction of new laws affecting the judicial branch. In short, while the branches of government in the United States are clearly less integrated than they are in the United Kingdom, they are also less separate than simple models of the United States political system might suggest.

PRESIDENTIAL APPOINTMENTS TO THE SUPREME COURT

There are no ordained routes by which a man reaches the Supreme Court. Indeed, no legal or constitutional requirements for any federal judges exist. Recruitment to the humblest district court is not, as in Britain, delineated by traditions and practices which keep judicial posts within the strict confines of a part of the legal profession, but is open virtually to anyone whom the President and his advisers would like to see appointed. Nor are the courts of appeal perceived as higher courts staffed on a hierarchical pattern of recruitment from the members of inferior courts. Promotions do take place, but they are by no means the norm; of 139 judges serving, or eligible to serve, on the courts of appeal in January 1973 only 57, or 41 per cent, had been promoted from a district court. Similarly, Justices of the Supreme Court are not normally drawn from the ranks of the judges of the circuit courts of appeal. Only 22 of the 101 men to have sat on the

Court were actually judges of inferior federal courts when they were promoted, and four of those were on the Supreme Court in 1979, all appointees of Republican Presidents. The American federal system allows judicial experience (that is, taking part in the process of judging) to be acquired in state courts and forty-two Justices of the Supreme Court have acquired their knowledge of the bench in that way. Even so, no fewer than forty-two had no judicial experience prior to their service on the country's highest, and most prestigious, court. Since the turn of the century only twenty-two of the Justices appointed had any judicial experience (Abraham, 1974, pp. 45-7).

This is not to say that they have no legal experience. It would be unthinkable for a nomination to be made to the Court of a man without even a Ll.B. degree. Many Justices have acquired their legal experience in private practice or by teaching at a university or in government service. Congressmen regularly introduce Bills requiring future Justices of the Supreme Court to have judicial experience, but Congress has never passed them. It is widely accepted that the tasks of a Justice are much broader and much more philosophical than the task of a trial judge or even a circuit court of appeals judge and that experience outside the confines of the courtroom is almost essential for a great Justice. This was Felix Frankfurter's view, as it was Learned Hand's; certainly the names of the great Justices contain very few whose major qualification was judicial experience.

The backgrounds of the last six Chief Justices illustrate the immensely broad range of experience possessed by the senior figure of the nation's judiciary. Warren Earl Burger, Nixon's nominee in 1969, is only by comparison with his predecessors somewhat inexperienced; a lifelong Republican, he helped to organise the Young Republicans in Minnesota, played a leading role in Harold Stassen's successful campaign for the governorship of Minnesota, served on two state statutory boards for a decade, was the floor manager for Stassen's campaigns for the presidential nomination at the Republican Conventions of 1948 and 1952, and was an assistant attorney-general in Eisenhower's administration until he was appointed to the court of appeals for the district of Columbia in 1956. His predecessor, Earl Warren, had a more distinguished career. After being involved in local California politics as a district attorney for nineteen years, he was elected the state's attorney-general as the nominee of the Republican, Democratic *and* Progressive parties whence he advanced to the governorship of California for an unprecedented three terms of office, and was actually Thomas Dewey's vice-presidential running mate in the 1948 election.

Harry Truman had appointed Warren's predecessor and had turned to one of America's most versatile and experienced public servants,

Fred Vinson. Vinson spent three years as Kentucky's attorney-general before coming to Washington as a Congressman, where his fourteen years' service was marked by major contributions to the New Deal programme; he was then appointed by Roosevelt to the circuit court of appeals for the district of Columbia, but he soon resigned to become in succession Director of the Office of Economic Stabilisation, Federal Loan Administrator and Director of the Office of War Mobilisation and Reconversion, and finally Secretary of the Treasury. Harlan Fiske Stone was Vinson's predecessor and he was one of only two Associate Justices to have been promoted directly to the Chief Justiceship. The other was Edward Douglas White, promoted by Taft in 1910; intriguingly both were appointed by Presidents of a different party from their own after careful political calculations. Before he was appointed to the Court by Coolidge in 1925, Stone had taught law at Columbia University Law School for a quarter of a century and then been the Attorney-General who had cleaned out the Justice Department following the Teapot Dome Scandal, thus aiding considerably Coolidge's successful presidential election campaign in 1924.

Stone had succeeded Charles Evans Hughes, who had in his time been professor of law, Governor of New York, Associate Justice of the Supreme Court (a post from which he resigned to fight, just unsuccessfully, a presidential election against Woodrow Wilson), a member of the Cabinets of both Presidents Harding and Coolidge, and a member of the Permanent Court of International Settlement in The Hague. Even more distinguished was Chief Justice William Howard Taft. For fifty years he was in the front line of public service, first as a public prosecutor and then as a member of the Ohio Supreme Court; thereafter, in succession, he held the posts of United States Solicitor-General, Judge of the Sixth Circuit Court of Appeals, Governor of the Philippines, Secretary of War under Theodore Roosevelt, President of the United States, no less, and professor of law.

A detailed study of Associate Justices would show similar patterns of broad experience. Few have not been involved in active party politics; indeed, even appointees to lower courts have their party identification publicised so that it is easily known precisely how many adherents to the party out of office a President nominates. Many Justices have served as Congressmen and many more have held high office in the federal government. Even those who seem to have been chosen from the academic community, or from a state legal system, have been very much more than merely professors or merely judges; they have almost invariably enjoyed close links with the President himself or powerful political figures in the state. Appointing a Justice is an intensely political operation in which a whole range of considerations will play their part. There is no single hierarchical road to the Supreme Court, for nomination is very much part of the American patronage system.

The first stage in the process of filling a vacancy on the Court is for the President to make a nomination. Immediately the vacancy occurs, a host of individuals and organisations move into action attempting to get the President's ear. Trade unions, the National Association for the Advancement of Coloured Peoples (NAACP), business corporations, church groups, state legislators, friends of the President and of aspiring nominees, even the Chief Justice himself on occasions joins in the lobbying (Murphy, 1961). Danelski's book on Herbert Hoover's nomination of Pierce Butler in 1922 gives a good idea of the intense activity triggered off by a Supreme Court vacancy as groups and individuals intercede to advance, or often to destroy, the claims of possible candidates (Danelski, 1964). In recent years the American Bar Association, through its Standing Committee on the Federal Judiciary established in 1945, has lent its voice to the process by expressing a collective view on the quality of candidates, although its favourable report, now assumed as a necessary precondition for senatorial consent, is not always taken seriously (Walsh, 1970; Grossman, 1975). Following a leak of the names of potential replacements for Justices Black and Harlan in October 1971 and the ABA Committee's low categorisation of the two top names put forward by Nixon as possible replacements, the President announced that he would no longer submit prospective nominees to the Committee. This did not dissuade the ABA from promising to issue post-nomination evaluations. In any case, the Committee's legal importance, and considerable power, lies in its role over appointments to inferior courts where it has been granted a virtual veto power. The White House will thus be deluged with letters, telegrams, delegations, promises and threats, sometimes spontaneously offered but more normally carefully orchestrated. This can, however, be overdone. When Felix Frankfurter was lobbying for Learned Hand, Franklin Roosevelt observed that he had had twenty callers pressing Hand's name on him, 'and everyone an emissary from Felix', and he was determined then *not* to give way to this concerted pressure; thus did one of America's most renowned and respected jurists not get on to the Court (Lash, 1974). For the most part, it is the Attorney-General who attempts to put some order into the chaos of Washington lobbying, but it is the President who makes the final choice (Abraham, 1974, pp. 22-31).

Vacancies in the Court happen at irregular intervals, on average about every twenty-two months. They occur sufficiently irregularly for the President to give his personal attention to the task of selection, a luxury he could not possibly afford for the far more numerous nominations to be made to the lower federal courts, where senatorial influence is much greater. Unsurprisingly, the two most significant criteria in the selection process are the nominee's philosophical position on the great issues currently dominating the Court's work and his personal relationship with the President (Scigliano, 1971). In the days before 1891 when the Justices had to travel enormous distances on appalling roads and stay in a series of seedy hotels and boarding houses while carrying out their secondary duties as circuit judges, the physical stamina of a nominee was an important consideration. Justices, like politicians, tended in the nineteenth century to be younger on appointment than their successors in this century and the need to be able to cope with the tough physical environment of Washington life was one factor. That they were tough is perhaps testified by the large number who survived more than twenty years on the Court (see Appendix 1). Such considerations are less important now, although Justices have to be virtually 'workaholics' to keep abreast of the demands made upon them. Generally speaking, however, the primary consideration for a President is that the nominee is known to him and the nominee's views on constitutional matters largely coincide with his own. Party links tend to cover both these factors and only 14 of the 101 Justices have been appointed by Presidents not of their own party. In recent years only Eisenhower, whose career had failed to provide him with a large number of political associates and connections, and Nixon, whose introversion denied him intimate access to the politicians with whom he had worked for twenty years, have needed to search far outside their coterie of acquaintances for candidates.

For most Presidents, however, there are several potential candidates for the nomination. Other calculations therefore come into play. When a Catholic leaves the Court, Catholics lobby for another member of that religion, normally successfully; similarly, there was, for more than five decades, a Jewish seat held by a succession of distinguished and often liberal men—Brandeis, Frankfurter, Goldberg and Fortas. There are usually attempts to strike a balance between the regions and there is considerable pressure on a President to avoid the dominance of the eastern establishment. Apparently the most powerful opposition to the appointment of Earl Warren as Chief Justice in 1953 came from those who believed that insufficient patronage had come North Dakota's way! Careful considerations of political advantage are never far away from a President's calculations and nominations have often been used to soothe ruffled feelings or to cement developing alliances. Sometimes, the political considerations outweigh the two fundamental principles of ideological conformity and personal acquaintance. When Eisenhower was faced in 1956 with the task of replacing the liberal Catholic, Frank Murphy, his instructions to his Attorney-General were to find another Catholic, and preferably a Democrat from the pivotal state of New Jersey in order to rally some Democrat-inclined voters round the local Republican banner. William Brennan happened to be a Catholic and was a well-respected judge on the supreme court of New Jersey. Thus the conservative Eisenhower came to appoint the most liberal Justice sitting on the Supreme Court in 1979.

Because there is no prescribed route for reaching the Supreme Court and because different Presidents use different criteria for deciding on nominations, the experiences and qualities of the Justices over time inevitably provide no stable and common pattern. Attempts have been made to prepare a portrait of the typical Justice, but such attempts end up with generalisations of such simplicity that they do not substantially add to our knowledge (Schmidhauser, 1959). It would indeed be curious if the Justices had no legal experience; and it would be almost as curious if they had not been involved to some extent in political activity. Only Shiras in 1892 and Harry Blackmun in 1970 came to the Court without any prior political experience. It would also be curious if the majority of Justices had not come from essentially middle-class and professional backgrounds. Yet the Court, like the presidency, is not the preserve of the establishment; apart from Kennedy, none of the postwar Presidents, neither Truman nor Eisenhower nor Johnson nor Nixon nor Carter, was born into a family of high economic and social status. Earl Warren's father was an immigrant store-keeper who was murdered and Warren Burger sold insurance policies to pay for his legal education. By the time Warren and Burger reached the Court, however, they were obviously men of standing and substance. There have now been 101 Justices of the Supreme Court confirmed in office throughout its history, during which so much has changed that the virtue of comparing the social background of those who sat on the bench before the Civil War with those who have been Justices since the New Deal is questionable. The formal procedures, however, have not altered; it remains the prerogative of the President to nominate a candidate and the task of the Senate to confirm, or withhold confirmation.

There is a subcommittee of the Judiciary Committee whose prime responsibility is to vet presidential nominations in the judicial field. In cases of nominations to the Supreme Court it is more usual for the whole Committee to consider the names and make a report to the Senate, which then votes on the nomination. It is only recently that nominees have appeared in person before the Committee (Thorpe, 1969). Harlan Fiske Stone was the first to do so, in 1925, and the practice slowly became the norm. Some, like Sherman Minton, refused on the grounds that to do so would weaken the constitutional principle of the separation of powers by allowing a part of the Congress to delve into the possible stand a member of the judicial branch might take. Every nominee since Earl Warren has appeared, usually to his advantage and normally without fuss. But Senator Joe McCarthy's crusading interest in every public figure's attitude towards what he considered to be subversive activities and southerners' worry about the constitutional principles and practical consequences of the *Brown* decision have made the appearance of some nominees very uncomfortable. Thurgood Marshall suffered several gruelling days of questioning and Abe Fortas spent twice as long even as Marshall before the Committee in 1968. There is a genuine problem here, for the Senators want to know precisely the sort of things which adherence to the separation of powers prevents the nominee from answering. Once the Senators take their confirmation duties seriously and consider the ideological position, rather than the ability or morality, of the nominee relevant, they are bound to ask hypothetical questions about the nominee's performance on the bench which he cannot yet answer. When they do discover his position, it is too late to do anything about it. When Fortas refused to be drawn on discussing past cases, which reflected the current interpretation of the Constitution he had sworn to uphold, or future cases, on which no judgement had yet been made, it reminded many observers 'of some of the anti-subversive hearings of a decade ago when witnesses were forced to plead the Fifth Amendment against self-incrimination again and again in response to questions about their associations' (*New York Times*, 19 August 1968).

Broadly speaking, there has been a presumption that the President has a right to put on the Court men of whatever ideological stance he chooses. Presidents unquestionably see it this way. Nixon made this quite clear on the campaign trail of 1968 and in his press conferences introducing his nominees. Theodore Roosevelt, emphasising the primacy of ideology even over party loyalty, expressed this view to Henry Cabot Lodge in 1912 when discussing the possible nomination of Horace Lurton. 'The nominal politics of the man', he wrote, 'has nothing to do with his actions on the bench. His real politics are all important ... He is right on the negro question; he is right on the power of the federal government; he is right on the Insular business; he is right about corporations, and he is right about labour' (Scigliano, 1971, p. 116). Every President attempts to some extent to pack the Court; that is the prerogative of patronage. Only very few do not attempt to place men of distinction on the Court, if only for the pragmatic reason that men lacking distinction make little impact on the Court's output and such an appointment would thus be wasted.

The Senator's duty is thus to advise on and consent to nominations in terms only of the nominee's fitness for such an important post. When Nixon wrote to Senator Saxbe in March 1970, implying that the President had a constitutional right to have his nominees confirmed, he was constitutionally and historically incorrect. But, when others claimed that their refusal to consent to his nomination of Harrold Carswell was merely a matter of measuring his qualifications, they were being less than honest and more in accord with their predecessors who had denied confirmation to earlier Presidents' nominations. The precise facts surrounding several of the earliest nominees remain disputed, but it is probably correct to say that there have been twenty-five nominations in the United States' history on which the Senate has either taken no action or expressed its rejection—one in the eighteenth century, nineteen in the nineteenth century and five this century (Swindler, 1970). That is to say, one out of every five nominations has failed to find senatorial approval, the nineteenth century showing the lowest rate for successful nominations.

The reasons have generally been twofold. In nearly all cases of rejection, the Senate has been at loggerheads with the White House and Supreme Court nominations have become their battleground. This was especially the case in the nineteenth century when the American parties were frequently in the process of dissolution or when death brought to office a Vice-President who had originally been consciously selected to appeal to a minority; in either case, Presidents found not merely that they had no party majority in the Senate but that they had there a bitterly partisan faction personally opposed to them. In the five twentieth-century cases this situation also existed; John Parker, denied the opportunity to appear before the Judiciary Committee himself, was in part the victim of the hostility between the conservative republicanism of Herbert Hoover and the growing, and frustrated, radical populism of several powerful and confident Senators. Parker's failure to be confirmed was theoretically linked to his allegedly anti-black and anti-labour attitudes, even though locally prominent blacks and the North Carolinian AFL actually supported him, but in reality it is explicable basically in terms of the senatorial-presidential relations during a congressional election year. Ironically, the man who was successfully nominated, Owen Roberts, proved less liberal than Parker, if his subsequent career as Chief Judge of the Fourth Circuit is a proper yardstick for comparison. The Senate's relations with Lyndon Johnson in 1968 and with Richard Nixon in 1970, when the other failures took place, were also fraught.

In the twentieth-century instances, however, the second factor becomes predominant; this is the hostility on the part of a majority of Senators to the political philosophy of the nominee himself. This hostility was by no means absent in the nineteenth century—indeed, nominations tended to reflect presidential ideology and thus exacerbate the divide between dissident Senators and the President—but it became more open in the twentieth. Nor should it be forgotten that Senators are men of pride and standing; certainly in the nineteenth century many of them considered themselves at least the equal of some of the Presidents and in the twentieth century they still resent presidential attempts to steamroller them into acquiescence. This accounts, for instance, for the somewhat rough ride Eisenhower's nominations received, since the Senators took ill the President's habit of making appointments when the Senate was in recess. When Brennan appeared before the Judiciary Committee, he had already participated in some Supreme Court discussions. Not all Presidents have been as fortunate as Eisenhower in this assumption of confirmation; John Rutledge, George Washington's nominee for Chief Justice in July 1795, had already taken up his post and made judgements before the Senate refused to confirm his appointment in December.

Although the Senate unquestionably has the constitutional authority to refuse confirmation to presidential nominations, it is probably true to say that only the most imprudent or unfortunate Presidents will not get their nominee safely over the senatorial hurdle. The Senate may have the power of veto but it cannot foist its choice on to an unwilling President. Having chosen a personal acquaintance whose political philosophy is congruent to his own, a President, one might think, could expect to see his own vision of the Constitution stoutly maintained by the man for whose elevation he is responsible. And in 75 per cent of cases Presidents are not much disappointed. But, once appointed, a Justice is no longer obligated to anyone and is accountable only to his own conscience and God. 'If conscientious, able, and independent men are put on the bench,' Charles Evans Hughes wrote, 'you cannot predict their course as judges by reference to partisan motives or to personal or party loyalties' (Hughes, 1928, p. 49). Independence and the aura of the robe can release unforeseen energies and unperceived values in a man. Most of the great Justices have admitted that putting on the robe alters the man and, over time, they change their views about the proper relations between federal and state governments or between government and individual citizens. If the Constitution is seen as an evolving document, then, as Earl Warren has said, a Justice must be ready to rethink his earlier suppositions. Although some Justices have continued to keep in personal contact with the Presidents who appointed them, there is little evidence to suggest that they act as the President's poodle. It has been suggested that Warren Burger had conversations with Richard Nixon and then his Attorney-General, John Mitchell, on important issues, if not specific cases (Kohlmeier, 1972, p. 259). But, if this did in fact occur, it is rare; more common is the sort of relationship Abe Fortas had with Lyndon Johnson, where the topics for conversation were concerned with national policy-making rather than judicial policy-making.

Since ideological conformity is not always the guiding principle behind nominations, it is not surprising that some Justices follow a line clearly not to their patron's liking. This would be true of Benjamin Cardozo and William Brennan. It was also certainly the case of Eisenhower's nomination of Earl Warren, a decision he admitted regretting more than any other. Later in his life, and conscious of what Warren had done, Eisenhower wrote of appointments to the bench: 'My thought was that this criterion [being on a lower bench] would ensure that there would then be available to us a record of the decisions for which the prospective candidate had been responsible. These would provide an inkling of his philosophy' (Eisenhower, 1965, p. 297). Harry Truman, too, was far from satisfied by the performance of all his nominees. Like Eisenhower, he reckoned that his biggest mistake had been a Supreme Court appointment and his observations about Tom Clark ('He hasn't made one right decision that I can think of') were couched in the most basic language this very basic President could summon up (Miller, 1976, pp. 242-3). Theodore Roosevelt was scarcely more complimentary about the great Oliver Wendell Holmes, whose opinions in anti-trust cases were entirely unexpected, and he observed: 'I could carve out of a banana a Judge with more backbone than that' (Abraham, 1974, p. 62). If Richard Nixon had thought that his four appointees would have backed him in the Watergate tapes case he was badly disappointed. Frankfurter's distinguished career on the Court disappointed the liberals who had championed him in the 1930s and Byron White's restrained conservatism in recent years has been contrasted with the alleged liberal views of his presidential sponsor, John Kennedy. In Frankfurter's case, the issues before the Court changed and the liberal principle of giving preference to legislators' decisions rather than a Justice's conception of prudent policy validated laws very much less progressive than those the Hughes Court had struck down; but there is some evidence that this self-restraint acted as a smokescreen for a fundamental conservative streak in his philosophy (Grossman, 1962; Spaeth, 1964). With Byron White, the personal attachments which are so often at the nexus of Supreme Court appointments may well have blinded Kennedy to his innate caution; and only time will tell whether John Paul Stevens is going to continue and develop the independence of view which has already resulted in his casting several votes which Gerald Ford surely would not have applauded.

The independence which Justices effectively enjoy can ensure a healthy disregard for the more emotional and unthinking shifts of public opinion. But it also leaves them unaccountable for their actions to anyone other than themselves. The 1937 Retirement Act, allowing Justices at the age of 70 to retire on full pay, was designed to limit the number of particularly elderly members of the Court, some of whom in the history of the Court had manifestly stayed on longer than their failing faculties should have permitted. Before this Act, it needed all the diplomatic skills of fellow Justices to persuade members to retire. In 1869 Justice Grier had been called upon by his colleagues to resign; Stephen Field was one of those whose unpleasant task it had been to intimate that he should go and he was himself approached by his brethren nineteen years later and urged to resign; Field's successor, Joseph McKenna, ironically suffered the same fate. McKenna had reached the stage not merely when he voted in a way logically contradictory to his stated position but also where he had written an opinion deciding the case one way when there had been a unanimous vote the other! His colleagues first agreed not to hand down decisions in cases where his vote was pivotal (Taft had already sometimes cast his own vote to produce the correct result when McKenna had inadvertently cast his against his own position) and then persuaded him to resign from the Court he loved so much and from which he derived his happiness and his social pleasures (Murphy, 1961, pp. 165, 184-5).

Justices have traditionally been singularly unenthusiastic about leaving the Court, once appointed, even though the financial inducements have always been great. Samuel Miller once turned down the offer of four $25,000 retainers, preferring his $10,000 salary on the Court. Political inducements have taken some Justices from the Court; Hughes, for instance, resigned to accept the Republican nomination to fight Woodrow Wilson in 1916 and others, like Douglas and Vinson, have been mentioned as possible presidential candidates this century; Presidents like Franklin Roosevelt and Lyndon Johnson have persuaded some Justices, like Burnes and Goldberg, to return to the overt political fray; a few, like Whittaker, have found the task of being a Justice unattractive and have resigned to undertake more satisfying employment. But these are the exceptions. Nor has the possibility of substantial pensions to all of those retiring at 70 after ten completed years of service encouraged a habit of early retirement. Most Justices keep at work until death, or the premonition of death, or manifest incapacity effectively makes the decision for them. Hugo Black was 85 when he finally retired and John Harlan was virtually blind when he retired, both in 1971, and both were dead within a few weeks; William Douglas was partially paralysed by a stroke but attempted for several months to do the impossible, even though he was 76 and had sat on the Court for 35 years. In 1979 five members of the Court were over 70; by the end of the 1978 Term Burger had, like Brennan and Marshall, completed ten years of service, but it is unlikely that any of them will quietly leave their colleagues and the exhausting labour of being a Justice.

Two things appear to keep Justices active beyond their time. First, the job itself is clearly very satisfying. It may be extraordinarily onerous, but a Justice knows the power he wields, the significance of his every action, and experiences at first hand the enormous variety of human and corporate conditions. The passage of time breeds familiarity with colleagues, both fellow Justices and other Court personnel, which are intimate and fundamentally important; for the Court *is* an isolated institution whose members must form a rather exclusive part of Washington's vibrant political life and exercise a discretion and self-restraint unusual in America's capital. A few, of course, retain close links with their presidential nominators; Frankfurter continued to deluge Franklin Roosevelt with memoranda while Vinson and Fortas, employing the more effective means of personal contact, enjoyed mutually satisfying relationships with Harry Truman and Lyndon Johnson respectively. Not only is the job satisfying, it is also often seen as acutely important. Since the majority of Justices have been active in politics before their elevation and are often acute political animals, they prefer to time their resignations to give their party or political ideology maximum advantage. The clearest expression of this determination to prevent the appointment of dangerous newcomers to the Court was perhaps made by Howard Taft in a letter to his brother in 1929:

> I am older and slower and less acute and more confused. However, as long as things continue as they are, and I am able to answer in my place, I must stay on the Court in order to prevent the Bolsheviks from getting control . . . the only hope we have of keeping a consistent declaration of constitutional law is for us to live as long as we can . . . The truth is that Hoover is a Progressive just as Stone is, and just as Brandeis is and just as Holmes is. (Quoted in Schmidhauser and Berg, 1972, p. 74)

The President, then, has to gamble to some extent if he wishes to pack the Court and fill it with distinguished Justices. The two do not always ride hand in hand. Once on the Court, his nominees are their own men if they choose to be; the President can have no hold over them. But he can, in a few instances, still thwart their actions. The Court, as we shall see, has no coercive powers of its own to enforce its decisions. If force is needed, the federal marshals responsible to the President must exercise it. Although the President is obliged by the Constitution to see that the laws be faithfully executed, Presidents have frequently chosen to ignore the Supreme Court's rulings or to accept them with such lack of applied enthusiasm that they have no effect. The separation of powers is thus seen in all its complexity; the executive nominates, the legislative confirms or denies confirmation, the unaccountable judiciary judges, and the executive enforces or fails to enforce those judgements. Many of these factors are illustrated in the detailed study which follows of Richard Nixon's nominations to the Supreme Court.

THE NIXON NOMINATIONS

On 31 March 1968, Lyndon Johnson announced that he would not be a candidate for the presidency in the coming November election. This knowledge immediately turned many people's minds to the question of his successor, especially among Republicans who saw the vision of their party's recapturing the White House after eight years' relegation to the background of national politics. For eight years without the patronage associated with the presidency and being a minority in both Houses of Congress, the party quite naturally saw Johnson's withdrawal amidst the national turbulence over the Vietnam War, civil rights and law and order as a sign that their star was in the ascendancy. With Richard Nixon in the White House, the highest office in the land would once again become a Republican preserve. This vision had immediate relevance in June when Earl Warren, for fifteen years Chief Justice of the United States and now approaching his seventy-seventh birthday, offered President Johnson his retirement 'effective at your leisure'; when Johnson announced this offer, he also announced that he was nominating Associate Justice Abe Fortas to succeed him. If, therefore, Republicans could postpone confirmation of Fortas until after the end of the year, there was every possibility that the fifteenth Chief Justice of the United States would be a Republican appointed by Richard Nixon.

Calculations of this kind were only one factor of significance in the summer of 1968. In several quarters the reputation of the Supreme Court, or the Warren Court as it was called, was at a low ebb. A series of decisions had antagonised important individuals and vocal groups. The desegregation of public schools in the south had been extended to desegregating all public places; the rights of suspects had been con-siderably enlarged and the arbitrary behaviour of many law enforcement officers strictly regulated, though at the cost of freeing some singularly unpleasant criminals; other stands had been taken extending individual freedoms against those who valued censorship, wished prayers to be said in public schools and believed all radicals to be security risks. The greater the distance from the liberal establishment centres on the eastern seaboard and parts of California, the greater the disquiet about the crumbling of an ordered society. The events of 1966 and 1967, with their black riots, looting, arson and Vietnam demonstrations smacking in many people's eyes of anti-American disloyalty, only served to exacerbate the feeling of moral crisis. To those who shared this view of America, the Supreme Court, and particularly its liberal wing, of which both Warren and Fortas were members, was in part responsible.

Within this general political climate, exaggerated by the fact of its also being an election year, the nomination of Abe Fortas did little to ameliorate the already unhappy relations between President and Congress. Although Fortas came from a comparatively poor background in Tennessee and had to work himself to the top of the legal tree, he epitomised three factors peculiarly antipathetic to the growing conservatism of the day. He seemed very much part of the liberal establishment with his beautiful home, attractive wife and musical soirées, at which the most distinguished string players joined the Justice in classical quartet playing. He was also an intimate friend, indeed crony, of the President, having become friendly with him when they were both young New Dealers in Washington before the Second World War and having adroitly rescued him from the consequences of charges of ballot malpractices in the 1948 Texas senatorial primary; he was a regular, and welcome, visitor and advisor to the White House. Finally, he was a liberal, not as absolute as Douglas or even Brennan and Warren, but a definite liberal, whose vote could normally be counted upon to defend the individual against the excesses of the state machines. In normal years, these factors would have been comparatively unimportant. His admitted abilities and the recent tradition of presidential success in appointments to the Court were in his favour; nor did he lack supporters in the Senate. But 1968 was not normal times.

The Senate Judiciary Committee, as was proper, went into session under its chairman, James Eastland, the senior Senator from Mississippi, an arch-conservative and a persistently hostile critic of the Warren Court. At first, objection to Fortas's nomination was moderately unexceptionable, but two major lines of complaint soon emerged (Schmidhauser and Berg, 1972, pp. 103-26). First, there were powerful objections to Fortas's judicial philosophy, especially where it was supposed to favour suspect rights. In one dramatic moment Senator Strom Thurmond shouted at Fortas: 'Mallory! Mallory! I want that name to ring in your ears.' He was referring to a black, Andrew Mallory, whom the Supreme Court had unanimously reprieved from the electric chair in 1957, eighteen years before Fortas became an Associate Justice, on the grounds that the confession extracted from him in 1954 had been improperly coerced (*Mallory* v. *United States*, 1957). Senator McClellan of Arkansas stated that 'the Court has become the enemy of all the law officials in this country. We are reaping the whirlwind.' And another Senator kept a crime clock in the committee room, on which the nation's crimes were carefully recorded, as though there was a direct causal link between Supreme Court decisions and the ever-mounting crime statistics. In the summer of 1968, despite Earl Warren's earnest pleas, entirely in line with his own early career as a public prosecutor in California (that the Court wanted not to set criminals free but to see them tried fairly), few Senators were prepared to face their electorates having voted to confirm a man who was widely thought to have been the ally of criminals, pornographers and atheists. Just as the Court's decisions affect politics, so political undercurrents reverberate on the Court.

The second line of attack concentrated on Fortas's close links with the President. Some professed that it was improper in a system of government which claimed to be founded on the principle of separation of powers for a member of one branch to be so intimately connected with another. Yet Justice Owen Roberts had served on the Pearl Harbour investigation; Justice Robert Jackson had been a prosecutor at Nuremburg; and Chief Justice Earl Warren, albeit reluctantly, had chaired the Commission on the Assassination of President Kennedy. Harry Truman had actually suggested to Chief Justice Fred Vinson that he should follow Truman as the Democratic Party's presidential candidate. To the attacks on his relationship with Johnson, Fortas defended himself with dignity: 'I am a Justice of the Supreme Court', he said, 'but I am still a citizen.' Taft fifty years earlier had been conscious of the ethical problem of involving himself in politics while still Chief Justice, but his justification echoes Fortas. 'I presume I have a legitimate right', he told a friend, 'to possess the President of such information as I think useful, if he desires to receive it' (Murphy, 1961, p. 163). Fortas's fault, however, was to be associated with an unpopular President, though the complaint was usually of constitutional impropriety or of cronyism, an attack not difficult to mount seeing that Johnson had nominated another old friend, the Texan Homer Thornberry, to fill the vacancy that would have been caused by Fortas's elevation. It was also asserted that there was something improper in a lame-duck President actually exercising his constitutional power; but this argument, which lacked historical foundations as well as constitutional authority, was merely another cloak under which to hide the primary objection that conservatives on Capitol Hill did not want Fortas as Chief Justice and another liberal appointed to the Court.

Friends of the President managed to extricate the nomination from Senator Eastland's Committee before the autumn elections. When in the Senate, on 1 October after more than three months of bitter filibustering debate, a cloture vote mustered only forty-five, twenty-two short of the necessary sixty-seven, Fortas asked the President to withdraw his name from consideration. Thus Lyndon Johnson became the first President since George Washington to fail in winning consent for his nominee as Chief Justice. Earl Warren stayed on for another year but, once it became clear that the likelihood of his surviving whole and hearty until another Democrat occupied the White House was slim, he resigned and thus presented Richard Nixon, as Republicans and conservative Democrats had hoped, with the opportunity of appointing the new Chief Justice.

In the spring of 1969 a furore broke about Fortas's head because of his recent financial connections with a crooked businessman serving a prison sentence for violations of the Securities and Exchange Act. This association was generally regarded as a clear breach of the standards of judicial propriety, even though Fortas had not participated in any cases involving the financier and had eventually returned the retainer as a result of public criticism. The public outcry whipped up by his opponents, his own less than candid response, and concern among supporters of the Warren Court that its prestige would be irreparably tarnished if he remained an Associate Justice, led Fortas to resign, the first Justice in the history of the United States to be driven from office (Shogan, 1972). Within a few months of entering the White House, then, Richard Nixon was fortuitously presented with two vacancies—a replacement for the liberal Chief Justice and a replacement for the liberal Fortas. Franklin Roosevelt had had to wait five *years* for his first vacancy.

Nixon's first nomination was for the Chief Justiceship. In an unusual off-the-record press conference, he explained his processes to correspondents (Mackenzie, 1969). He was aware, first of all, that a Chief Justice ideally required skills in addition to those of the intellectual ability and integrity required of an Associate Justice; he should also be an administrator and a leader. There was to be no political clearance from Senators nor, in this case at least, clearance from the American Bar Association; neither did he approve of the unspoken convention held by some people that a Catholic should replace a departing Catholic, a Jew replace a Jew, or a black a black. Furthermore, mindful of the accusations made against Lyndon Johnson that his nominees in 1968 had been personal friends, or cronies as his enemies described them, Nixon claimed that he was naturally looking for a man of distinction likely to command widespread support in the nation and in the Senate, but also for a man whom no journalist, no antagonistic Congressman, could label as the President's crony. The ideal man should be about 61 or 62 and share those views of the Constitution which Nixon had elaborated along the campaign trail in 1968.

Nixon consulted only his close friend, political advisor, campaign manager and Attorney-General, John Mitchell. Five men widely canvassed for the office were dismissed. Charles S. Rhyne, a fellow law student of Nixon's, a former president of the American Bar Association, and head of the citizens' drive for Nixon in the presidential elections of 1960 and 1968, was passed over because he was a personal friend. Herbert Brownell, Nixon's closest advisor next to Mitchell and formerly Eisenhower's Attorney-General, asked not to be considered since he feared that he would produce bitter controversy in the Senate. Thomas Dewey, the defeated Republican presidential candidate in 1948, was disqualified on account of his age. Potter Stewart, already an Associate Justice, had told Nixon that the Court's interests would not be served by elevating one of its members to the Chief Justiceship. It had happened only twice in the past—with Edward White in 1910 and Harlan Fiske Stone in 1941—and neither had quite managed the change from one among equals to the first among equals. Finally, John Mitchell had disqualified himself because he was so clearly a political friend of the President's. This, of course, pre-dates the Watergate scandals and Mitchell's subsequent conviction for perjury, perverting the course of justice and accepting illegal contributions to his master's campaign fund, so that Nixon's public judgement that he was 'superbly qualified' rings somewhat balefully in the ears.

Nixon turned to Warren Earl Burger, Chief Judge of the district of Columbia Court of Appeals. His virtues, the President said, were five-fold. Nixon had been thinking of an existing federal judge of experience and reputation: Burger had been appointed by Eisenhower to the court of appeals of the district of Columbia circuit in 1955 and had thus had fourteen years of face-to-face contact with some of the constitutional issues whose determination by the Warren Court so offended Nixon. Secondly, his opinions on most of these sensitive matters, which he had been free in publicising in his lucid and confident style, coincided largely with those of Nixon and the conservative forces which had carried him to the White House. Thirdly, he was precisely the right age, being 61½. Fourthly, Burger was both a known quantity, yet also neither a political nor a personal friend. Nixon and Burger had first met in 1948 at the Republican National Convention in Philadelphia, when Burger was leading the Minnesota delegation in favour of Harold Stassen, and they had met again in 1952 when Burger helped to bring the Stassen delegation over to Eisenhower. These first favourable impressions had been strengthened over time by the publicity given to some of Burger's opinions, which mirrored much of Nixon's own thinking about the Constitution. Finally, Burger not only looked the part with his imposing presence and distinguished looks, but he had also expressed a keen interest in Court administration. While he clearly lacked the distinction of some of his predecessors, Burger was rapidly confirmed by a vote of seventy-four to three in the Senate.

With Fortas's resignation, Nixon had a second vacancy to fill. Mitchell suggested the name of Clement Haynsworth, a South Carolinian then Chief Judge of the fourth circuit Court of Appeals. He met most of the President's requirements about judicial experience, a 'strict constructionist' philosophy and the added specification of coming from the south. In this instance, however, political considerations were very much at work (Evans and Novak, 1971). Nixon's so-called 'Southern Strategy' in 1968 had not only ensured him victory in the November presidential election; it had also left him indebted to the immensely strong-willed, Democrat turned Republican, Senator from South Carolina, Strom Thurmond. The Senator had every intention of cashing in on this political debt and a surprisingly large number of South Carolinians were recipients of presidential patronage. Thurmond had one of his political assistants, Harry Dent, well placed in the White House to bring pressure on the administration to redeem the promises Nixon had made, about, among other things, easing up on the programme of school desegregation in the south. Dent campaigned fiercely, and successfully, against the Secretary for Health, Education and Welfare, John Finch, whose department was doing its best to translate the fourteen-year-old *Brown* decision into reality. Part of the strategy for insulating the south from Washington and liberal pressure was to place conservatives on the bench, at the district level where senatorial courtesy played an accepted role, and also at the highest level if possible. As the Eisenhower appointees, mostly moderates, retired from the circuit courts, the Nixon replacements, in effect the Mitchell nominations, were extremely conservative, men like Charles Clark, who had been a leading strategist in Mississippi's resistance to desegregation, or Harrold Carswell, who had been repeatedly reversed and reproached by his circuit court while still a district judge. In these circumstances the name of Haynsworth was passed up from Dent to Mitchell, and from Mitchell, who was well aware of the debt owed to Strom Thurmond, to Nixon.

Initially, it seemed as though this nomination would be as routine as had other twentieth-century nominations of Associate Justices. But it was not. Liberal Democrats had not forgotten how Fortas had been denied the Chief Justiceship and then hounded from the bench. After some fairly unscrupulous ferreting, they discovered that Haynsworth had invested, in a cemetery of all things, in partnership with a business friend of very dubious reputation, and that he had failed to declare his pecuniary interest in some of the cases he was actually adjudicating. Liberals played these aspects of impropriety to the utmost, in effect challenging the Senate's integrity to treat Fortas and Haynsworth by similar criteria. The bulk of those who voted against confirmation were also ideologically opposed to the nomination, attacking Haynsworth's apparent insensitivity over civil rights, his seeming prejudice against labour, and a dissenting opinion he had written backing the labyrinthine attempts of Prince Edward County, Virginia, to avoid desegregating its state school system. The determination of liberals to wreak their vengeance was strengthened by the administration's patent unconcern for some of the values they held so dear; in the middle of the hearings, the administration, with Nixon's knowledge, actually filed a suit to halt desegregation of many southern schools and Congressman Gerald Ford announced the start of impeachment proceedings against William Douglas, the most libertarian of Associate Justices. On 21 November, the Haynsworth nomination was voted down by fifty-five to forty-five, with seventeen Republicans joining the majority.

President Nixon was furious. He blamed his nominee's defeat upon 'anti-Southern, anti-Conservative, and anti-constructionist' prejudice and promised to nominate another man from the south with conservative and constructionist views. The name he sent to the Senate was G. Harrold Carswell, a singularly unknown and undistinguished judge from Florida who had been elevated from a federal district court to the court of appeals for the fifth circuit six months earlier. The appointment, Henry Abraham wrote, 'was an act of vengeance—one intended to teach the Senate a lesson and down-grade the Court' (Abraham, 1974, p. 6). Commentators assumed that, with the American Bar Association endorsing Carswell, the Senate would not spite the President again. But they were wrong.

Two basic objections to Carswell quickly surfaced. First, he was an even less distinguished public figure and jurist than Haynsworth. The Dean of the Yale Law School observed that he had 'more slender credentials than any nominee for the Supreme Court put forth in this century' and the Dean of Law at Duke University, North Carolina, who had been a vocal backer of Haynsworth, confessed: 'There is, in candour, nothing in the quality of the nominee's work to warrant any expectation whatever that he could serve with distinction on the Supreme Court of the United States.' Some of his supporters made a virtue out of his ordinariness. Senator Roman Hruska, for instance, went on public record as saying, 'even if he were mediocre, there are a lot of mediocre judges and people and lawyers. They are entitled to a little representation, aren't they, and a little chance?' But this did not impress moderate Republicans or the establishment, normally pro-Nixon, legal fraternity, who held the Supreme Court in high regard and genuinely minded about the quality of its personnel. The President did not share their esteem; when the Republicans' Senate whip had visited Camp David earlier to ask Nixon to withdraw Haynsworth's name, he came away unsuccessful, telling journalists that the President simply did not understand the gut feeling in Washington that the Court was something sacred and should not be used for political ends. Nixon had gained no new understanding by the spring of 1970.

The second complaint was ideological in that Carswell was even more insensitive over civil rights than Haynsworth. Some early statements of his publicly espousing white supremacy, and his role in transferring a public, federally supported golf-course into the status of a private club to circumvent a Supreme Court ruling proscribing segregation in public recreational facilities, were publicised. Indeed, his record spoke for itself. Of Carswell's eighty-four published decisions while a federal judge, about 60 per cent had been reversed, twice the average rate of his admittedly conservative circuit. His whole record showed a 40 per cent reversal rate, the seventh highest rate of the sixty-seven district judges in his circuit, and a steadily increasing rate of reversal at that. The plethora of accusations that his court had been noted for its improper delays and racially biased decisions, exaggerations though these were to some extent, made a mockery of the American Bar Association's criteria for recommendation. One southern Senator has been quoted as saying that, if the vote had been by secret ballot, Carswell would have been lucky to have won ten affirmative votes (Harris, 1971, p. 127).

But each Senator's vote would be public and the Carswell nomination was only one factor in senatorial politics in the first months of 1970. It was Birch Bayh who felt that something ought to be done to prevent the United States being foisted with Carswell on its Supreme Court but he, and his fellow liberals, were even more concerned with extending the life of the 1965 Voting Rights Act, which was coming under attack from southern Democrats and conservative Republicans alike. Consequently, he had little time to lobby himself. A pressure group like the NAACP, which might have taken a leading role in opposing the nomination, was also concerned primarily with the Voting Rights Act and, indeed, was alarmed when other civil rights groups tried to bring pressure on to the Republican Senate leader,

Hugh Scott, whose help they needed for a bi-partisan defence of the Act. The protracted struggle over Carswell's nomination was in fact carried on by senatorial aides and the outcome was largely determined by their work. One response soon became clear; many Democrats would only vote publicly against Carswell if the Republicans themselves were split, because they had no intention of laying themselves open to attack for voting on partisan grounds. Since 1970 was also an election year and the feedback from some states was strongly in favour of Carswell (Senator Spong received literally thousands of letters, many vituperative and obscene, as well as six assassination threats if he voted against Carswell's nomination), several Senators tended to look to their political careers before their consciences. Furthermore, the southern Democratic Senators either favoured Carswell or dared not vote down another nominee from their part of the Union.

Much, therefore, depended on the Republican Senators. Their immediate instincts were to close ranks and back their nominal leader. Certainly Hugh Scott feared that his position as minority leader would be jeopardised if he voted for a second time against his President and other moderate Republicans felt obliged to back Scott's line lest their more conservative fellows ousted him from leadership. But two distinct forms of pressure began to affect the unity of Republicans. First, the legal fraternity, both conservative and radical, entered the fray, approaching eminent lawyers, bar associations and law school deans throughout the country so that a well-orchestrated crescendo of opposition arose to convince Senators that they should think very seriously about confirmation. This elite voice was augmented by a careful campaign of letter-writing which made the scale of pressure-group activity almost unprecedented; Senator Saxbe, for instance, received 4,000 letters on the issue, eight to one against Carswell. Secondly, the administration displayed an insensitivity and incompetence only accountable for by unconcern for and ignorance of congressional norms. No attempts were made to woo the moderate Republican Wednesday Club; on the contrary, Senators were threatened, if they failed to back the President's nomination, with reprisals like strong opponents in primary elections, slowdowns or cut-offs in funds and patronage. Consequently there were no Republicans of standing prepared to lobby on the President's behalf and this left the running to the anti-Carswell group. On 1 April, Nixon wrote to Saxbe demanding a presidential right to unimpeded power in nominating procedures, which was manifestly no part of the Constitution as construed by Senators: 'What is centrally at issue in this nomination is the constitutional responsibility of the President to appoint members of the Court—and whether this responsibility can be frustrated by those who wish to substitute their own philosophy or their own subjective judgement for that of the one person entrusted by the Constitution with the power of appointment' (Murphy and Pritchett, 1974, pp. 172-4). This aggressive, non-conciliatory line was epitomised by Mitchell's public statement that Senator Margaret Chase Smith, the strong-willed and fiercely independent Senator from Rhode Island, would vote for Carswell when she had yet to make up her mind. She promptly voted against confirmation.

Finally, the Bayh group was much better informed and organised than the administration and its supporters, such as they were. For Bayh to fulfil his ambitions, he had to save the Voting Rights Act and postpone the vote on Carswell until his friends' concentration could be directed towards that nomination and the public campaign convert a few waverers. In this he succeeded. The opponents of the Voting Rights Act occupied so much of the Senate's time that it allowed Bayh, by making full use of the parliamentary techniques available to him, to postpone the vote on Carswell until after the short Easter recess. When the Senate reconvened, Bayh once more outsmarted the White House by giving its congressional linkmen the impression that the crucial vote would be on whether to recommit Carswell's nomination to the Judiciary Committee. While Bayh had struck a bargain with those Republicans who were opposed to Carswell that they could follow their party's line on the recommittal vote so long as they held firm on their negative vote on the nomination itself if it should come to the floor of the Senate for a vote, the administration was busy pressurising its possible supporters to vote against recommittal and ignored the vote on the nomination itself. The vote to recommit the nomination to the Judiciary Committee was lost by fifty-two votes to forty-four, figures which Bayh had calculated more accurately than the White House, and so a vote was promptly taken on Carswell's nomination. This Bayh won, by fifty-one votes to forty-five, and Nixon had lost his second successive nominee.

Both Carswell and Nixon were distinctly upset. The nominee soon entered the Republican senatorial primary in Florida, campaigning under the angry motto: 'This time the people will decide.' They did: 62.7 per cent of the voters supported his opponent. The President assailed the Senate with some vigour, accusing it of standing irrevocably in the way of any federal judge from the south who shared 'strict constructionist' views (a judgement almost certainly incorrect, since there were several men who met the President's requirement and were infinitely more distinguished than Haynsworth or Carswell; indeed, the Senate confirmed the Virginian Lewis Powell twenty-one months later by eighty-nine votes to one). And soon afterwards he claimed that the Senate had uniquely denied him the right to see his choices

appointed in contravention of the Constitution's *pro forma* requirement of consent, a historical appreciation and constitutional interpretation manifestly and obviously devoid of factual support. Nixon then
turned to the new Chief Justice, Warren Burger, for advice and
offered the name of Harry A. Blackmun to the Senate. Blackmun's
closest friend in elementary school had been Burger and he had acted
as best man at Burger's wedding, as indeed had Burger at Blackmun's
own. The response to this nomination was very different. Both the
liberal Senators from Minnesota, Hubert Humphrey and Eugene
McCarthy, added their approval and the NAACP, while hesitating to
applaud the tenor of his judgements, nevertheless acknowledged his
fairness; conservatives liked his far from activist view of the
Constitution and the American Bar Association, while slightly
worried that his cautious habits might slow him down on the Supreme
Court, found him 'thoroughly qualified'. And so did a unanimous
Senate.

Nixon was soon blessed with further good fortune, when two more
vacancies in the Court occurred, permitting him to nominate four
Justices within a period of only three years. In September 1971 both
Hugo Black and John Harlan resigned from the court—within a few
weeks both were dead—and left the Court intellectually a very much
barer place. Although often on opposite sides, these two Justices, the
populist from Alabama with the fervid belief in the rights of the
individual, and the urbane easterner with a deeply inbred concern for
judicial non-involvement, had graced the Court by the clarity and
conviction with which they expressed the eternal conflicts of that
institution. To replace such men would be hard indeed. Nixon's
response, however, was not to search widely for men of stature,
experience and intellectual standing, but to announce a short-list of six
names which drew forth the criticism that the President's nominations
continued to show a relentless pursuit of mediocrity. Even the
American Bar Association urged Nixon to add some people with
stature and publicised its ranking of the administration's two top
choices as 'unqualified' and 'not opposed'. For once, Nixon did not
press on in his determination to spite the establishment forces of the
press, Senate inner club and eastern intellectual community. He
produced, rather as though he had kept their names purposely hidden,
two candidates of distinctly higher quality, although even they were
hardly in the mould of Hugo Black or John Harlan.

Lewis Powell, already 64, came from Richmond, Virginia, but he
belonged to the new south rather than to the unreconstructed south
with whose members Nixon had been previously concerned. He was a
past president of the American Bar Association, was Chairman of the
Richmond Public School Board during the 1952-61 period when the

Brown decision was slowly, but peacefully, implemented, and had been a member of Lyndon Johnson's 1967 National Crime Commission, to which he had written a minority report advocating Constitutional Amendments to correct what he termed an imbalance between the rights of the accused and the rights of citizens. Although his experience had otherwise been limited to the private practice of law, his essentially conservative view of the judicial role sufficiently appealed to Nixon to make him eligible for promotion to the highest court of the land. Even more ideologically conservative was Nixon's second nominee, William H. Rehnquist. He was, at the time, Assistant Attorney-General and had been involved in conservative Republican politics for many years. He was active on Barry Goldwater's behalf in 1964, had supported Nixon strongly in 1968, and was not averse to suspending normal arrest procedures if he felt the occasion demanded, as he did when clearing the arrest of 7,000 Vietnam War demonstrators in May 1970. Although essentially a politician, he was not inexperienced in the field of law, having been clerk to Justice Robert Jackson for the 1952 Supreme Court Term. He stood to the right of Powell and, conceivably, of the President himself. Not unnaturally, liberal groups like the American Civil Liberties Union fought the nomination, but nothing like the moves to prevent the nominations of Haynsworth and Carswell developed. On 10 December 1971, six days after the Senate had consented to Powell's nomination, he received its blessing by sixty-eight votes to twenty-six. Rehnquist was only 47 when appointed to the Court, one of the youngest Justices in recent years, and is thus the only Nixon appointee likely to survive into the twenty-first century.

The events of 1968 to 1971 exemplify in a somewhat exaggerated form many of the cross-pressures at work when a vacancy on the Supreme Court arises. Each appointment reflects to some extent not merely the presidential view of the criteria relevant for Justices of the Supreme Court (and Richard Nixon, it must be said, is unique among Presidents in this century in his openly scornful and derogatory attitude towards the institution) but also the relationship between Congress and President at the time and the constitutional conventions then prevalent. The rhetoric of much of the debate hides some of the realities. While southerners were much more open in their ideological motivations, northerners of both parties tended to clothe their partisan feelings not in ideological justifications but in constitutional arguments as Republicans did in 1968, or ethical standards as Democrats did in 1969 or standards of competence as occurred in early 1970. Except when the relations between Congress and the President are singularly strained, as they were in 1968 and to some extent in the period of revenge after the Republican victory that year, the presumption remains, outside the south, that a candidate's ideological stance is a presidential matter. In this period, then, the nomination of a Justice became an ideal battleground for the deeply felt struggle between the conservative coalition of southern Democrats and Republicans against the northern Democrats over the proper policy outputs of the Supreme Court and the whole place of liberal legislation and executive action in modern America.

But the norms of Congress seem to dictate that attacks on the Court and using the Court for ideological purposes are only permissible under very special circumstances. The Fortas, Haynsworth, Carswell drama seemed to have spent its emotional force by the end of 1971, so that William Rehnquist, whose views approximated very closely to those of Haynsworth and Carswell, survived in part because he was clearly a man of some distinction, an extreme conservative, maybe, but an exceptionally able one. When his opponents failed to uncover examples of ethical irregularities or manifest lapses from accepted judicial standards, they accepted the convention that it is a President's right to delineate as far as he can the ideological composition of the Court. He has the right, in normal circumstances, to pack the Court. If Hugo Black and John Harlan had lived another two years until the summer of 1973, when the Watergate saga had served to sour relations between Congress and President, then Rehnquist, hailing from the Justices Department, might well have failed to be confirmed.

CONGRESS AND THE COURT

The Constitution of the United States is singularly sparing of any clear exposition of what the Founding Fathers expected the judicial system to look like. It left much of the important fleshing out of Article III to the Congress; it did not establish the number of Justices who were to sit on the Court; it explicitly left to Congress the task of defining those classes of cases in which appeals could lie with the Supreme Court; it made no mention of lower federal courts; and it left to the mercy of Congress the provision of money and human assistance for the Court's work. Apart from the positive statement that a small, but significant, class of cases must constitutionally be heard at the outset of litigation by the Supreme Court—its original docket (Article III, s. 2.2)—and the negative provision that the Justices' salaries could not be diminished (Article III, s.1) the Constitution gave birth to a judicial branch like a nearly empty container into which Congress was to pour its own preferences.

The number of Justices of the Supreme Court is settled by statute and convention as nine and has been so since 1870. But it was not always thus. Under the 1789 Judiciary Act, which established the basic framework of the judicial branch for more than a century, there were to be six Justices, who divided their time between hearing appeals in Washington and riding circuit; that is, travelling hundreds of miles through that particular part of the Union designated 'their' circuit and sitting as a member of an intermediate court between the lower district federal courts at one level and the Supreme Court itself at the other. One advantage of this system was that Supreme Court Justices became familiar with local conditions, state laws, regional problems spawning litigation, and so acquired a more vivid understanding of the background to cases coming to the Court; yet, as Gouverneur Morris observed at the time, riding rapidly from one end of the country to the other is not necessarily the best way to study law (Frankfurter and Landis, 1926, p. 17). The Justices themselves regularly bemoaned the necessity of this inconvenient travelling and, as the Union increased in size and population, either the circuits and the ensuing travelling had to be increased or some circuits, together with new judges, had to be created. Until 1869 there was a statutory requirement, under the 1802 Judiciary Act, for a new Justice to be added to the Supreme Court as each new circuit was established following the country's westward expansion. The Court thus grew in size, not because it was felt that six was an inappropriate number for its functions, but because an Act tied the Court's numbers to the number of circuits.

The first addition occurred in 1807 when the accumulated demands of the new states of Kentucky, Tennessee and Ohio were satisfied by the establishment of a seventh circuit and a seventh Justice, who was required, it should be observed, to reside within the circuit. Throughout the first quarter of the nineteenth century, new states were admitted to the Union—Louisiana in 1811, Indiana in 1816, Mississippi in 1817, Illinois in 1818, Alabama in 1819, Maine in 1820 and Missouri in 1821. Congress prevaricated and refused to countenance any radical alteration of the system itself; its response was to settle for more of same, to continue the practice of circuit-riding, and merely to increase the number of circuits and the number of Justices. But even this essentially inadequate response was postponed for several years, since powerful personalities in the Senate and the House of Representatives refused to compromise over the details, and the normal incentives to produce a congressional package—economic gain, patronage opportunities, and so on—were lacking. Politicians were acutely aware of the political consequences of appointments to the Court and during this period of America's history there were powerful forces in several of the states who wanted in any case to diminish federal authority; such people were thus not averse to arguing that the problem of administering federal justice might best be served by limiting the extent to which the federal judicial branch needed to be present in the states. In the earliest days of the Union some of the Justices had not hesitated to express their political views on judicial occasions and had thus made powerful political enemies for themselves. No one was more outspoken against the Jeffersonian Republicans than Samuel Chase, whose public stand on issues of current debate led the House of Representatives to pass eight articles of impeachment against him in March 1804. In January 1805 Chief Justice Marshall, high on the list of future candidates for impeachment proceedings, presided over the trial in the Senate but the Republicans, though enjoying a twenty-five to nine majority over their Federalist opponents, managed to muster a majority on only three counts and the necessary two-thirds majority on none. On no occasion since then has any Justice reached the trial stage and none has appeared in danger. This particular congressional power, very much thought of in the bitterly divided America of the nineteenth century, has now become virtually a dead letter as a means of punishing political and judicial figures; yet the attempt to impeach Richard Nixon is a reminder that it is not yet buried.

The divisions which plagued early American history, and surfaced with Jefferson's presidential victory in 1800 and again during and after the Civil War, sometimes were sufficiently subdued for concerted action to take place. In 1837 the partisan and regional demands of Congressmen were satisfied and the United States was divided into nine circuits, to each of which a Supreme Court Justice was assigned. But this was only a palliative. The burden of circuit-riding, particularly in the new ninth circuit where in 1838 Justice McKinley travelled 10,000 miles through Alabama, Louisiana, Mississippi and Arkansas in the days before the steam engine or the motor car, remained heavy. Congress, however, was itself deeply divided and what the Senate liked the House of Representatives rejected, or what satisfied the politicians of the east antagonised those from the new states in the south and west. The Court consequently fell further behind in its work. Consensus was achieved in 1863, when the number of Justices and circuits was increased to nine; but soon the bitterness felt by Congress towards President Andrew Johnson spilled over in the Court's affairs. In 1866 an Act was passed to provide that no vacancy on the Court should be filled until the number of Associate Justices was reduced to six, so that, when Justice Wayne died in July 1867, the Court was reduced in size to eight. In 1870, Congress turned its attention to numbers again, this time not to spite a President but to spite the Court itself. The eight-man Court had divided along party lines (Chief Justice Salmon Chase was by then seeking to erase his historic links with the Republican Party and forge new ones with the

Democratic Party), invalidating the Legal Tender Act of 1862 and thus making the $450 million of greenbacks effectively valueless (*Hepburn* v. *Griswold*, 1890). A Republican Senate hastily followed President Grant's lead and reinstated the ninth Justice; since Justice Grier had retired, Grant was able to nominate two Justices, loyal Republicans both, and fifteen months after *Hepburn* the constitutionality of paper money, and thus a basic crutch for the nation's economy, was assured (Ratner, 1935; *Knox* v. *Lee*, 1871). The question of numbers did not occur again seriously until 1937; President Roosevelt, chafing at the series of blows struck at his New Deal legislation by a Supreme Court lavish in its use of judicial supremacy to invalidate several laws central to the President's programme, proposed to increase the size of the Court by the addition of an extra Justice for each one over 70 years of age, up to a maximum of fifteen. This proposal ultimately failed. Although there were other factors at work in 1937, the convention that the size of the Court should not be partisanly altered carried some weight. Yet it remains true to this day that Congress could, if it so decided, create additional Justiceships or put into abeyance a Justiceship when it fell vacant.

Associated with the increase in the membership of the Court in the nineteenth century was an increase in the work-load of the individual Justices. This work-load is largely delineated by Congress. The 1789 Act remains the central pillar of the nation's judicial system, for it set out for the first time the structure of the judicial system and the rules affecting the right of appeal to the Supreme Court (Warren, 1923). The United States was divided into districts, at least one of which had to exist in every state, and each district had a federal court with a federal judge. For nearly 100 years appeals from district courts went to circuit courts composed of the Justice responsible for that circuit and district judges. The enormous growth in the economy of the United States and the increasing complexity of an industrialising country expanding through virtually a continent gave rise to a veritable explosion of litigation. The system could not manage and the Supreme Court fell further and further behind in its work. The inflow of cases to the Supreme Court is always primarily conditioned by the quantity of cases in the lower courts. In 1880, 38,045 cases were pending in the district courts and by 1890 the number had risen to 54,194; the Supreme Court experienced a proportionately similar increase, from 1,212 cases on its docket in 1880 to 1,816 by 1890 (Frankfurter and Landis, 1926, p. 60). The backlog of litigation awaiting decision grew longer and longer, so that three years could pass before a suit reached final hearing in the southern district of New York, for example; similar delays occurred at the level of the Supreme Court. Clearly reform was overdue, as it was also overdue in another area. The duty of the Justices to ride circuit and preside over circuit courts had become a dead letter; they worked in Washington from October until May and this left precious little time for holidays, research work and circuit-riding. In any case, Congress had been moving in a somewhat random way towards severing the direct links between the circuit courts and the responsible Supreme Court Justice and had established a circuit in California without a presiding Justice; it had also, in 1869, created separate circuit judges to act in place of the Justices. Here, too, reform was required.

Throughout the 1890s public utterances of senior Justices, admonitions from Attorneys-General and the inescapable logic of necessity slowly pushed Congress towards action. In 1891, the concern for local patronage and personal disagreements were put aside and an Act was passed which did much to tidy up the whole judicial system and limit the inflow of cases to the Supreme Court. This Act established nine full-time intermediate courts of appeal to which the bulk of the litigation spawned by Congress's increased involvement in the economic and social management of the country could be appealed; the most significant issues were still reviewable directly by the Supreme Court from the district courts. The remedy proved decisive for the number of new cases coming before the Court halved within two years and the Court was soon able to reduce its backlog.

Congressional response to overload in the federal judicial system has thus taken two forms. One approach has been structural, creating more circuits and more tiers of courts. This approach has a long history with the establishment of new circuits, the division of districts, the creation of courts to deal with specific areas of federal laws, and with the ever-spiralling provision of manpower. Congress agreed in 1978 to the largest expansion of the federal judiciary in the United States' history, adding 117 district judges to the existing 281 and 35 appeals judges to the existing 62. The increase did not come without much internal argument about the precise allocation and size of so massive an addition to presidential patronage (judges are nominated by the President and confirmed by the Senate) and it needed intense bargaining in the Conference Committees to finalise the geographical location of the new district judgeships. For twenty years now there has also been an argument in Congress over the redrawing of boundaries of the circuit courts; in the 1950s liberals prevented the creation of a consolidated fifth circuit, which would have effectively been nothing more than a deep south circuit; in the 1970s conservatives thwarted attempts to break up the fifth circuit into two parts, each to be added to smaller and more liberal circuits. Political considerations thus still determine much of Congress's action in this field, just as they did a century ago. Despite the structural changes that have taken place, each circuit still has a member of the Supreme Court as its titular head and cases of immediate importance will be heard, when the Court is in recess, by the appropriate Justice in chambers.

The second approach has been to limit the number of cases entitled to be heard by the Court. The most significant reform in this area was the 1925 so-called Judges Act. Although the 1891 Act had eased the Supreme Court's burden considerably, the number of cases coming before the Court began to drift upwards, so that by 1923 nearly 750 appeals and petitions for review, on most of which the Justices were obliged to pronounce, were filed. Following intense lobbying by Howard Taft, at that time Chief Justice, Congress enacted legislation which permitted the Court itself discretionary power over virtually all its docket. Since most cases had already been heard at least twice, in a district court and a court of appeals, the power to choose only the most important cases for full review did not significantly diminish the rights of American citizens and certainly expedited the judicial process. It did not, however, reduce for very long the inexorable increase in people hoping to persuade the Court to hear their cases.

There have, in fact, been several occasions since then on which the work-load of the Court has become a matter of public discussion. In 1937 President Roosevelt rashly intimated that the Court, of whose decisions his New Dealers disapproved so strongly, was behind in dealing with its docket and therefore needed more Justices to help it out. Chief Justice Hughes's counter-attack, both on the substance of the accusation and on the time-consuming consequences of enlargement, made Roosevelt's dissimulation counter-productive. In the late 1950s the issue arose again and was again linked with partisan opposition to some of the Court's output. Henry Hart calculated even then that the Justices barely had enough working hours, let alone rest, to recharge their intellectual batteries as well as perform their functions properly (Hart, 1959-60). Hart's figures did not pass without comment (Arnold, 1959-60), but they contained an important truth within them. Since then the Court's docket has more than doubled.

Others have been much less impressed by the force of statistics, especially William Douglas, the longest-serving Justice in the Court's history. In 1960 he contended with characteristic vigour that 'I do not recall any time in my twenty years of service on the Court when we had more time for research, deliberations, debate and meditation' (Douglas, 1960). In the 1970s, too, he was to challenge the conventional wisdom, essentially on the grounds that the time taken up in hearing oral argument and writing opinions had not increased at all since 1939 but had in fact been significantly reduced. There was still plenty of time, he maintained, to do the work and enjoy 'hiking, which is good for judges as well as others' (Douglas, 1970a, p. 297).

In December 1972 he returned to familiar ground, even referring to the 'vast leisure time we presently have' (*Tidewater Oil Co.* v. *United States et al.*, 1972, at 174). No colleague would accept such an evaluation, but then no colleague worked with the same intense concentration, speed and decisiveness or shared his long years of experience and confident certainties. As Table 2.1 shows, there really has been a massive increase in the cases on the Supreme Court's docket and this must have some effect on the working of the Court.

Table 2.1   *The Supreme Court's Case-Load, 1968-1974 Terms*
(cases disposed of)

		1968	1969	1970	1971	1972	1973	1974
a	Original docket	0	2	7	8	8	4	4
b	Appellate docket	1,288	1,433	1,540	1,628	1,771	1,868	1,877
c	Petitions granted	101	95	101	131	133	166	155
d	c as % of b	7·8	6·6	6·6	8.0	7·6	8·9	8·3
e	Miscellaneous docket	1,829	1,922	1,771	2,009	1,969	2,004	1,966
f	Petitions granted	64	38	83	30	21	17	19
g	f as % of e	3·5	2·0	4·7	1·5	1·1	0·8	1·0
h	Total	3,117	3,357	3,318	3,645	3,748	3,876	3,847
i	Cases remaining on docket	767	793	894	888	892	1,203	821

Source: Harvard Law Review.
Note: In calculating *c, d, f* and *h* cases summarily affirmed, reversed or vacated are counted as instances where petitions for review have not been granted.

Such a growth cannot be explained purely in terms of an expanding and affluent population, although such developments have clearly contributed to the present state of affairs, nor by cultural arguments involving a progressively more litigious streak among American citizens (Grossman and Sarat, 1975). Three more factors have played a major part in this expansion. First, the types of dispute which the Supreme Court has been prepared to consider since the 1950s have widened enormously. The whole field of civil rights has now become amenable to judicial solutions and thus the number of individuals or groups who believe their interests will be served by litigation has increased. Secondly, the Court's own decisions, many of which have interfered with subject areas previously thought to be the exclusive preserve of state governments and elected officials, have generated increased expectations of what can be achieved in the federal courts. Not only has some of this expansion involved the Court in particularly complex and intricate calculations, as has happened since the 1962 decision of *Baker* v. *Carr* made the drawing of constituency boundaries a subject meet for judicial review, but it has also enlarged the category of petitioners able to bring their cases into the federal courts. Nowhere is this more true than in the case of prisoner petitions; it has been calculated that 83 per cent of the Court's 1971 docket was criminal cases so that, had there been no expansion of litigant rights, access to the Court and hopes of success, the Court's case-load might not have increased at all (Casper and Posner, 1974). What is more, new social services help; in 1968, for example, neighbourhood legal services, financed by the Office of Economic Opportunity, processed cases involving nearly 1 million people in a total of half a million cases (Douglas, 1970b, p. 62). Although the powerful economic interests continue to be regular litigants, the law is by no means the sole preserve of the rich. Finally, federal legislation itself, increasingly encroaching on hitherto unregulated areas of social and economic life, gives rise to an ever-expanding number of potentially litigious situations, which the American tradition of employing judicial remedies for political problems encourages.

Warren Burger, the present Chief Justice, had been perturbed by this expansion for some time. And in 1971 the Federal Judicial Center, of which Burger is chairman, set up a committee of seven practising and academic lawyers under the chairmanship of Paul Freund to make a report, with recommendations, on the case-load of the Supreme Court. The Committee concluded in its report of December 1972 as follows:

> The Courts of Appeal have encountered a dramatic rise in their own business, with a proportionate outflow to the Supreme Court; and the task of coping with the discretionary jurisdiction on *certiorari* overhangs all the Court's work ... If trends continue, as there is every reason to believe they will, and if no relief is provided, the function of the Court must necessarily change. In one way or another, placing ever more reliance on an augmented staff, the Court could perhaps manage to administer the docket. But it will be unable adequately to meet its essential responsibilities. Remedial measures comparable in scope to those of 1891 and 1925 are called for over again. (Freund, 1972, pp. 8-9)

The Committee made four major recommendations. The most controversial, and most commented upon, was that a National Court of Appeals be established to screen all petitions for *certiorari* and appeal and pass about 400 of the most 'review-worthy' (*sic*) to the Supreme Court. This suggestion provoked more comment outside Congress than on Capitol Hill and little more has been heard of it, although consideration was given to a new National Court of Appeals by a Commission on Revision of the Federal Court Appellate System under its chairman, Roman Hruska, but Congress had taken no positive action by the time it recessed for the 1978 elections. Several Justices, past and present, went on record in opposition to the idea of a National Court of Appeals and, although there were sitting Justices and academics who accepted the need for reform, even they were not certain that the Freund formulation was the most appropriate answer. If the 400 cases passed on to the Supreme Court are obviously of political and judicial significance, then there is no need for a further Court to pronounce on the obvious; if, however, they are not obvious, then the Supreme Court is being denied control over the very margin where its fundamental responsibilities lie and where imaginative and creative jurisprudence is developed (Ulmer, 1973; Hodder-Williams, 1976).

The other proposals were conceptually quite different. One involved the elimination by statute of certain procedures allowing appeals direct to the Supreme Court from three-judge district courts and in some other instances, mainly from the Interstate Commerce Commission and in anti-trust cases. The third proposal envisaged the creation of a non-judicial body to investigate and report on prisoner complaints. The final recommendation was that the Supreme Court should be granted more staff to assist in the Clerk's office, in the library, and in the Justices' chambers. After a few years legislation was passed which limited some of the instances where direct appeals to the Supreme Court from three-man district courts were permissible and in 1978 the House of Representatives gave its blessing to a Bill which would make the Court's docket almost entirely discretionary. But major changes have not occurred. Congress has continued to exercise its constitutional power warily and judiciously; as is so often the case, innovations run into the dominant fact of congressional life that it is easier, and politically safer, to prevent change than to innovate.

This is not to say that Congress always treats the Court with distant respect. On the contrary, throughout the United States' history there has been tension between the two branches of government, tension which has on occasions flared up into downright hostility (Nagel, 1965). There is likely to be tension between the elected legislators and the unelected Supreme Court whenever the Justices employ their power of judicial review to annul Acts which the legislators, or their close friends in their home states, have passed or to impose upon the states new requirements as a result of reinterpreting the Constitution.

In every Congress a large number of Constitutional Amendments are introduced to limit the Court's powers or to establish tight qualifications for appointments. These moves rarely progress far and are more expressions of individual frustration than serious preliminaries for reform; besides, it does the sponsor little harm in his home state to be able to say that he has introduced an Amendment. Much more common, and politically more sensible, are the attempts to reverse the Court by statutory means, either by redefining those areas where appeals may be taken to the Supreme Court for final adjudication or by redrafting laws to annul an unpopular statutory interpretation. This is not surprising, given the fact that the Court's decisions are, and must necessarily be, so political. While conflict is endemic, it is often dormant, but the potential for crisis is ever present, needing only a spark to blow a normal disagreement into a fundamental row, for the Court can so easily be used as a rhetorical target in ideological controversies raging in the country as a whole, as it did in the 1957-1960 period and again ten years later.

The decision outlawing segregation in state educational systems caused an enormous outcry in the south and the Court's popularity was not advanced by a series of decisions in 1957 which cut back sharply on the states' power to institute loyalty checks before hiring men. State politicians, closely linked as they are through party and personal connections to Congressmen, attempted to use their representatives in Washington to employ Congress's power to reverse the Court's decisions. This involved creating a climate of opinion which challenged the Court's authority and the propriety of its decisions, such as the report issued in August 1958 by the chief justices of thirty-six states doubting whether the United States still enjoyed a government of laws and not men; it also required the introduction of legislation in Congress, some of which was to use the Article III power to limit the range of matters permitted to be appealed and some of which was designed to reverse, through statute, those decisions of the Court based upon statutory interpretation. In the early 1960s the Warren Court decided a series of cases which further antagonised vocal sections of American society, for they outlawed the reading of the Bible and the saying of prayers before morning school, extended the rights of suspected criminals and forced states to redraw their constituency boundaries so that the vast advantage given to small rural constituencies was ended. The response in the 1960s was essentially similar to that in the 1950s (Pritchett, 1961; Murphy, 1964; Murphy and Tananhaus, 1967-8; Schmidhauser and Berg, 1972).

As Table 2.2 shows, Congress has been comparatively active throughout the postwar period in considering measures to curb the Court or cut back on its decisions. For all this activity, however, little

Table 2.2 *Congressional Action on the Supreme Court, 1945-1968:* (Number of roll call votes on Bills aimed at reversing Supreme Court statutory interpretations or aimed at the Court as an institution; the actual number of Bills involved is in parentheses)

	Statutory Reversals	*Institutional Attacks*
79th Congress	6 (2)	1 (1)
80th Congress	8 (2)	0
81st Congress	20 (5)	0
82nd Congress	12 (2)	0
83rd Congress	15 (2)	1 (1)
84th Congress	9 (1)	0
85th Congress	12 (4)	5 (1)
86th Congress	12 (3)	3 (1)
87th Congress	2 (2)	0
88th Congress	3 (2)	8 (2)
89th Congress	3 (1)	9 (3)
90th Congress	9 (2)	5 (1)

Source: Schmidhauser and Berg (1972), p. 144.

of substance actually emerged. In the 1950s only a single Bill passed both houses and the high emotion so evident on Capitol Hill soon died down. The readiness of the Supreme Court itself to backtrack somewhat, as it did in *Barenblatt* v. *United States* (1959), the tendency for Senators, well led and influenced by Lyndon Johnson, to take a less parochial and narrowly partisan view of their responsibilities, and an injection of less conservative members into Congress as a result of the 1958 election, all played their part. In a way, this episode was similar to other historical instances of clashes between Congress and the Court; an innovation from the Justices draws forth a response from the politicians which, in its turn, produces a withdrawal and partial retreat from the Court. The early 1960s saw a similar configuration of political activity; liberal decisions of the Court certainly triggered off a widespread condemnation and became grist to the politicians' mill in 1964, but the dire threats of politicians failed to produce concrete results, apart from a few parts of the Omnibus Crime Control and Safe Streets Act of 1968 and the rejection of Abe Fortas as Johnson's nominee for the Chief Justiceship. The partial retreat of the Court in the 1969 and 1970 Terms may well have assisted in dampening the ire of the Court's opponents.

Congress is also the ultimate provider of funds for the Supreme Court and, as the paymaster, is in a strong position to exercise leverage. For the fiscal year 1978 just over $9 million was appropriated, which is not a great deal when set against the total expenditure of the judiciary budget; the cost of the lower federal courts exceeds $400 million. The power of the purse has not been much used to bring direct pressure on the Court—that would be too crude and too obviously antipathetic to the principle of separation of powers—but it has been employed to indicate diffuse congressional disapproval of the Court's actions. In the second session of the 88th Congress in 1964, both the House of Representatives and the Senate passed the Government Employees Salary Reform Act which raised the salaries of Members of Congress and all federal judges, *except those of the Supreme Court*, by $7,500. The Justices were awarded a mere $4,500 increase. In 1965 Emanuel Celler, the liberal New York chairman of the House Judiciary Committee, introduced a Bill to restore the differential, but the Bill met with a surprisingly well-organised opposition and failed, by 203 votes to 177, to pass. Quite clearly, as the debate indicated, many Congressmen were antagonistic to the Court because of some of its recent decisions, most notably *Reynolds* v. *Sims* (1964), which was to force states to apportion their constituencies equally. And in the 1970s, too, Congress moved slowly to increase the Justices' salaries, indeed, to remunerate the whole federal branch in a generous manner. Warren Burger's hand in persuading the legislature to grant major increases in 1977 enhanced his standing considerably among the judges in the federal system.

It can be seen, then, that Congress not only has the constitutional power to exercise considerable control over the Supreme Court; it also exercises that power. Mainly, this power is employed in a non-partisan manner designed to create a judicial system appropriate for the United States. The 1789 Judiciary Act is the major landmark and section 25, which granted the Court appellate jurisdiction over state court judgements denying federal or constitutional rights, is its most significant legacy. Although the politics of Congress itself and national ideological differences have clearly affected the development of the Supreme Court's position in the American constitutional system, the most partisan and most overtly hostile criticism of the Court has rarely prevailed. The Court is well aware of this constant threat, as are its temporary friends (for support for the Court is linked more to personal judgement of its decisions than abstract philosophies about its role) and each acts within the constraints of Congress's potential power. And, just as Congress can legislate in a way which obstructs the Court's work and hinders the development of its jurisprudence, so the Justices have on occasions attempted to influence Congress into taking action which would assist its work and advance its notion of its own role. This is the final aspect of the interrelationship of the apparently separate powers to which we must turn.

THE JUDICIARY AS POLITICAL INNOVATOR

The principle of the separation of powers does not envisage the judiciary's playing an active role in the formulation of national legislation; nor, indeed, does the philosophy that the courts and their agents should be above the partisan political struggles of law-making. Yet, despite the constitutional barrier and the theoretical objections to judicial involvement in the process of making policy, the Supreme Court, and especially the Chief Justice, have not kept aloof from the public political fray. In its history, members have sought political office as Hughes did in 1916 or have waited in unfulfilled expectation of being called to high places. Justices have also given Presidents the benefit of their advice and friendship and have, on occasions, been given leave of absence from the Court to perform quasi-judicial functions on behalf of the President; such were Jackson's duties at Nuremburg, Roberts's on the Pearl Harbour Commission and Warren's on the Kennedy Assassination Commission. There is, however, nothing systematic about these instances and they do not exemplify attempts by members of the highest court to introduce specific legislative measures into Congress. However, many of the congressional statutes relating to the judicial branch trace their origins to lobbying by the judicial branch itself.

Warren Burger has been noticeably active in taking public stands on legislative matters and in employing his position and status to influence congressional action (Landever, 1971; Miller, 1973). In each year since he became Chief Justice he has presented an annual 'State of the Judiciary' message to the American Bar Association's conference; this is very much more than merely a comment on the state of the nation's judicial system, for it often contains explicit comments on legislators' inaction and it regularly calls for reform. Only a small portion, if any, of this address is primarily related to the Supreme Court's work; it is mostly directed at galvanising the Association's members into pressing legislators, both federal and state, to reform the cumbrous practices of state, as well as federal, court procedures. He is not afraid on these occasions to berate Congress explicitly; in 1975, for instance, he complained that Congress had failed to appropriate sufficient funds either to ensure the successful working of the newly passed Speedy Trial Act or to recruit and retain able lawyers as federal judges in a society where private practice can be so lucrative and in a period during which parsimony towards judicial salaries had prompted more federal judicial resignations for economic reasons in two years than had occurred in the previous thirty-five. These two public concerns of Burger's—reform at the state level and improvement in the number and remuneration of federal judges—have borne fruit.

An Institute for Court Management has been established and its graduates are now active in a large number of state courts; state-federal judicial councils have now been set up in nearly all the states of the Union; the National Center for State Courts was incorporated in 1971 and is active in a number of programmes designed to monitor the activities of the state courts. All these developments owe something, at least, to the constant call for more modern techniques in court management and a more national system of justice espoused by Burger. Increases in the salaries of judges have also been achieved and, after much wrangling and political procrastination, definite steps towards a very large increase in the federal judiciary. Once again, the Chief Justice's efforts in this respect were responsible at the very minimum for the continuing publicity given to the need for such an expansion.

Addressing the American Bar Association is perhaps a normal expectation of a Chief Justice; Earl Warren used to express himself to the American Law Institute. But Burger has played a much more active lobbying role, both in the positive sense of promoting legislation and in the negative sense of attempting to thwart congressional action (*New Republic*, 4 November 1972; *New York Times*, 27 April 1973; Murphy and Pritchett, 1974, pp. 273-5). He will, for example, engage in public debate through press conferences; thus, when the American Civil Liberties Union in April 1976 criticised what it took to be a conservative trend in the Court and complained that it was embarked upon a dangerous and destructive journey designed to dilute the power of the federal judiciary to serve as guardian of federal constitutional rights, Burger promptly defended the Court's action before the press. He will also make direct personal contact with congressional leaders. In September 1978 he asked Strom Thurmond to hold final action on a Bill to reform the bankruptcy laws and contacted its principal sponsor, Dennis DeLoncini; as a result the Bill *was* held up for a week and the final version accepted some, but not all, of Burger's requests. This kind of open lobbying did not endear him to several Congressmen, nor have his public statements such as the February 1976 complaint that the Senate's procrastination over the Judgeships Bill was due entirely to political considerations peculiar to a presidential year.

The only unique feature of Burger's forays into the realm of congressional action is his concern with modernising the state judicial systems. Howard Taft, when he was Chief Justice, was very active in advancing his ideas for judicial reform and he incorporated them into a draft Bill prepared in the Court itself. This Bill was indirectly floor-managed through Congress by a committee consisting of Justices Day, McReynolds and Van Devanter (Swindler, 1972, p. 248). One product of this lobbying was the 1925 Judges Bill which gave the Court so much discretion over its docket. Since that time, the Court has from time to time entered the hustings; Chief Justice Charles Evans Hughes in 1937 sent a letter to Burton Wheeler, chairman of the Senate Judiciary Committee, answering President Roosevelt's adverse comments on the Court point by point; in 1963, Earl Warren spoke out against the burgeoning of states' rights Amendments, which he interpreted as a major attempt to alter the fundamentals of the Constitution; most recently of all, the Justices of the Supreme Court unanimously informed the Senate Judiciary Committee early in 1978 that they favoured congressional action to limit further statutory rights of appeal and to grant the Court virtually complete discretion over its docket. Some progress had been made when the congressional session ended in October. As far as federal judicial matters are concerned, then, the Court, either as a collegiate body or as represented by its Chief, has been openly involved in part of the lengthy process needed in the United States to initiate and pass legislation. This role, it needs to be added, is one provided for by Congress.

In 1922, Congress created, at Taft's insistent prompting, the Judicial Conference of the United States, composed of federal judges representing the eleven circuits under the chairmanship of the Chief Justice. The Conference is intended to keep a running review of the rules of procedure and other court matters and it reports to the Supreme Court as a body; in turn, the Chief Justice has had since 1948 to submit an annual report to Congress. In 1939, following further lobbying from the judicial branch, Congress established the Administrative Office of the United States to take over from the Department of Justice the bureaucratic and executive functions of the Conference. By the end of the 1950s, a regular feature of the Conference reports was a systematic presentation of legislative recommendations. And a convention grew up in Congress that no Bill connected with organisational matters of the federal judiciary would be reported out of the Judiciary Committee until the Conference had commented upon it. Since procedural matters normally have substantive consequences, this tradition effectively granted considerable legislative influence to the Conference and its chairman, the Chief Justice. The Rules of Appellate Procedure and amendments to the civil and criminal rules of procedure, such as were adopted by the Court in December 1967, become operative as though they were law, unless Congress makes a determined effort to countermand them. Thus, through congressional legislation and the establishment, financed from federal funds, of organisations such as the Federal Judicial Center and the Administrative Office, the judicial branch is provided with the authority and the back-up expertise to consider improvements in the judicial system and recommend action. At the head of all these institutions is the Chief Justice (Swindler, 1972; Fish, 1973).

Warren Earl Burger differs from all his predecessors since Taft in his deep and abiding concern for judicial reform and, especially, his readiness to use his position and energies to advance it. In a system such as that of the United States, there can be no equivalent to the British Lord Chancellor, straddling the legislative, executive and judicial branches of government and acting as the integrator and innovator for the whole legal system. Warren Burger has attempted to be an American 'Lord Chancellor' and has done much to revolution-ise the antiquated procedures of the law throughout America; this may well be what history will remember him for. By his own admission, Burger spends at least one-third of his working day on extra-Court activities, monitoring the proposals of the Conference committees, sponsoring and lobbying for institutions to improve the state systems, and liaising closely with the director of the Administra-tive Office of the United States. In examining the Supreme Court, especially under Warren Burger, it is important always to remember that he is Chief Justice, not merely of the Supreme Court, but also of the United States.

3

Decision-making Within the Court

The Constitution and Congress, as has been seen, establish the range of cases which the Supreme Court may hear. Whether it *will* reach the merits of a particular piece of litigation is another matter. As a result of the 1925 Judges Bill, the Court in effect controls its own docket; even in those instances where the law appears to have granted the right of appeal, the Court has found ways of deciding to which cases it will give a full hearing. The first hurdle a litigant needs to overcome, therefore, is to persuade the Court to consider his case at all. The technical device used in more than 90 per cent of cases is the petition for a writ of *certiorari*; or, to translate the legal formula into more homely language, the losing party asks the Court to issue an instruction to the lower court to send the record of the case up to the Supreme Court so that its members can 'be made more certain' about the details. If the Court grants the writ, and thus agrees to consider the merits of the case, the first, and in some ways the most difficult, stage of successful litigation has been safely negotiated.

Having agreed to decide the merits of the case, the Court then settles to its task of adjudicating. The record of the case in the inferior court and briefs from the parties concerned (and briefs, too, from other parties whom the Court recognises as having a stake in the case or possessing special and useful knowledge helpful to them) are sent to the Justices for their perusal before oral argument takes place in the grand Courtroom of the Supreme Court. Soon after this short incursion into public, the Justices decide in the secrecy of the Conference Chamber whether to affirm or reverse the decision of the lower court.

The final stage in the process is for this basic decision on the merits of the case to be justified in an opinion of the Court. This opinion not only establishes which of the litigating parties has won; it also sets out the reasoning and the constitutional principles and precedents behind the decision. The Constitution, as Chief Justice Hughes once observed, is what the Justices say it is; its meaning may well change over time and these shifts are signalled by the arguments used in the Court's opinions. To the individual litigant, the general impact of his particular case is much less important than the fundamental decision to affirm or reverse the lower court's decision; to many thousands of others, however, the case also has relevance as a new principle is often forged and thus becomes applicable in a much wider context. Few Americans cared for Ollie McClung and his café; but many millions were affected by the Court's upholding of the 1964 Civil Rights Act.

REACHING THE COURT

The Supreme Court stands at the apex of the American judicial system. It is indeed the highest court, the court of last resort, for the litigant who loses here has no other court to which he can turn. Decisions of the Court can only be reversed in three ways—by a Constitutional Amendment in those instances where it has interpreted the Constitution, by an Act of Congress in those instances where it has interpreted a federal statute, or by its own resolve to reverse itself. These things do happen, but they do not happen very frequently. Only four decisions have been reversed by Constitutional Amendment; those of *Chisholm* v. *Georgia* (1793) by the Eleventh Amendment, *Dred Scott* v. *Sandford* (1857) by the Fourteenth Amendment, *Pollock* v. *Farmers' Loan and Trust Co.* (1895) by the Sixteenth Amendment and, most recently of all, *Oregon* v. *Mitchell* (1970) by the Twenty-Sixth Amendment. The overruling of statutory interpretation, as the last chapter indicated, also takes place on occasions but is hardly a regular feature of legislative-judicial relations. In more than 150 cases the Court has publicly overruled itself and in many more cases its decisions have so refined, or indeed ignored, precedents that some degree of reversal has in reality taken place. But these are all rare instances; for all practical purposes, what the Supreme Court decides becomes the law for the foreseeable future. It is the court of last resort, beyond which the losing litigant has nowhere else to appeal.

Although the Court may be thought of as the highest court of the land, by no means every legal conflict is entitled to be carried to it for final adjudication. In a federal country like the United States, there are two distinct sets of courts. Each state, responsible as it is for its own constitution and laws covering a wide range of human activities, has its own system of courts. All cases concerned with state law (like burglaries, murders, breaches of contract, and so forth) are tried in the state courts. In most instances it is possible for the party who has lost the case in the court of first instance to appeal to a higher court within the state; and for many crimes it is open to the defeated party to appeal right up to the state's supreme court. Parallel to the states' system of courts is the federal system, designed to hear cases and adjudicate on controversies arising under federal law. At the lowest level, there are ninety-one district courts distributed throughout the country roughly so that at least one district court is to be found in each state and more in the more populous and litigious states. From these courts, except in instances specifically provided for by Congress, appeals are taken to one of the eleven circuit courts of appeal (see generally Richardson and Vines, 1970). The final stage of the appellate process then becomes an appeal to the Supreme Court.

It might seem from this simple description that the two court systems are watertight and that no litigation can pass from one system to the other. But this is not so. Because the United States is governed under a written Constitution, conflicts can arise in states about the meaning and reach of the Constitution, which is, as the Constitution itself makes clear, the supreme law of the land. The Supreme Court has become the final arbiter of the meaning of the Constitution, so that individuals who believe that state laws or the actions of state officials transgress the requirements of the Constitution can ultimately appeal to the highest national court for a definitive judgement on the matter. Clarence Earl Gideon was convinced when he was charged in the circuit court of the fourteenth judicial circuit of Florida with breaking and entering, very much a state matter, that he was entitled to a lawyer under the Constitution. Judge McCrary told him that he was not so entitled, carried out the trial and sentenced Gideon to jail. Gideon appealed, first within the Florida system, and then to the Supreme Court. Such an appeal may only be considered because the issue at stake is a constitutional issue, the plaintiff raised the issue in his state trial, and the Supreme Court is the final judge on the Constitution.

The road to the Supreme Court is likely to be long and also expensive. It is long because the normal processes of the law must be followed and the hierarchical principles of the judiciary clearly followed. It may take more than two years in the lower federal courts, for they are severely overworked and have a long backlog of pending cases, and anything up to five years in the state court system even to reach the Supreme Court. Within the Supreme Court, final decisions are handed down in most cases within a comparatively short period of time and only a few particularly complex cases are held over for more than a year. Occasionally, however, things can move more quickly, for the Court is empowered to reach down to the lower courts within the federal system to expedite a matter of particular importance. The

Steel Seizure Case of 1951 provides a good example of this; the steel companies sought a temporary injunction to restrain the government's control of them in the district court of the district of Columbia and on 30 April 1952 the court issued the preliminary injunction, only for the court of appeals of the district of Columbia to stay the injunction on the same day, pending argument. On 3 May the Supreme Court by-passed the court of appeals' action by bringing the case directly on to its docket; on 12 May it heard oral argument; on 2 June the decision of the Court, confirming the injunction and thus asserting the unconstitutionality of President Truman's nationalisation, was issued. Similarly, the attempt by the Nixon administration to prevent the publication of the Pentagon Papers was foiled by the most rapid consideration of the *New York Times*'s and *Washington Post*'s lawsuits. The urgency is well expressed in Justice Hugo Black's passionate opinion: 'I believe that every moment's continuance of the injunctions against these newspapers amounts to a flagrant, indefensible, and continuing violation of the First Amendment.' But these instances, much-publicised though they may be, are rare. The need to adjudicate on the constitutional status of rival delegations at a convention or the right of a convicted murderer to be hanged or the right of a President to withhold evidence from a grand jury, to take three famous recent examples, are not the normal fare of the Court.

It is not easy, in fact, to state precisely what is the Court's normal fare. The Constitution specifies one set of cases which should have their first chance of judicial resolution before the Supreme Court. Article III, section 2.2, states that 'in all cases affecting ambassadors, other public ministers and consuls, and those in which a state shall be party, the Supreme Court shall have original jurisdiction'. The reality is less simple than this wording might suggest, for the Supreme Court has chosen to interpret the second sentence of that section of the Constitution in such a way that cases involving states, for instance, have first to be considered in a district court. Section 2.2 continues as follows: 'In all the other cases before mentioned the Supreme Court shall have appellate jurisdiction, both as to law and fact, with such exceptions and under such regulations as the Congress shall make.' In many instances to which a state may well be party, Congress has legislated provision for the lower federal courts to make the original judgement and the Supreme Court has tended, as a consequence, to allow the lower courts first chance to untangle the legal and factual complexities. The Court's original jurisdiction is invoked sparingly. Even in so important a matter as a complaint against the motor manufacturers, in which eighteen states alleged a conspiracy to limit the development of equipment designed to control air pollution from motor vehicles, the Court refused to accept original jurisdiction.

Indeed, it is rare for more than two or three cases each Term to bother the Justices; the vast majority of cases thus reach the Supreme Court on appeal from another court.

The Constitution in effect granted to Congress, in the second section of Article III, the power to delimit the Supreme Court's appellate jurisdiction. The American equivalent of the man on the Clapham omnibus may announce with fervour that he will appeal his case all the way to the Supreme Court, but there is a range of legislative barriers and conventions which make such an announcement more symbolic than real. The 1st Congress quickly made use of this power and passed the 1789 Judiciary Act which broadly established the conditions under which cases could be carried to the Supreme Court; since then, most notably in 1891 and 1925, Congress has further refined the regulations governing appeals to the Supreme Court, as was described in the previous chapter. Broadly speaking, there are now two routes by which a litigant can reach the Court. The first route is the appeal route, when a litigant is entitled by statute to appeal directly to the Supreme Court. The appeal is either against the decision of a three-judge district court, as established by congressional law, or against the judgement of a state's highest court where the federal—or constitutional—interest has not prevailed. Thus, a state court decision finding unconstitutional a federal law or finding constitutional a state law claimed to be unconstitutional can be appealed directly to the Supreme Court. But the only state court decisions reviewable by the Supreme Court are the final judgements or decrees by the highest court of a state in which a decision *could* be had. The highest court is usually, but by no means always, the state supreme court. In 1960, the Court reversed the judgement of the police court of Louisville, Kentucky, which imposed two 10-dollar fines on a man named Sam Thompson, or 'Shuffling Sam' as journalists came to call him; the reason why this was possible was that, under Kentucky law, fines under 20 dollars could not be appealed to any higher court in the state, so that Shuffling Sam's lawyer was forced to appeal directly to the Supreme Court, where his conviction was found unconstitutional (*Thompson* v. *Louisville*, 1960). A literal reading of the relevant Act would suggest that the Court was obliged to consider all these appeals on their merits, hear oral argument and issue a full opinion. But this does not in fact occur, and the Court retains discretion even over these cases. The numbers are not in fact particularly large and have averaged just under 300 each Term during the 1970s, but they would occupy a great deal of the Justices' time if they were all granted full review. On average about 15 per cent have 'probable jurisdiction noted', the formal way of indicating acceptance of the case, and this figure seems to have remained fairly constant for the last two decades

(Douglas, 1960, p. 410; Rohde and Spaeth, 1976, p. 119). The remaining 85 per cent are dealt with briefly. A tiny handful are summarily reversed; others are 'vacated and the case remanded' back to the lower court to be decided in the light of a specified Supreme Court decision; yet others are summarily affirmed; the remaining cases, half the total, are dismissed for a variety of singularly uninformative reasons such as 'want of a substantial federal question' or 'want of jurisdiction'. These bland phrases are merely formal expressions of the Court's decision not to grant full review. In effect, therefore, appeals are treated very much like petitions for writs of *certiorari* and the discretion which the Court has actually applied was being recognised by Congress in 1978. Proposals to dispense with the appeals route altogether, except for a few clearly stated types of litigation, made considerable progress through the congressional legislative obstacle course.

In numerical terms, then, the second route must be the most important. This is the *certiorari* route, by which an unsuccessful litigant petitions the Supreme Court to hear his case, even though he has no statutory right of appeal. The 1925 Judges Act, it will be recollected, had given the Court a large discretion in choosing which of the cases to hear. This discretionary power is a very real one and enables the Justices to control not only the volume of litigation on which they must adjudicate—a control which must necessarily be done by some means or another—but also the subject matter of the litigation. There are two points here. First, however much an aggrieved party may feel he ought to have a constitutional right to 'appeal right to the Supreme Court', it would be wholly impracticable for such a right to be granted in a way which required the Court also to hear argument on the appeal. Chief Justice Taft explained to Congress in 1925: 'Litigants have their rights sufficiently protected by a hearing or trial in courts of first instance and by one review in an intermediate appellate Federal Court. The function of the Supreme Court is conceived to be not the remedying of a particular litigant's wrong, but the consideration of cases where decisions involve principles, the application of which is of wide public or governmental interest' (quoted in Schmidhauser, 1960, p. 122). One of the main functions of the Justices is thus to distinguish the issues of general importance from those of parochial and personal concern. Secondly, the precise criteria by which this distinction should be made are not self-evident but are the subjective calculations of the Justices themselves. Although, as we shall see, there is considerable unanimity on a large number of cases not deserving review and some unanimity on a few cases manifestly worthy of review, in that area of doubt where the Court's discretion is crucial there are genuine and major differences of opinion within the Court. The decisions that are made, not surprisingly, sometimes fail to satisfy the outside academic commentator (see especially Harper and Rosenthal, 1950-1; Harper and Etherington, 1951-2), but there is no alternative to some human process, inevitably subjective, sifting the applications down to a manageable size.

To limit the number of *certiorari* petitions that are granted, a series of devices has been developed whereby the Court can refuse to consider the cases because they fail to pass the tests of jurisdiction and justiciability. Article III of the Constitution asserts that the jurisdiction of the Supreme Court is limited, first of all, to cases and controversies. In other words, there must be a concrete dispute between two parties, each of whom is personally involved in the dispute, requiring adjudication. This requirement excludes hypothetical cases, whether presented as a plea to prevent possible future losses, or presented merely as questions to the Court about the constitutionality of hypothetic situations on which no litigation has yet been initiated. George Washington's request in 1792 for the Court's comments on the constitutionality of twenty-nine points he had raised was firmly refused, but this principle does not prevent individual Justices from conferring privately with Presidents and giving them the benefit of their friendship and advice. Fred Vinson was frequently in the White House and Abe Fortas's close relationship with Lyndon Johnson has already been discussed. Indeed, Justices have often been involved, as individuals, in extra-Court activities (Wheeler, 1978). But the principle that there should be a case or a controversy also precludes the Court from taking the initiative in declaring that an Act of Congress exceeds the authority granted to Congress under Article I or a piece of state legislation infringes some provision of the Bill of Rights. It must wait until an individual brings a case into the courts claiming substantive personal damage through some government either imposing an unconstitutional burden on him or depriving him of his constitutional rights. As Robert Jackson observed: 'We have no self starter'; and the Supreme Court may wait not months, but some years, before a genuine dispute finally reaches it for ultimate disposition.

In the second place, a case must be ripe for judicial solution. This involves two things: first of all, there must still be a wrong to be righted, so that the Court will sometimes declare a dispute 'moot' because it is no longer possible to fashion a genuine judicial remedy. Potter Stewart tends to limit the number of issues he would want the Court to consider in part by excluding cases where time has rendered the dispute merely hypothetical. This is no absolute rule; the cases which found that state laws forbidding abortions were unconstitutional (*Doe* v. *Wade*; *Roe* v. *Bolton*, 1973) could never have been decided if the principle of mootness were rigorously adhered to, since, by the time a genuine conclusion would have been reached by the Court, the baby would be born and an abortion irrelevant. Secondly, it is sometimes held that genuine cases may be 'political questions', not amenable to judicial resolution at all. This tactic has both a philosophical and an instrumental basis (*Baker* v. *Carr*, 1962; 'Note', 1969-70; Strum, 1974). The separation of powers may be thought of as a principle enjoining upon the Court a restrained attitude towards matters clearly and explicitly reserved to the political branches. This may be thought of as the 'classicist' view and is only applicable when there is a textually demonstrable constitutional commitment of an issue to a co-ordinate branch of government. Deciding questions involving the recognition of foreign governments, the authority of foreign diplomats, or the validity of treaties fall under this rubric. The philosophical base merges into the instrumental base with the 'prudential' view of political questions; this extends the range of issues coverable by the concept to those cases where adjudication would explicitly denigrate co-ordinate branches of government, or stir up a hornet's nest which would weaken the standing of the Court, or unquestionably be ignored by those to whom a judicial order might be directed. In the 1970s, the Court refused to face the claim that the Vietnam War was unconstitutional since it had not been declared by Congress (*Mora* v. *McNamara*, 1971; *Massachusetts* v. *Laird*, 1972). This was clearly a prudent use of the 'political questions' device to avoid entering a dispute with which, in practical terms, the judicial process could not cope. William Douglas dissented in *Mora* on the fundamentalist grounds that interpretation of constitutional powers was clearly at issue, while Potter Stewart wanted to make it explicit that the constitutionality of the issue was a political question. The remainder of the Court kept silent and dismissed the application for a writ of *certiorari*, though their reasons for doing so were clearly prudential.

The prudential view itself, whether explicit or implicit, merges into the functionalist view which holds that the doctrine of political questions should be applied whenever one of the Court's judicial objectives is thought likely to be adversely affected. This conscious subjectivity means that the 'definition of a political question can be expanded or contracted in accordion-like fashion to meet the exigencies of the time' (Roche, 1955, p. 768). Since the Court's ability to ensure conformity to its judgements depends upon a public willingness to accept its authority and the executive branch's willingness to enforce its edicts, the Court tends to ensure a close relation between its calculation of enforcement problems and the proclamation that a particular conflict constitutes a political question. Those like Frankfurter or Stewart, who believe that the Court should avoid constitutional adjudication whenever possible, are the quickest to employ the political questions doctrine because their perception of judicial objectives is a self-denying one. But such judicial abnegation was no part of Warren's judicial philosophy. In *Powell* v. *McCormack* (1969), he chose to sweep away the prudentialist and functionalist views because of their manifest imprecision and stick to the classicist, and least limiting, view. The argument in the *Powell* case was thus reduced to the question of whether Congress had an absolute right to control its members and thus bar Adam Clayton Powell, the duly elected representative from Harlem, from the House of Representatives. Not finding this absolute right, and mindful that the electorate's votes would be meaningless if Congress could remove unpopular, or even corrupt, members at will, Warren had to find for Powell. The consequences of this decision, however, were that the district court below had to tackle the really problematic issue of relief, of deciding whether Powell was properly denied his seniority rights, in short, of forcing Congress to produce back pay and go back on its earlier policy of exclusion (Weeks, 1971). A more prudent Court might have hidden behind the political questions doctrine and avoided the likelihood of issuing an unenforceable decree.

In limiting its docket, then, the Court will ensure that a case meets the constitutional requirements of being a case or controversy; it will check whether it is amenable to judicial resolution and may shy away from a case either because it presents a question which is thought to belong more properly to another branch of government or because a decision on the merits would in all probability be unenforceable; it will make certain that the case meets jurisdictional requirements in that congressional legislation permits appeals in the particular instance to come to the Supreme Court; and, finally, it will determine that the plaintiffs actually have standing to sue.

To have standing to sue necessitates a genuine, personal interest in the litigation; thus, the constitutionality of an Act can only be tested after it has been applied and can only be tested by an individual who shows that he has been injured by its operation. In Connecticut a law existed in the 1950s which forbade the sale or use of contraceptives and the constitutionality of that law was challenged by a doctor concerned to encourage some of his clients to use contraceptives. But the Court would not face the challenge to the state law's constitutionality because it had not actually been enforced and the appellants had no personalised grievances to air (*Poe* v. *Ullman*, 1961). Linda Brown had been denied access to desegregated schools; Clarence Gideon had been denied a lawyer; Ollie McClung had been arraigned before a federal court. Yet there are some governmental actions which, if the rule of standing were absolute, would be beyond the reach of the ordinary citizen to challenge. In 1923, the Court had decided that it could not entertain taxpayers' suits, that is suits instigated by a taxpayer, on behalf of other taxpayers, claiming that the *use* of their taxes was unconstitutional (*Frothingham* v. *Mellon*, 1923). But in 1968, Earl Warren wrote an opinion which softened the absolute and argued that the requirement for standing was that there should be a logical nexus between the status asserted and the claim sought to be adjudicated (*Flast* v. *Cohen*, 1968). It is not only taxpayers who are assisted by this extension, but other groups who can show a logical nexus between themselves as a specific category and the governmental action they seek to challenge. This is a considerable development, given the fundamental principle of American jurisprudence that lawsuits are adversary proceedings between two individuals personally involved in a controversy. The Burger Court, however, has refrained from expanding the right. In 1972, for instance, it did not permit the Sierra Club, an organisation devoted to preserving the environment, to litigate against the Secretary of the Interior because its members could not show personal injury sustained as a result of the Secretary's action (*Sierra Club* v. *Morton*, 1972).

The personalised nature of the adversary proceedings at the heart of the American legal system, however, merges imperceptibly into group interaction as groups sponsor, and otherwise assist, the litigation of individuals. The tradition of American politics which envisages politics as essentially a process of group accommodation is extended into the judicial process, and increasingly openly. The rules of standing bear witness to that. So, too, does the possibility of instigating a class action. This device permits an individual who has a personalised claim in the courts to bring an action on behalf of 'all others similarly situated' and was introduced to ease the burden of the courts in instances where a myriad succession of individuals would have to litigate to assure themselves of their own rights. Desegregation litigation was largely framed within the context of class action, so that individual blacks could assert and gain rights on behalf of all blacks. The Burger Court, however, has begun to limit the ease with which individuals can successfully assert standing and instigate class actions, partly by stressing the personalised aspect of standing and partly by requiring that the representative of a class incurs the costs of informing all other members of the class about the proposed litigation. There is no simple rule delineating the criteria, but the Court has used its discretion palpably to control the influx of cases on to its docket. The concertina-like use of 'political questions' is now mirrored by the concertina-like requirements for standing; in both instances, the Court had its own very cogent reasons for wishing to limit the number and nature of cases on which it wished to adjudicate and in both instances it was a matter of will rather than law which predicated the conclusion (Yarborough, 1978).

DECIDING TO DECIDE

The control that the Court effectively has over its docket is almost complete and its consequent ability to determine which issues it will adjudicate and which it will ignore provides it with a formidable power. For the significance of this sifting process is that it greatly influences the issue areas in which the Court will formulate national policy and determines, in part, what that policy will actually be. The Court itself offers little illumination on the criteria employed to decide to which cases *certiorari* will be granted or which appeals will be given a full hearing. The Court's Rule 19 states that 'a review on writ of *certiorari* is not a matter of right, but of sound judicial discretion, and will be granted only when there are special and important reasons therefor', but the rule actually provides very inadequate guidelines as to the Justices' conception of special and important reasons. These change as the composition of the Court changes and as new areas of litigation arise and new values begin to command widespread support in the Court and the country.

The formal position is clear enough. All documentation goes initially to the Clerk of the Court's office. Here petitions are divided into two categories—the appellate or paid docket (that is, those for which the petitioner pays the considerable cost of filing and printing the necessary documentation) or the miscellaneous docket, which is made up of petitions filed under the *in forma pauperis* (i.f.p.) statute, a procedure allowing federal courts to grant leave to persons to continue litigation 'in the style of a pauper' without paying expenses once they have testified to an oath of poverty. This practice goes back to 1892, when the costs involved were met from the fees paid by lawyers for their admission to the Supreme Court bar, but since 1964 they have been financed by an appropriation from Congress. One need not be destitute to qualify; one must just show that payment of fees would seriously impair the normal necessities of life. The Clerk's office goes out of its way to stretch the Court's limited requirements if it believes that a petition is serious; a single, ill-spelt application in pencil from a state penitentiary, as with Gideon, may be as carefully processed as the generally required forty copies of printed document-ation. All cases on the appellate docket are immediately circulated in blue folders to each Justice; each case on the miscellaneous docket, now the 5,000 series, is sent to the office of the Chief Clerk, where the relevant documentation is copied so that each Justice can then receive his own individual record of the case in its traditional red folder. Originally merely carbon copies, the so-called 'flimsies', the papers are now Xeroxed, which hastens the distribution but enlarges the bulk of such cases.

The nine Justices meet regularly in the Conference Room to conduct their business, one major part of which is to sift the petitions and decide which to consider in detail. The Chief Justice naturally takes the leading role in this process. Until recently, he would, after discussion with the Clerk of the Court, place on the special or 'dead' list those cases he considered to be unimportant and not worthy of review. A surprisingly high number of cases has normally been treated in this way; in the days of Vinson and Warren more than half the petitions were disposed of in that way and the proportion has since increased; it was then open to any Associate Justice to delete cases from the list if he wished to consider them for review. Recently, however, the procedure has been reversed and now the Chief Justice circulates a 'discuss' list of those cases he considers require Court attention. Apart from the beginning of the Term, when the Conference can last for several days as the accumulated business of the long vacation is dealt with, the Justices meet most Fridays under the chairmanship of the Chief Justice. He will have circulated about a fortnight in advance an agenda, together with the relevant papers for the listed cases; at this stage any Justice can ask for a case to be held over or for further information to be collected. The Chief Justice is very much *primus inter pares*; although he enjoys several prerogatives as Chief Justice in the way of Court patronage, he is nevertheless merely one member of a nine-man collegiate Court and his voice and vote count no more and no less than any of his brethren (Mason, 1968). He gets paid marginally more—$75,000 rather than $72,000—a differential which was half as large before February 1977. But this distinction has always been regarded askance by many people; when a proposal was once made to increase the differentiation between Fred Vinson and the rest of his Court to $5,000, some Congressmen thought it a long step in the wrong direction and left him with a mere $500 more than his colleagues' $35,000. Associate Justices can be equally determined to assert equality; when Hughes sent a message to MacReynolds asking him to hasten to the Conference because he was already late, a sharp reply was sent to remind the Chief Justice that MacReynolds did not work for *him* (quoted in Rehnquist, 1973).

It is, indeed, the independence of the individual Justices which is immediately striking about the Supreme Court. Each Justice has his own suite of rooms, his own secretarial staff, his own personally chosen law clerks to help him out; each petition is considered by each Justice separately and, although there is some intercommunion between Justices, they tend very much to be their own men. They operate, in short, like nine little law firms. It is only at the weekly Conferences and during oral argument that they operate together as a single Court.

Until recently, the precise process leading to the decision to grant a petition for a writ of *certiorari*, although it differed marginally from chamber to chamber, was broadly similar. Until the vast growth in the Supreme Court's docket, most Justices looked at all the petitions filed; Felix Frankfurter, for instance, would take a full load home once a week and leaf through them while lying in bed. This apparently casual treatment of so fundamental a part of the Court's work was buttressed by the work of the Justices' law clerks. These young men (there had only been four female clerks by 1977), usually in their mid-20s, are some of the ablest graduates of America's most distinguished law schools and, in recent years at least, have often had some experience of being a clerk in a lower federal court or in a state supreme court. They would spend a high proportion of their time examining the documentation and checking appropriate Court precedents before writing a brief memorandum summarising the facts of the case and setting out the constitutional or statutory issues involved. With the recent growth of petitions, the Justices have taken on more law clerks so that now each Justice employs three, while the Chief Justice has four. Since more than 100 sets of documentation arrive at the Supreme Court each week, it is no longer practical for a Justice to have a serious look at all the petitions. Early in the Term he will look at a high proportion of them, but as the Term goes on he will have enough confidence in his clerks to leave the initial screening to them and concentrate on the difficult cases and the preparation for the cases on which the Court has decided to consider the merits. With nine sets of chambers working on each case, the chances of a substantial question failing to be filtered out was infinitesimal; if *certiorari* were not granted, it was because the Justices deliberately chose not to do so.

In 1972, however, their process was somewhat altered. Lewis Powell, newly appointed to the Court, felt that his law clerks were too occupied with the routine, although important, business of writing memoranda, and thus could not spend enough time helping him to come to terms with the legal precedents relevant to the Supreme Court's work. He suggested that a pool of law clerks should be established to sift the *certiorari* petitions, each Justice providing his clerks in alternate weeks. Four of his colleagues, the other three Nixon appointees and Kennedy's sole surviving appointee (Byron White), joined the scheme. What then happened was that the petitions for review were divided each week into three batches of about forty and were sent in the first week, for example, to the chambers of the Chief Justice, Justice Blackmun and Justice Powell respectively. In the second week, 120 petitions would be divided up again and sent to the chambers of Justice White, Justice Rehnquist and the Chief Justice, whose four clerks were augmented for this task by the single law clerks assigned to the retired Justices, in the early days of the scheme Tom Clark and Stanley Reed. The memoranda produced by the clerks are somewhat longer than in the other chambers, because the law clerk is writing not only for his own Justice, whom he soon comes to know and understand and who can always summon him for elaboration, but for four others whom he cannot know so well. Justice Stevens, who replaced William Douglas in 1975, has chosen to continue the traditional practice where each chamber does all its work independently. Instead of nine chambers examining each petition individually, in effect only five do so now. While this may have some administrative advantages for the Justices involved in the pool, in that their clerks have more free time to assist with looking up citations and considering opinions (an argument some clerks in the traditional chambers do not accept), there remains the slight disadvantage that each petition is looked upon by fewer eyes. Nevertheless, since it still only requires a single Justice to indicate his wish for a case to go on the discuss list for it to be considered at Conference, the likelihood of a major issue not being discussed at all remains infinitesimal.

By 10 o'clock on most Friday mornings, the nine Justices will have arrived in the Conference Room, complete with two or three little handcarts each full of memoranda, briefs, notebooks, indeed all the information they think will be needed for their taxing day-long session. The Conference Room, which leads out of the Chief Justice's chambers, is simply furnished with a long mahogany table, nine high-backed chairs individually tailored to each Justice's requirements and a portrait of the great Chief Justice John Marshall looking down on its proceedings. The room used to be very much neutral territory; but Warren Burger, in an attempt to stamp his own personality on to the Court, has partially integrated it into his own suite of rooms, installing a desk there and also a secretary. For the Conference itself, however, no assistants, no clerks, no messengers are allowed. Once each Justice has shaken hands with all his colleagues and the great oak doors are closed, the Justices are on their own. If any one of them needs some information, it is the duty of the most recently appointed Justice to open the door and pass the request to one of the messengers waiting outside.

At the beginning of the Term in October the backlog of petitions is so great that the first Conference of the year, dealing with more than 1,000 applications, may take a few days. A quarter of the year's sifting will then have been completed and the weekly Conferences become more manageable. Nevertheless, since time must be set aside for discussion on the cases actually argued before the Court and for agreement on a wide range of subsidiary matters that make up the complete Supreme Court diet, there is no doubt that time is short if every case is given full collegiate treatment. Furthermore, as Table 2.1 (p. 51) indicated, the odds on getting one's cases fully reviewed are singularly daunting. Only 8.3 per cent of the paid docket were granted review in the 1976 Term and a paltry 1.1 per cent of the miscellaneous docket.

It is not as if the requirements are, at first sight, onerous. Only four of the Justices are needed to vote in favour and a writ of *certiorari* will be automatically granted. This was a promise Taft gave to Congress when he was lobbying for the 1925 Bill. For four decades after that a petition might be granted if three Justices felt strongly enough about a case (Westin, 1958, p. 88). More normally a fourth Justice would vote affirmatively merely to please his colleagues or to acknowledge the strength of their views. But in the busier times of today, it does not seem to apply, and, even when the Court was reduced to seven after Hugo Black and John Harlan had stepped down from the Court in 1971, the rule of four remained sacrosanct (*Donaldson* v. *California*, 1971). Four members, of course, are normally only a minority and it is possible for the majority to prevent a full consideration of a case merely by the expedient of voting, at a later Conference, that the writ had been improvidently granted. This happened in 1976, in *Burrell* v. *McCray*; a brief unsigned opinion of the Court announced that, after further reflection, a majority of the Court agreed that the writ had originally been improvidently granted. As Brennan noted in dissent, the rule of four would become a nonsense if this practice became common, since the remaining five would always have a majority to frustrate the principle of the 'Rule of Four'. Indeed, it would; but it is only in exceptional cases (*Burrell* is not unique) that the principle is violated and then only in instances where the Court is deeply divided over its proper role.

Fortunately for the Justices, a very high proportion of the petitions can be easily disposed of, either because they do not meet the Court's own basic requirements or because they are clearly frivolous. In fact only about 30 per cent of cases even reach the discuss list (Brennan, 1973, p. 470). This has always been broadly true. For many prison inmates, appeals and other legal procedures seem to provide a form of occupational therapy. It seems also that even the paid docket has its fair share of litigants who use legal procedures to postpone the inevitable or continue their litigation out of sheer bravado. The bar may sometimes have difficulty in advising clients not to appeal, for they

cannot be quite certain what the Court will do next, while unscrupulous lawyers may also advise appeal for personal financial reasons,
although they know the chances of success are nil. Certainly the costs
of litigating a hopeless case may well be less than the two years of
profits a company falling foul of federal anti-monopoly legislation
would expect to make. Yet the Court refuses to decide a dispute
simply because someone has money enough to hire a lawyer; there
must be a constitutional or statutory point of substance.

In 1937 Chief Justice Hughes estimated that less than half the
appellate docket was of sufficient merit for a Justice to spend his time
considering and a study of the 1950s confirmed these figures
(Tanenhaus *et al.*, 1963). The i.f.p. docket contains a much higher
proportion of trivia and of claims which fall outside the Court's jurisdiction. Many, Justice Frankfurter once wrote, 'are almost unintell-
igible and certainly do not present a clear statement of issues necessary
for an understanding' (*Brown* v. *Allen*, 1953, at 493). When the actor,
John Kornhauser, protested in 1970 that his civil rights had been
violated in his dressing room ('I was just standing there naked,' he
said, 'and they would not arrest me; they *compelled* me to put on my
clothes'), the Court felt his complaint was not serious enough nor of
sufficiently general applicability to concern them. Even those that are
intelligible are often clearly frivolous. Are blacks in fact Indians and
therefore entitled to Indians' exemption from federal income taxes?
Are the federal income tax laws unconstitutional in so far as they do
not provide a deduction for depletion of the human body? Does a ban
on drivers turning right on a red light constitute an unreasonable
burden on interstate commerce? (Brennan, 1973, p. 478.) The testimony of several former Justices, Earl Warren, Tom Clark and Arthur
Goldberg, agrees that a good third-year law student could deal easily
with a very high proportion of the applications for review (Keeffe,
1973, p. 184; Goldberg, 1973, p. 15; Warren, 1973). Certainly there is
a high level of agreement on what is not worth consideration; in the
decade 1947-56, Chief Justices Vinson and Warren dead-listed 53.4 per
cent of all *certiorari* petitions; by 1973 the figure had risen to about 70
per cent (Ulmer, 1971a, p. 439; Brennan, 1973, p. 479). In other
words, slightly less than a third of all cases on the docket actually
occupy any of the Justices' time at Conference. To some observers,
this seems a cavalier practice and grotesquely irresponsible; Henry
Hart in the 1950s felt that the Court was skimping all its duties,
including the detailed perusal of *certiorari* petitions, because of a lack
of time, and Alexander Bickel fifteen years later was reminding liberal
readers of the *New Republic* that somebody's fate hung in the balance
in all the cases appealed and none of them should be regarded as
trivial (Hart, 1959-60; Bickel, 1973). But some of them *should* be

regarded as trivial. Furthermore, as Fred Vinson told the American Bar Association in 1949, 'to remain effective, the Supreme Court must continue to decide only those cases which present questions whose resolutions will have immediate importance far beyond the particular facts and parties involved' (Murphy and Pritchett, 1961, p. 55).

That still leaves a very large number of non-frivolous cases on the docket. Normally, the Court grants between 160 and 180 of these applications, often consolidating a number of cases presenting the same question into a single concern. Some cases are obvious, but they are surprisingly few. Only 9 per cent of petitions in the 1972 Term were unanimously granted and approximately 60 per cent of those actually granted only received four or five votes (Brennan, 1973, p. 481). The Justices are, with notable exceptions like William Douglas in his last years on the Court, remarkably restrained in their readiness to grant petitions. Clearly the number of non-frivolous cases which do not get heard is increasing. In the 1955 Term, according to Harold Burton's papers, 474 petitions were considered for review; in the 1970s the number had risen to about 1,200. Yet, broadly speaking, only slightly more petitions are now granted than twenty years ago, so that the decline in the proportion of petitions granted is very considerable. It may be, of course, that the cases which were considered in the 1940s and early 1950s were intrinsically less substantial than those given full review in the 1970s; certainly there were fewer opinions in fewer cases. And it may also be that a large number of serious cases currently before the Court may relate to areas of the law which have been well ploughed and which a majority of the Justices has no intention of disturbing; denying the appeal then confirms the lower court's judgement and there is no need to spend time on, say, a tactical case designed to procrastinate over school desegregation. Having said this, however, it still remains likely that some cases of substance which might have been considered by the early Warren Court cannot get a hearing before the Burger Court. The constraints of time dictate an upper limit of around 160, the figure accepted by the Freund Committee, and it is logical to conclude that, as long as the Court's docket of non-frivolous cases continues to expand, an increasing number of significant disputes will not receive the Court's full attention.

Whichever period since 1925 is being examined, however, the selection process has always occurred. A growing literature has been devoted to analysing the calculations behind the Court's granting of *certiorari* (Schubert, 1962; Tanenhaus *et al.*, 1963; Hamus, 1967; Ulmer, 1971a; Ulmer *et al.*, 1972). Much of this work suffers from the inevitable weakness of deducing factors from aggregate data over time during which the personnel of the Court changes and from ignorance of individual Justices' perception of the actual issues at stake. Judicial biographies to some extent confirm the broad generalisations that have emerged from the study of the *certiorari* process, but they also add to the complexity of explanation by highlighting the vast range of calculations and values which seem to determine the Court's grant of *certiorari* which needs, after all, only four affirmative votes.

The cue theory of *certiorari* 'maintains that justices of the Supreme Court employ cues as a means of separating those petitions worthy of scrutiny from those that may be discarded without further study' (Tanenhaus *et al.*, 1963, p. 121). The evidence adduced by Tanenhaus and his associates, updated by Ulmer and others, and checked against the increasing tendency for Justices to publicise their dissents from a Court decision to deny *certiorari*, certainly suggest that for several Justices there are certain types of case which trigger a positive response. These issues are not randomly selected or pre-ordained; they follow the conscious decision of Justices and these decisions follow logically from the values of the Justices. In the 1920s, when Pierce Butler, the former railway company lawyer, epitomised the majority's ideological stance, cases against railroads were always taken; Hughes stemmed this tendency; in the 1940s Hugo Black persuaded his colleagues to take federal employees' and liability cases whenever the railway companies *won* in the lower courts. Butler consciously favoured the companies, Black the employees. The controlling values, however, can cover quite different criteria; they can relate, for example, to the subjectively determined importance of the issue, the importance of the parties involved, conceptions of the judicial role itself and the areas in which Justices believe the Court ought, or more often ought not, to be involved. Whether there are clear cues or not, the Justices have to employ some criteria to distinguish between the importance of cases before them and to enunciate, if only implicitly, their own priorities. The selection of cases is thus a matter of great delicacy, in which competing values are not easily reconciled.

A Justice's values are very much more than his own estimation of what the Court *ought* to decide. Conflicts between circuit courts are normally automatically considered, as the Supreme Court's own rules suggest, but there are occasions when the Justices consciously choose to wait a year or two until the particular issue has been agonised over by more judges and the crucial points of difference in constitutional interpretation become clearer. Just as they sometimes like to wait upon the maturing wisdom of their colleagues in the lower courts, they sometimes use the rulings of a respected appeals court judge as a guide to granting *certiorari*. When Judge Edgerton of the district of Columbia court of appeals wrote the majority opinion, *certiorari* was rarely granted (nine times out of sixty-eight), but when he dissented *certiorari* was granted twenty-three times out of thirty-seven and his dissent confirmed by the Court in 80 per cent of the cases (Rosenzweig, 1951, pp. 165-6).

A host of other factors can come into play, many of which are essentially tactical. In the furore which followed the school desegregation cases of 1954 and 1955, the Court carefully avoided passing on the constitutionality of state laws prohibiting inter-racial marriage. By 1967 this emotive issue could be dealt with more calmly and a unanimous Court found such state laws unconstitutional (*Loving* v. *Virginia*, 1967). The flow of appeals can also, in effect, force the Court's hand, especially if the lower courts have decided the issue variably; such was the situation in 1961 when the rash of writs claiming that the constitutionality of the gross malapportionment common in many states of the Union should be judicially determined. The differing responses to this in the lower courts virtually forced the Court to meet the issue head-on (*Baker* v. *Carr*, 1962). On other occasions, the Justices try and control both the timing and the particular facts of the case in an area calling for the Supreme Court's authoritative pronouncement. By 1960, for example, it was clear to most Justices that the principle enunciated in *Betts* v. *Brady*—that states were obliged to provide lawyers for indigents in capital cases, and other 'unspecified' special circumstances—was a shambles; there had been so many special cases pleaded successfully that the time had come to overrule *Betts*. John Harlan was one of the Justices who kept his eye on the prisoner petitions, looking for a suitable case. He passed over several where the offence committed might have provoked a public reaction or where the convicted offenders might stir up public opprobrium; *Gideon* v. *Cochran* provided, quite fortuitously, the perfect vehicle by which *Betts* could be overruled, because the crime was merely one of breaking, entering and stealing and Clarence Gideon was an unexceptionable middle-aged white man. (The case began as *Gideon* v. *Cochran*; by the time the case reached the stage of opinion-writing Wainwright had replaced Cochran as superintendent of penitentiaries.) Similarly, when the Burger Court agreed to hear a case to decide whether death was a constitutionally permissible punishment for rape, they carefully chose *Coker* v. *Georgia*, which concerned a white rapist and his white teenage victim, rather than two cases involving black rapists, also from Georgia. While these tactical considerations relate to calculations on the likely response to particular decisions, other tactical considerations can relate to the internal politics of the Court.

Since the vote to grant or deny an appeal for review is a fairly clear indication of how many of the Justices will vote on the merits (Ulmer, 1971), a policy-oriented Justice will sometimes refrain from voting to grant *certiorari* because he knows that, even if granted, there is a majority against his position and it is better, in his view, that the *status quo* remains as the public position of lower courts rather than the authoritative pronouncement of the Supreme Court (Murphy, 1964; Brennan, 1973). It can also be a sensible tactic to pass over an instance where the facts of the case are likely to have a disproportionate effect on fellow Justices and public response and wait for a more suitable vehicle by which to raise the same constitutional point.

The art of culling the petitions for review—for it is an art rather than a science—grows on a Justice. Earl Warren always used to speak of the 'feel' for deciding whether a petition was worthy of review; William Brennan has used much the same language and John Harlan once told the Bar of the City of New York that frequently 'the question whether a case is "cert-worthy" is more a matter of "feel" than of precisely ascertainable rules' (quoted in Gressman, 1973); every Justice admits that the longer he sits on the Court the easier the sifting process becomes. The reasons for this are many: familiarity teaches what has already been covered and what duplicates existing or past issues for judgement; the passage of time strengthens the values which guide the criteria, the 'cues' indeed, through which decisions are taken; as with any new occupation, repetition simplifies what seemed complex as the functions and responsibilities of the job become clearer to its practitioner. Although the art is learned and becomes easier for the Justices, explaining the form of that art remains a subject of informed speculation. The very lack of unanimity, or even near-unanimity, in the granting of petitions points to immensely varied sets of values, judicial and ideological, which guide the Justices' work. The increasing tendency to publicise dissent from the ultimate decision to grant or to refuse review merely emphasises the difference of opinion between the Justices.

The differences have to be resolved in Conference and the final result is ultimately determined by voting. The Chief Justice presides and normally starts the discussion; thereafter the senior Associate Justice makes his contribution, and so on, down to the latest appointee. Sometimes the verbal involvement of Justices is slight; at others, a major debate generating heat and passion may ensue. When discussion is ended, the voting takes place, the most junior Justice voting first and the Chief Justice last. Hughes was, by all accounts, a masterful chairman; his conduct of the Court, Frankfurter recalled in a metaphor indicating unfamiliarity with musical language, 'was like witnessing Toscanini lead an orchestra' (quoted in Westin, 1958, p. 126), and his respect for Hughes was only increased by his experience of Harlan Stone's management of the Conference, which was singularly less dominant. Stone tended to carry on a running debate with any Justice who expressed views different from his own, so that the Conference not only dramatised the internal disagreement but spilled over into the Saturday following. It was not only Frankfurter who complained about Stone's penchant for a continuing seminar, but it was Frankfurter who came to utilise the opportunities for participating in a seminar to the fullest and often lectured his colleagues on points of constitutional law like the professor he had once been or agonised aloud about his personal dilemmas or personal experiences, especially in cases affecting naturalisation or discrimination against minorities, for Frankfurter never forgot he was a Jew. Hughes has his detractors who claim that he controlled the Court too rigidly. But Hughes was a formidably effective chairman, prodigiously well informed on every case on the agenda as well as potentially relevant precedents, confident and clear in his presentation, and with the demeanour that countenanced only cogent and constructive comment (McElwain, 1949-50). 'One just did not drool or needlessly talk if Hughes was around,' Frankfurter noted in his diary, observing at the same time that Hughes's control did not preclude a thorough consideration of each case (Lash, 1975, p. 275).

It is during the Conferences that the maximum of personal intellectual interaction takes place between the Justices. Although private conversations and attempts at lobbying do take place and memoranda often pass from chamber to chamber, the only regular meeting of the nine Justices is on Fridays in the Conference Room. Lewis Powell had imagined the Court to be a collegial body in which the most characteristic activities would be consultation and deliberation, but he found a court which was a bastion of jealously preserved individualism ('We stay at arm's length,' Byron White told a reporter) and in which a Justice could go through an entire Term without once being in the chambers of the eight other members of the Court. Like the Freund Report, comment has not always been favourable in this respect and the disciples of Felix Frankfurter still hanker after a Court where decision-making processes should resemble the academic seminar and be the product of long intellectual and intra-collegial bargaining; Frankfurter believed that the unanimity of *Brown* was primarily achieved by the amount of time spent discussing the issues and arguing about the appropriate wording of the opinion and the relief granted and he tried unsuccessfully to persuade his colleagues to consider fewer cases in much greater depth. Tradition, the press of work, the former experiences of Justices, all strengthen the intensely individualist traditions of the Court. This is why the Conferences are so significant; here Justices must defend their positions, attempt to convert others to them, resolve their doubts and finally make a public expression by vote of their considered judgement in a case before the Court.

When the decisions have been made, the junior Justice joins the Chief Justice and the Clerk of the Court to draw up the order list summarising the day's decisions. This is soon published and the parties are rapidly informed by the Court's bureaucracy of what the Justices have decided. As a quick perusal of the list will indicate, the subject matter of the Friday Conferences can be very varied, for it is concerned with more than merely whether to grant *certiorari* or not. However, that gate-keeping function is its primary one and to persuade the Court to hear a case is the first, and, in many ways, the most difficult hurdle success-fully cleared. Now the time has come actually to consider the merits.

NON-JUSTICE INVOLVEMENT IN DECISION-MAKING

Justice Brandeis used to say, 'We do our own work'; he thus con-trasted the Supreme Court with the Congress and the White House, both of which employed large numbers of assistants, advisors and other staff, and stressed the personal responsibility of each Justice for all the decisions made collectively by the Court. On the question of responsibility, he was quite correct and would still be correct today. But he was being somewhat ingenuous in suggesting a monastic purity on the part of the Justices when it came to fulfilling this personal responsibility. On a very practical level, the permanent Clerks of the Court take an immense administrative burden off the Justices them-selves and the printers perform miracles of speed and accuracy in the bowels of the building. But this assistance, crucial as it is for the effective functioning of the Court, has little or no impact on the processes by which decisions on substantive issues are taken. Yet the Justices now need considerable assistance to familiarise themselves fully with the documentation on each and every case which is appealed to the Supreme Court. The responsibility for the decision on all these petitions remains the Justices', but the information on which that decision is reached is normally a digest of the complete record provided for them by one of their assistants, the law clerks. Any consideration of the decision-making process within the Supreme Court, therefore, must concern itself with the law clerks.

It was in 1886 that Congress approved the funding of assistants for Justices of the Supreme Court. In the early days, when Justices mostly worked in their own homes, these assistants were as much social props as legal helps; some, indeed, stayed with their Justices for many years, building up strong ties of affection and sympathy. But over time tenure gradually decreased in length and now the norm is twelve months, timed to correspond with the Court's judicial year (Newland, 1960-1). As the work-load of the Justices has increased, the number of law clerks has also increased. In 1977 each Justice had three clerks, except for the Chief Justice who had four; since retired Justices still 'hold office' technically, they can retain office space and a clerk as a government courtesy, as Tom Clark did until his death and Stanley Reed did until he was 92. At the beginning of 1978, only William Douglas of the living ex-Justices retained a presence in the building, Abe Fortas and Arthur Goldberg enjoying prosperous law practices in Washington. Law clerks are widely used throughout the American judicial system, in both federal and state courts. Just as appointments to the staff of Congressmen are eagerly sought after by graduate social scientists, so appointments as law clerks are popular among law graduates, especially among those whose conception of the legal profession goes beyond the means of acquiring wealth. Most prestigious of these appointments are those to the Supreme Court.

There is no universal route to such posts. Each Justice appoints his own according to his own procedures and there are almost as many methods of recruiting as there are Justices. Traditionally, the brightest of the law school graduates from the most distinguished law schools found their way to the Court on the personal recommendation of professors well known to a particular Justice, but now the link is as often a lower federal judge or a state supreme court judge. Indeed, an increasing number of law clerks seem to have had experience of clerking in a lower court and this is unquestionably useful experience for the demanding task of a Supreme Court law clerk. While this may be a trend, it is certainly not the rule. Douglas used to leave selection to three of his former law clerks, who decided between the two nominations from each of the law schools in the western states of the ninth judicial circuit, of which Douglas was the titular head and in whose wildernesses he had built his home and found much of his happiness; Minton always chose one law clerk from his own university, Indiana; Black's practice was quite clear, an Alabaman from an Alabama law school first and an Alabaman from Harvard second, but preferably a tennis player from whatever source; Marshall continues personal links with Yale and Harvard; Stewart recruits by application, references and interview as if for any other post. Most clerks are white and male; Felix Frankfurter appointed the first black in 1948, William Coleman jnr, who later became the chief counsel for the NAACP; William Douglas appointed the first woman in 1944 and only Black and Fortas appointed women in the years between then and 1972, when Douglas appointed his second. Many a clerk has gone on to higher things, in the academic community as might be expected (Professors Freund, Bickel and Reich are merely three of the best known), into politics like Elliot Richardson and Dean Acheson, and indeed Alger Hiss, and even into the judiciary itself, as Byron White,

William Rehnquist and John Paul Stevens, all of whom were law clerks before becoming Justices of the Supreme Court.

Law clerks perform a number of functions, but they remain fundamentally their masters' servants. Some are consulted widely and join with their Justices in preliminary discussions on the Thursday evenings before the weekly Conference; all are involved in summarising the petitions for review so that the Justices can quickly decide which ones need careful scrutiny; most are involved to some extent in the preparation and writing of opinions, whether this be the production of a preliminary draft, detailed criticism of the Justice's draft, or merely checking citations. On one occasion in Conference Douglas demanded to know the weather conditions in upstate Minnesota to see whether there were mitigating circumstances to explain the late filing of a petition and a law clerk had to seek out the Minnesota Weather Bureau to inquire about snowfalls. The work can thus be very varied. It can, however, also become something of a drudgery as month after month of petitions have to be read, frivolous though so many of them are, checked and summarised. It may be good for the *curriculum vitae*, but it is rarely glamorous. Nevertheless, without the law clerks the work of the Supreme Court would overwhelm its members. Douglas may have told one of his clerks that he could do all the work himself, but in 1972 even he had to take on an extra clerk to catch up with the petitions before the October Term began. Earl Warren put it like this: 'Despite what others may say, it's really the law clerks who deal with the cert. petitions.' But that is, in fact, an exaggeration, for the final winnowing is done by the Justice himself, though often after consultation and discussion with his clerks.

The crucial position of the law clerks in the working of the Supreme Court has naturally raised the question of the extent to which they influence the Court's output. Unfavourable estimations of this influence tend to come from conservative quarters, especially when they dislike what the Court is doing. At the height of the McCarthy hearings in the 1950s the Court began to hand down a series of divided decisions widely interpreted as being soft on communists (*Watkins* v. *United States*, 1957; *Yates* v. *United States*, 1957; *Sweezy* v. *New Hampshire*, 1957), and William Brennan, recently nominated by President Eisenhower as an Associate Justice, ran into a hostile hour of questioning from Senator McCarthy implicitly attacking him for softness on communists. Shortly afterwards the Commission on Government Security reported, suggesting that law clerks were a security danger and should become subject to some form of congressional control. Justice Robert Jackson observed the suspicion among some members of the bar at the time that the law clerks constituted a kind of junior court which decided the fate of *certiorari* petitions and noted sardonically that 'this idea of the law clerk's influence gave rise to a lawyer's waggish statement that the Senate no longer need bother about confirmation of Justices but ought to confirm the appointments of law clerks' (Jackson, 1955, p. 20). Joe McCarthy would not have appreciated the quip, nor would the conservative weekly *US News and World Report*, which ran an inspired, but provocative, article based upon the Commission on Government Security's singularly evidence-free report suggesting that the law clerks were the real power behind the judicial thrones and ought to be subject to the security and loyalty checks of most government employees. In December 1957 William Rehnquist drew upon his experience as a law clerk for Robert Jackson and wrote an article broadly in line with the conservatives' view that law clerks could influence their Justices, that their values were more liberal than either the American people's or their own Justices' and, therefore, by implication they were to some extent responsible for the liberal rulings of the Supreme Court (Rehnquist, 1957).

Although the Court weathered the congressional storms of 1958-60, it was not long before conservatives were once more attacking its personnel and, as they saw it, powerful forces behind the scenes. In 1966 conservatives in California discovered that one of Justice Brennan's prospective law clerks was one of the most radical, but able, of the students whose political activities they abhorred. Their horror found journalistic coverage and an article linking radical Court decisions with radical law clerks was actually written into the congressional record. Ultimately, for reasons not wholly unconnected with the liberal Justices' appreciation of the public's opinion of the Court, this particular law clerk was not appointed (Kopkind, 1966). It is natural that the views of the law clerks on matters of political debate may differ from those of the Justice for whom they work since the selection procedure does not seem to be designed to test ideological positions. The tradition that American law schools produce conservative lawyers has had to bow to the consequences of the new behaviouralism in jurisprudence and thus the present-day law clerks are likely to be more activist than their senior professors and even some members of the Court itself. Certainly the law clerks to Burger and Rehnquist during the 1972 Term were no conservatives and broadly shared the views of their fellow law clerks working in other chambers. Despite the political nature of the work and the strong political views held by some of the Justices, there is an unspoken assumption that every effort must be made to retain the image of impartiality and distance from the current political fray. When some law clerks approached their Justices in October 1969 asking for permission to attend the Vietnam moratorium demonstration, they were faced with an almost blanket response that everyone connected with the Court must eschew public stands on sensitive issues (Sarshik, 1972). There is, then, no escaping the point that law clerks do have political views of their own and judicial philosophies which may be at variance with those of their masters and that opportunities exist for these views to enter the process by which disputes reaching the Court are finally disposed of.

Rehnquist's 1957 articles on the subject, which he substantially endorsed during the hearings over his nomination to the Supreme Court, provoked some sharp ripostes. A contemporary of his argued that he had overestimated the liberalism of the clerks, ignored the overwhelmingly legal basis of their training, failed to perceive that the vast majority of cases was just not open to ideological decision-making, underestimated the ability and confidence of the Justices themselves, and forgot that the clerks' duties were mainly the boring routine task of summary and research (Rogers, 1958; Cohen, 1958-9). Rehnquist's reply was confined to three points—that the clerks were more liberal than their masters, that memoranda-writing on *certiorari* petitions does provide a chance for personal prejudices to be expressed, and that the new legal training also inculcated values which happened to be different from his own (Rehnquist, 1958). Rehnquist was not an Ivy League product as most of the other law clerks were at the time and this may have strengthened his philosophical antagonism. In any case, his three points remain valid as indicators of potential influences, but they conveniently ignore the form of relationship which usually develops between Justice and clerk.

There is no pattern common to all chambers. Some clerks are relegated to the unexciting task of sifting through the *certs* and looking up citations; some are more involved with their Justices and even, after consultation, pen the first draft of some less important opinion. But their work is exhausting; they lack secretarial assistance; they take some months to get on top of the routine work involved; they stay for only a year. By February they have probably mastered their job and by July they are gone; in any case, as Rehnquist himself admitted after he had been elevated to the Court, they tend to become more like their boss the longer they stay. Such people can have little opportunity for controlling a Justice's output, especially in those few but famous cases which quite clearly break new ground. Nobody could have persuaded John Harlan to have voted in favour of extending the equal protection clause of the Fourteenth Amendment to redistricting at the local level; nobody could have persuaded Hugo Black that the government had a right to restrain the *New York Times* from publishing parts of the Pentagon Papers. Justices are men of confidence and pride; while occasionally a man like Charles Whittaker may find the responsibility too heavy a burden to carry, even he would want to face his colleagues at the Friday Conferences or meet them in the dining room with the knowledge that his views were his own. The clerks could only wreak their baneful influence if an ideologically co-ordinated trio worked for a Justice who was the pivotal figure in a divided Court as well as a man of weak convictions and unconscientious habits. The possibility of such a constellation of factors is slim indeed. To those who hold conspiratorial views of society, however, such arguments fall on deaf ears. This has been much compounded by a remarkable ignorance of Supreme Court procedures among much of the American legal profession. Justices frequently have to make public statements emphasising that *certiorari* petitions are not divided up among the Justices according to the circuit from which they originate or the nature of the complaint or any other criterion. Tom Clark was once actually asked by several prominent lawyers to intercede on their behalf with his clerks to ensure that their petitions were granted (Clark, 1957, p. 304).

But this does not mean to say that the law clerks exercise no influence at all. Even to be the sounding board for White or Stewart while they discuss the issues before the Court is to play some constructive role in the clarification of judicial minds. It is clear from Harold Burton's papers that his clerks provided a considerable amount of input into his decisional processes, but it is equally clear that, in the last analysis, Burton was his own man. Yet it would be absurd to argue that clerks are merely subordinate factotums whose bright minds and avid researches provide nothing to the end result. When Alexander Bickel carried out the historical research on the Fourteenth Amendment in preparation for the argument in the *Brown* case, he must have influenced Felix Frankfurter's thinking to some extent; writing first drafts, even if in the style of their masters, can often settle the framework within which the opinion will develop and thus influence in a marginal way the development of the law. It is said that Chief Justice Vinson did all his 'writing' with his hands in his pockets, outlining to his clerks generally what he wanted, and then criticising it in parts before making suggestions for revision (Frank, 1958, p. 118). In the 'great' cases or those which particularly interest the Justice, the opportunities open to the law clerks seem small and, in so far as they do exist, probably conducive to a clearer appreciation of possible lines of argument on the Justice's side. In the 'minor' cases, it may well be that at the margin law clerks create the law. While these may seem minor to the Justices and to constitutional lawyers and political scientists, they are not necessarily minor to the parties involved or the interests represented in the litigation. Tax law may excite little enthusiasm inside the Supreme Court; the consequences of its decisions affect many bank balances a great deal.

These are the obvious sources of assistance to the Court. But in making its decision, its members depend very much on the briefs which the parties present. Since the cost of taking a case right to the Supreme Court is so high—even in 1954, the cost of *Brown* v. *Board of Education of Topeka* came to $250,000 for one side alone and that excluded fees which were waived—it is rare indeed for the particular individual named in the suit to be solely responsible for the financing and direction of the case. One group of litigants which clearly needs assistance are those who come to the court *in forma pauperis*; these people, often inmates of some state penitentiary, not only have the normal costs of printing elaborate briefs and records of the case waived, they are also provided with a lawyer. The Supreme Court itself usually appoints a senior figure of the Washington Bar and such an appointment, costly honour though it is, is rarely refused. For the poor litigant, it can often be a decided advantage, for the expertise and facilities available to a partner of a successful eastern law firm are often superior to those provided for state or county attorneys. Clarence Earl Gideon may have been at a disadvantage in the Florida county court; when his case came to be considered by the Supreme Court, he enjoyed a decided advantage (Lewis, 1964).

For other litigants, outside organisations often provide the legal expertise and the financial support. Since the issues involved in so much of the Court's docket have far-reaching implications for American society, it is not surprising that some groups are extremely interested in its proceedings and eager to use the judicial branch to advance their political aims. This is especially true of those who find their causes unsympathetically considered in the executive branch and ignored in Congress; it also applies in particular to those seeking to extend their civil rights rather than their economic advantage, since the Court is peculiarly the guardian of civil rights. Foremost among the groups who have employed litigation as one method of promoting their political demands have been the National Association for the Advancement of Coloured Peoples, the Jehovah's Witnesses and, in recent years, women's rights organisations (Vose, 1958; Barker, 1967; Johnston and Knapp, 1971; Vose, 1972; Getman, 1973; Cook, 1977). Group activity is not limited to celebrated cases on civil rights, though it is very much in evidence there; rather, as Clement Vose has written, 'litigation is a flow of pressure group activity that is old, common, and essential to the judicial review of the most controversial policies of municipal government' (Vose, 1966). Indeed, sometimes the reason for granting *certiorari* is precisely because the groups associated in a case represent important sections of American society. Yet the point needs to be made that the groups who are most regularly involved in litigation either, like the American Civil Liberties Union, are primarily concerned with civil rights or, like the NAACP in the 1950s and

1960s, have failed to advance their cause in the open arena of group politics within the executive and legislative branches of the federal government.

The NAACP, or rather its Legal Defence and Educational Branch, has been perhaps the most active group of all, for obvious reasons. There was a clear strategy leading up to the school segregation cases of 1954 and the cases to be appealed and supported were carefully chosen. Although the NAACP leaders were too few, and the organisation's funds too meagre, to launch a massive and concerted attack on discrimination throughout the southern states, the NAACP was certainly seen by segregationists to be a dangerous threat to their cherished society. Harassment of NAACP supporters and lawyers was common and often vicious; it was sufficiently successful in much of the south to dissuade any individual black from starting the litigation necessary before the NAACP could get involved and thus limited the number of cases or controversies from which the NAACP could choose (Peltason, 1961). Virginia, like other states, attempted to throttle the Association by a variety of legislative means and so prevent it from providing that assistance without which the ordinary black could never have surmounted the formidable barriers against successful litigation in the south. But in 1963 the Supreme Court found that the state's attempts to prevent groups like the NAACP from using the courts was unconstitutional (*NAACP* v. *Button*, 1963).

The involvement of groups on the side of individual litigants is merely a development of the old practice of inviting third parties, whose knowledge and information might be useful to the Court, to provide supplementary briefs as 'friends of the court'. These *amicus curiae* briefs began as genuine assistance to the Justices on a point of law or fact, but they gradually became used by groups whose interests might be advanced by a judicious input into litigation before the Court, so that the *amicus* brief 'is no longer a neutral, amorphous embodiment of justice, but an active embodiment of the interest group struggle' (Krislov, 1962-3, p. 703). As pressure groups became more bureaucratised, so their tactics became more formalised. The NAACP filed its first *amicus* brief in 1915 and other groups followed suit as federal legislation and the growth of regulating agencies affected more and more classes of people. Lawsuits thus began to concern a wide range of groups who showed an interest in the outcome of a specific piece of litigation. Take *Liberty Mutual* v. *Wetzel* (1975), for example; this case potentially affected the finances and profits of many of the largest employers in America, since it concerned the Sex Discrimination Act and the extent to which women had to be treated in precisely the same way as men. Twenty-one major airline companies, who employed more than 100,000 women, filed *amicus* briefs;

the nation's largest private company, American Telephone and Telegraph Co., did likewise; so also did the National Association of Manufacturers, the United States Chamber of Commerce, Westing-house Electric and General Motors. The fundamental significance of the *Bakke* case is well represented by the record number of *amicus* briefs filed, on both sides, to influence the Court's decision.

Third-party involvement is now much greater than it was fifty years ago as a result of a more regulated national economy and greater congressional concern to legislate for rights. Furthermore, the sort of material deemed relevant to the process of judging has also altered. The practice of including sociological and psychological data, insti-gated by Louis Brandeis when he was a leading labour lawyer, is all part of the growing complexity and sophistication of third-party submissions. In time, the Court accepted the relevance of such inform-ation. Footnote 11 of Warren's *Brown* opinion referred to a consider-able body of social science literature as backing for the argument that racial discrimination of itself limited the full development of black children; this non-legal reference, in fact unnecessary to Warren's interpretation of the Constitution, sparked off loud cries of criticism from conservative jurists and politicians alike. But it was part of the Warren Court's growing interest in ascertaining the actual conse-quences of laws, an interest which spilled over in its requests, especially of government, to provide it with data not strictly and narrowly legal. The 'Brandeis brief' thus radically altered the type of material which lawyers could usefully include in their presentations to the Court. The federal government will sometimes voluntarily associate itself with private litigation by filing an *amicus* brief. In 1962, the government's brief presented for *Baker* v. *Carr* carried considerable weight; in 1969, however, its request for a slowing-down in the pace of school desegregation in the south was largely ignored.

The growth of *amicus* briefs in the 1940s presented the Court with certain problems, since many of them were either no more than duplicates of the litigants' briefs or crude attempts to influence the Court by reminding it of the group's numbers and importance. Now, *amicus* briefs can only be filed if both parties to the case agree, or if the Supreme Court itself grants permission. The most appropriate roles for the *amicus* brief are the imaginative presentation of new approaches to the judicial problems facing the Court and the expres-sion of the consequences of different decisions for particular groups of people. The individual's lawyer will not risk novel interpretations of the Constitution, but will prefer to keep his argument as close to existing precedents as he can; the *amicus* brief is the vehicle to suggest creative jurisprudence. The NAACP suggested overruling *Plessy* v. *Ferguson* in 1941, but only persuaded the Court actually to do so in

1954; the line of argument which seems to have predominated in *Regents of the University of California* v. *Bakke* was derived from an *amicus* brief filed in support of Allan Bakke. The second role, which disturbed Hugo Black in the 1940s when it was no more than a show of political muscle, indicates to the Court the sorts of considerations they might have when deciding on the appropriate relief to grant. It is a reminder, if yet another should be needed, that the Court's role is inevitably political and that groups in the United States use the judiciary in order to advance their political interests.

These political considerations are, of course, only one set of factors that weigh with the Justices. As Justices, they are also the most visible and prestigious members of the legal fraternity and they are consequently conscious of their own standing and the current developments in legal thinking among that fraternity. For the Court, it should be remembered, is still a court, and its members judges, however political the consequences of its decisions may be. Thus, another input into the thinking of the Justices derives from the rest of the legal community. It is not only the law clerks who replenish annually the Justices' understanding of current thought in the country's great law schools; articles from the major law journals are read, sometimes as a self-imposed regular requirement, sometimes under the suggestion of clerks or colleagues. These find their way on occasions into the opinion of the Court, and into dissents, buttressing an argument with the weight of scholarly support. It was Brandeis who began this habit in his 1917 dissent in *Adams* v. *Tanner*, and he was, in the 1920s, the chief user of journal articles, not all of which came from the law journals. Others began to follow suit; to academics like Stone such a tendency came naturally; to legal realists like Cardozo, who believed that the meaning of the law was closely intertwined with the current 'facts of life', the development also came easily since they believed that a judge was 'free to draw upon these facts wherever he can find them, if only they are helpful' (Newland, 1959-60, p. 140). Earl Warren cited articles or pamphlets twelve times in the footnotes of his opinion in *Reynolds* v. *Sims*. Articles can also suggest new approaches; both *Gideon* v. *Wainwright* and *Baker* v. *Carr* were probably decided in the way they were because a number of articles had argued that the *status quo* was no longer defensible and that the time had come to reconsider the precedents of *Betts* v. *Brady* and *Colegrove* v. *Green*.

When briefs have been read and perhaps discussions with law clerks have taken place, the time has come for oral argument before the nine Justices. On alternate fortnights, from Monday to Wednesday, the Court sits to hear argument on the cases it has granted full review. At 10 o'clock promptly, the curtains behind the high bench in the velvet curtained Courtroom part and the Justices purposefully enter, as if on to a stage, to take their places on individually tailored chairs, the Chief Justice at the centre, the senior Justice at his right hand, the next senior at his left, and so on. The session lasts for precisely two hours, when, even in the middle of a presentation, the Court adjourns; it foregathers at 1 o'clock after the hour break for lunch (recently extended from half-an-hour, to Hugo Black's grave disquiet) and adjourns again at 3 o'clock. Gone are the days when the Court might sit for a week or more listening to the impassioned pleading of the greatest advocates of their day. As one response to the ever-lengthening backlog of cases in the nineteenth century, oral argument was limited in 1849 to two hours for each side; in the 1960s the norm became a single hour for each side and in some cases only half an hour was permitted. The summary calendar, as this innovation of Earl Warren's was called, then became the norm under Warren Burger and only cases of special importance or complexity are allowed more time. Not only has the time devoted to oral argument been diminished since the dramatic days of a century and a half ago, when the greatest advocates of the age graced the Supreme Court stage, but the quality of the advocacy has also deteriorated. With the possible exception of the morning-coated Solicitor-General, who usually presents the government's case in those disputes in which it is involved, there is no regular Supreme Court Bar composed of advocates regularly and famously employed to argue cases before the Court. The lawyers who come, attracted often by the unique opportunity of actually appearing before the Court, may be astonishingly inexperienced or inarticulate. An advocate may prepare his presentation carefully but, given the shortage of time, it is the Justices who actually dominate the proceedings.

Oral argument is essentially a grand seminar. No sooner has counsel begun to present his case than the Justices interrupt, bombarding him with questions of law and fact, concentrating on the particularly difficult or novel aspects of the case, worrying about the sort of judicial relief that might be appropriate or the probable consequences of affirmation or reversal. To witness such a session is fascinating and illuminating, for the Justices use it not only to clarify their own minds or reinforce positions already reached previously but also to conduct their own advocacy, whether by assisting counsel with helpful comments and warnings or by arguing through him with a colleague. Frequently, as in the *Brown* and *Gideon* cases, the Court directs the attorneys to consider a particular question and oral argument will revolve around that. Although oral argument makes few conversions, it sharpens the focus on the central issue of the controversy (Douglas, 1970, p. 294); an excellent presentation may not win a case, but incompetent handling of the brief may lose it.

The Justices for their part operate in their own special ways. The Chief Justice presides and ensures that the limitations of time are properly kept; it is said that Hughes once cut an unfortunate counsel off in the middle of the word 'if' when his allotted time was up. Some participate eagerly in argument with counsel, overwhelming him with questions and comments. Felix Frankfurter, as might be imagined, was a particularly active participator, once making ninety-three interruptions in two hours (Frank, 1958, p. 104); dominating the time in this way must have been frustrating to counsel and colleagues alike. Others, like William Douglas, seem hardly to participate at all. There is a continual movement of messengers to and from Justices and Justices are not averse to carrying on private conversations during oral argument. Frank Murphy often talked about non-Court matters with his neighbour on the bench, Felix Frankfurter, and at one period lobbied strongly with Frankfurter to intercede on his behalf with Franklin Roosevelt to obtain an ambassadorial post in India (to be followed by the Secretaryship of War) or France, even going to the extent of discussing possible successors (Lash, 1975, pp. 301, 310-11).

Oral argument is the only time when the Justices appear in public while performing their judicial role. Once the time for the attorney appearing in a case is over, the decision-making process reverts once more to the Justices' chambers and the Conference Room. The decision-making process is thus markedly different from that current in British appellate courts. The dependence on written briefs, often provided by groups not themselves actively involved in the litigation, the involvement of law clerks, the overtly political function which litigation performs, and the short and much interrupted excursion into the public domain, are all practices alien to the British courts.

DISPOSITION AND OPINION

The moment has now arrived for the final disposition of the case. At the regular Friday Conference following oral argument, the Chief Justice will open discussion and set out the issues as he sees them, each Justice in order of seniority then making his contribution. The right to initiate deliberations can, especially in the hands of a man like Hughes, give the Chief Justice a distinct advantage, since his preliminary remarks usually establish the agenda for discussion. The other Justices contribute a variable amount to the ensuing debate; sometimes they merely state their preferences to affirm or reverse; sometimes they pass; sometimes, as with Felix Frankfurter, they may embark on a long homily about the constitutional principles involved, though few would copy Frankfurter's example of once reading a whole article out verbatim! (Berry, 1978, p. 130). Some Chief Justices play the part of a strong chairman, limiting discussion and reaching the voting stage rapidly; others prefer to allow much longer and more discursive debate. While the Stone seminar went on interminably, with the converted talking to the differently converted, Douglas would sometimes wander away from the table and relax in a comfortable armchair, as the testy MacReynolds had done twenty years earlier (Lash, 1975, p. 241). When the Chief Justice calls the discussion to a halt, unless any Justice asks for the case to be held over or put down for re-argument—and by convention such requests are normally granted—the Court then votes on how to dispose of the case. As usual, the junior Justice is the first to make his position known and the other Justices follow in order of seniority. The Chief Justice votes last and a bare majority is all that is needed to affirm or reverse the decision of the lower court.

It is not always the case, however, that a Justice's vote represents accurately his personal preferences. The extent of tactical voting should not be entirely ignored. On occasions, of course, a Justice may be genuinely doubtful about the proper course to take and 'pass' when his turn for voting comes or vote to preserve the *status quo*. For the senior Associate Justice and the Chief Justice, however, other considerations come into play. By the time it is their turn to vote, it is usually clear what the result will be and thus they know that their own votes will not materially alter the basic disposition of the case. Hughes would, on these occasions, sometimes add his vote to the majority, even against his personal preferences, in order to give the Court's position greater respectability and thus enhance the illusion of certainty of law which he felt it was one of the Supreme Court's functions to uphold. Certainly, as Table 3.1 shows, Chief Justices have dissented from the majority position less frequently than the average; whether this is because their powers of leadership establish them as the dominant Justice, or whether it is because they often vote to strengthen an existing majority, is not clear. But there is a second reason for such a tactical vote. If the Chief Justice is in the majority, he assigns the writing of the Court's opinion; if he is in the minority, the senior Associate Justice assigns the opinion. Warren Burger by all accounts has followed the practice of his predecessors (Miller, 1973). In both the first abortion cases and in the school busing cases, he seems to have changed his vote in order to be in the majority. In *Swann* v. *Mecklenburg School Board*, he chose to assign the opinion to himself. Perhaps the power of Brennan's original dissent persuaded him that his original instinct to limit busing was wrong; or perhaps he followed the practice of Chief Justice John Marshall, who was not averse to writing the Court's opinion in cases with whose disposition he actually disagreed. Whatever the facts in these particular instances, the possibility for tactical voting is clearly there and the importance of being able to assign the opinion should not be underestimated.

Table 3.1   *Comparative Rates of Dissent at Three-Yearly Intervals, 1949-1976 Terms*

| | | | | | Term | | | | |
	1949	1952	1955	1958	1961	1964	1967	1970	1973
Number of Court opinions	87	104	82	98	84	91	110	106	140
Rate of dissent	137.9	190.4	179.3	193.9	154.8	137.4	128.2	214.2	210.0
Chief Justice's rate of dissent	2.3	17.3	15.9	24.5	16.7	5.5	6.4	17.9	14.3
Average rate of dissent	15.3	21.2	19.9	21.5	17.1	15.3	14.3	23.8	23.4
Highest rate of dissent	34.5	51.9	26.8	38.8	32.1	30.8	29.1	37.7	50.0
Lowest rate of dissent	2.3	5.8	12.2	11.2	4.8	2.2	0.9	16.0	9.3

Note: Because a different number of opinions was handed down in each of the Terms, rates of dissent have been calculated. These represent the number of dissenting votes that would have been cast per 100 opinions in any given Term.

The vote on the merits in Conference is assumed to have decided the basic question facing the Court, whether to affirm or reverse the decision of the lower court. But this is only part of the decision-making process, for the precise grounds on which the decision is justified have still to be spelled out. It is at this stage that the policy-making potential of the Court is seen at its clearest. Each case must represent a genuine conflict between two directly interested parties and the Court's decision at first sight merely decides that particular piece of litigation. In *Gideon* v. *Wainwright*, the Court decided that Clarence Earl Gideon *had* been unconstitutionally denied a lawyer in his trial and so Gideon was then released. But the opinion often—though by no means always—goes further than this; it sets out the fundamental principles and reasoning through which the particular case was resolved and so, by implication if not by direct assertion, sets a precedent for all similar cases. It creates law; it establishes, for instance, the right to a lawyer for all the host of men and women like Clarence Earl Gideon. It is this expression of the general significance of a single, isolated legal conflict which makes Supreme Court opinions so immensely significant and so widely influential.

In Britain, and in the United States before John Marshall set his magisterial seal on the Court, judges of the highest courts write individual opinions for each case. This is no longer the practice of the United States Supreme Court, although occasionally this occurs by chance. In the Pentagon Papers case (*New York Times Co.* v. *New York*, 1971) and in the first of the recent cases grappling with the constitutionality of the death penalty (*Furman* v. *Georgia*, 1972) all nine Justices wrote separate opinions. Marshall believed that several opinions delivered *seriatim* detracted from the majesty and stature of the law and weakened the impact of the Court's decision, and he tried as far as possible to enforce a unanimous acceptance of a single opinion setting out the Court's reasons for its decision. There are occasions when the Court believes a case is so straightforward or the reasons for not reaching the merits require so little explanation that a brief, unsigned opinion appears announcing the judgement of the Court. *Per Curiam* opinions, as they are called, tend to be unanimous, but even these nowadays frequently call forth expressions of dissent. Difficult questions naturally produce divided Courts and it does happen, of course, that there is no majority view of the proper reasons that lie behind a decision which itself has majority support, or indeed of the actual issue before the Court. Indeed, it can happen that there is a majority *against* each of the grounds offered as the basis of an agreed result; in *National Mutual Insurance Co.* v. *Tidewater Transfer Company Inc.* (1949), the case was decided for one party despite the fact that a majority of the Court rejected each individual reason as to why that party should prevail! In such a case, of course, there *is* no Court opinion as such.

The responsibility involved in opinion assignment seems clearly to provide a means by which the Chief Justice—or senior Associate Justice if the Chief Justice is in the minority—can enhance his own policy preferences. The opinion, by articulating the principles upon which the decision rests, also establishes a precedent for future cases of a similar kind. The Conference vote on the merits does not imply in itself anything about the individual Justices' reasons for reversing or affirming the lower court's decision and a particular result is often reached by diverse paths. Precisely which path is going to become the intellectual and precedential support for the new law of the land emerges from the Court's opinion for the majority. Sometimes a case can be the means for enunciating a new, sweeping constitutional principle, sometimes it is merely a vehicle for a narrow differentiation from an earlier precedent. The results as far as the litigants are concerned are the same, but the consequences are very different. Douglas would go through a draft opinion and take out specific facts and legal points quite deliberately in the hope that the opinion would be interpreted broadly and lead to further changes in the law (Lamb, 1976,

p. 64 fn.). It follows, therefore, that a policy-oriented Chief Justice is likely to assign the writing of the opinion to himself (than whom nobody could possibly be closer!) or to a colleague who most nearly shares his preferences. Up to a point, this is indeed what happens (Rohde and Spaeth, 1976). But there are too many other calculations and pressures for this to be anything like an absolute rule.

The Chief Justice is extremely unlikely to act in such a partisan way for long, since there are many other considerations which militate against a sustained policy of ideologically motivated opinion assignments. As the chief administrator of the Court, he is by convention obliged to share out the work of the Court as evenly as practicable. Sometimes this is difficult. Willis van Devanter, for instance, was an exceptionally able and useful critic and participator in Conferences, but he found it difficult to produce opinions of his own and averaged only three opinions a year during his last decade on the Court; Charles Whittaker thirty years later also found the strain of opinion-writing very considerable and tended to write fewer than his colleagues. Further, it is not always easy to distribute the writing of majority opinions evenly and according to personal preferences if one member of the Court is constantly in the minority. The opportunity for Burger to assign an opinion to William Douglas in the 1969-74 Terms was obviously limited; they voted together only 240 times out of 696. Had Douglas not been the senior Associate Justice and thus able to assign the Court's opinion to himself when Burger was in the minority, the position might have become extremely difficult. Not only should the load be evenly shared but there is an expectation that the distribution of important cases should also be fair. The frictions in the Stone Court were not eased by Frank Murphy and Wiley Rutledge believing, almost certainly correctly, that Stone was underassigning the significant decisions to them. Nor were the spiky personal relations between Earl Warren and Felix Frankfurter unconnected with Warren's tendency to assign less cases to Frankfurter.

Precisely how a Chief Justice uses the assigning power depends very much on his own priorities, which may well alter over time. All Chief Justices have chosen to write the Court's opinion in particularly significant cases, as their colleagues expect, for it gives added weight and authority to the Court's pronouncement. Warren's assignment to himself of *Brown* v. *the Board of Education of Topeka*, which outlawed racially segregated state schools, and *Reynolds* v. *Sims*, which asserted the constitutional necessity for states to establish legislative districts of equal population, come immediately to mind. Burger, too, has followed the practice; in both *United States* v. *Swann* and *Nixon*, which forced President Nixon to hand over confidential White House tapes to the special Watergate prosecutor, the importance of the cases effectively required self-assignment. Considerations of this kind lay behind Fred Vinson's change of mind in *Sweatt* v. *Painter* and *McLaurin* v. *Oklahoma State Regents*, two important cases which began the erosion of the 'separate but equal' principle, for he originally assigned the opinion to Hugo Black but later chose to write for the unanimous Court himself. Considerations of a decision's impact will sometimes encourage the Chief Justice to assign the opinion to a particular member of the Court. In the later years of the Warren Court, John Harlan was not infrequently assigned cases which decided in favour of suspects' rights in an attempt to impress upon the observing public that even the leading conservative on the Court approved what would be vulgarly interpreted as a pro-suspect decision. Tom Clark, the Presbyterian lay preacher, was given the case which outlawed the compulsory reading from the Bible at the beginning of the school day in the state educational systems. Stone originally assigned *Smith* v. *Allwright*, the case which found unconstitutional the practice common in the south of excluding blacks from Democratic Party primaries, to Felix Frankfurter. Robert Jackson, admitting the matter was delicate, wrote a brief note to the Chief Justice pointing out that Frankfurter, who in southern eyes was not only a hated liberal easterner but also a Jew presumably sympathetic towards minority groups in general, was probably an inappropriate choice. Jackson, who had mentioned his thoughts to Frankfurter and discussed them with some of the other Justices, suggested that, if possible, the opinion should be assigned to a southerner who had had connections with the Democratic Party (Mason, 1956, p. 614). Stone did precisely that; he reassigned the opinion to Stanley Reed, a white Protestant who had been a Kentucky Democratic Congressman before his appointment. A Chief Justice can also be concerned with his own public extra-Court image and assign opinions to himself only in those cases with which he wants his name to be associated in the public mind. There is some evidence that both Hughes and Warren proclaimed their liberalism, but hid their conservatism by writing most of their opinions in cases in which they were part of the liberal majority (Ulmer, 1970, pp. 64-5).

Some Justices are clearly more conscious than others of the political reaction to the Court's decisions; some feel that such political considerations are entirely inappropriate. When the Court struggled with the school desegregation cases from 1952 to 1955, most of its members were acutely aware of the political angle; Robert Jackson, who had once been Roosevelt's Attorney-General, saw the issue clearly as one of politics and was searching for a legal basis for an essentially political conclusion; the southerners on the Court—Hugo Black, Stanley Reed and Tom Clark—all believed that the precise form the judgement took was of critical importance if it were to be obeyed. The

1955 decision to remit the oversight of desegregation to the local district courts and to frame the requirements to desegregate in the context of 'all deliberate speed' was consciously based on political calculations (Ulmer, 1971; Berry, 1978, pp. 154-61). Since most Justices have been active in politics before nomination to the Court, calculations of this kind are second nature. But some, and Frankfurter was often one, can be determined to ignore the political implications of Court action. In *Pendergast* v. *United States* (1943), the Court's decision freed a Democratic Party political boss; immediately after that, the Court decided against a Republican Party political boss and confirmed his prison sentence. Douglas felt strongly that, as the author of *Pendergast* and an acknowledged Democratic Party stalwart who might actually have presidential ambitions, he should not author the opinion keeping Republican Nucky Johnson inside. Frankfurter became very excited about even considering such things as relevant (Lash, 1975, pp. 178-82), but in this he showed either naïvety or an excess of other-worldliness, because the effectiveness of Supreme Court decisions can hinge on considerations other than the purely legal. All the great Justices have realised this; and most of the greatest Justices have had considerable political experience.

These are essentially extra-Court limitations on a Chief Justice's unfettered use of his assignment power. Just as important are intra-Court considerations. An equal and fairly apportioned number of opinions is one such consideration. Even more important, however, is the Chief Justice's need for his majority to hold. The vote at the Conference after oral argument is a tentative one, not a binding commitment. The initial opinion is the vehicle through which a majority may be enhanced or, as frequently happens, a majority may disintegrate and become a minority. In choosing a colleague to write the Court's opinion, the Chief Justice may sometimes seek a larger majority at the expense of an opinion written closely to his preferences; he may sometimes ask the least-committed to write the opinion to ensure that a slender majority holds; or he may feel that an argument to his liking is more important than a large majority. Consequently there is a tendency to assign the opinion in a closely divided case to the pivotal fifth Justice of the majority but, in cases where there is a larger majority, to a Justice ideologically closer to the assigner; the larger the majority, the greater the freedom of the writer to follow his own preferred courses since the need to hold a majority is far less limiting. Earl Warren's assignment practices support the idea that he consciously discriminated against himself and Hugo Black in 5:4 decisions and favoured the more pivotal Justices in order to keep them in the majority. The indirect evidence on opinion assigning can support all these positions (Abraham, 1968; Ulmer, 1970; McLauchlan,

1972; Rathjan, 1974; Rohde and Spaeth, 1976; Slotnick, 1978).

The Justice to whom the opinion has been assigned must hold his majority. And this involves writing an opinion which will satisfy not only his own personal preferences but also the requirements of others. Thus, a considerable amount of discussion takes place between the Justices; a first draft is printed by the Supreme Court printers in the building's basement and circulated for comment; passages get added or amended by request; references to some cases may be removed and references to others included; analogies are left out and different comparisons introduced; personal visits and a stream of memoranda are all means by which Justices try to persuade their colleagues to remain faithful to their initial vote or to alter their position and join the majority (Mason, 1956; Howard, 1968; Berry, 1978). In Louis Brandeis's private papers is the thirty-fourth printed draft of one of his opinions. Some Justices value the freedom of expressing their own personal views higher than the value of massing the Court; Felix Frankfurter, for instance, was prone to write separate concurring opinions to make public the precise reasoning by which he had reached the same substantive decision as a majority of his colleagues and, in the eyes of some Justices, did the Court a disservice by his unwillingness to give some ground in order to create an opinion which would speak more for the Court as a whole. Harlan Stone, who, like Frankfurter, had been a law professor, was well aware of the problem of personal probity involved. But it became more important to him to write an opinion to which five or six of his fellow Justices would sign their names than to prepare an opinion entirely to his own satisfaction, but which would only corral two or three of his colleagues. This need to compromise, he once wrote to a friend, 'proves that the university professor is the only free man who can develop legal doctrine in his own way and travel the road he chooses in accounting for his conclusions' (Mason, 1956, p. 308). This need to present the opinion of the Court in such a way as to achieve maximum support inevitably leads to some blurring at the edges and on occasions to a confusion as to the basic principles on which the decision rests. This lack of absolute clarity and internally consistent logic in some instances lays the Court open, unsurprisingly, to attack from law professors and others for whom the collegiate nature of opinion-writing is not always fully appreciated.

There is another dimension of opinion-writing which is markedly different from British practice. Although the Court is deciding a case presented to it in an adversary format and judging on the merits of the arguments in the briefs and further articulated orally, the Court's opinion can, and does, go beyond the facts of the case. Thus decision-making can operate rather like a legislative subcommittee, with the

Justices and their law clerks doing their own investigatory work and the Court often outbidding the subscribed briefs and calling, in oral argument, for counsel to go further. New legal data are often incorporated, and they are not subjected to adversary scrutiny. The final argument in the opinion may well be largely self-generated and depend upon sociological and demographic facts which form no part of the record (Lamb, 1976). Harry Blackmun's opinion in *Roe* v. *Wade* is a particularly fine example of this practice. Blackmun spent much of the long summer recess at the Mayo Clinic, Rochester, researching into the facts and figures of abortion and his opinion establishes, in a way not presented by counsel at all, quite distinct constitutional rights for each trimester of a foetus's existence.

Writing the opinion for the Court is no easy matter. At the absolute minimum, four fellow Justices must be persuaded to sign the final draft and any self-respecting Justice would like to carry as many of his brethren with him as possible. Sometimes, it is impossible to muster a majority at all. In 1978 Lewis Powell announced the decision of the Court in the case of the *Regents of the University of California* v. *Bakke* and wrote an opinion; but the opinion was not the Court's opinion because he failed to get his colleagues to sign it. An opinion authored by Stevens for himself, Burger, Stewart and Rehnquist in effect accepted half Powell's argument and a joint opinion of Brennan, Marshall, Blackmun and White accepted the other half. It is rare to find an opinion co-authored as happened in this case; it only occurs if special emphasis wants to be made as, for example, when all nine Justices signed the opinion of *Cooper* v. *Aaron* in 1958 establishing that problems of 'riot and tumult' were no reason for halting the desegregation of schools. An even greater divergence appeared in *Terry* v. *Adams* (1953) where the Court found unconstitutional the exclusion of blacks from the Jaybirds, an all-white association which regularly held its own election some weeks in advance of the Democratic primary regulated by the state in Texas. In Conference, the Court divided 4:4 with Frankfurter passing. Because the Court was evenly divided, the Chief Justice as usual assumed the right to assign the opinion and asked Black to write an opinion for the Court, but Black could not hold Clark and capture Frankfurter's vote and ended up with only Douglas and Burton agreeing that the black had been deprived of his Fifteenth Amendment rights; Frankfurter, typically, authored an opinion of his own; and Tom Clark persuaded the Chief Justice, Jackson and Reed, as a result of his draft opinion, to change their votes and sign his opinion, which was less absolutist than Black's. Ultimately, then, the Jaybirds' cornering of the nomination process was outlawed by eight votes to one, but it was impossible to reach a consensus on the reasons for this nearly unanimous decision.

But the consequences of seeking one, as Brennan found after he had laboured to create a 6:2 opinion in *Baker* v. *Carr* (1962), can often be to write an opinion which appears somewhat confused in its line of argument, imprecise in its intellectual thrust, and perhaps contrary to the main implications of several earlier decisions.

The price a Justice pays for this sort of opinion is twofold. At one level, he lays himself open to attacks from the legal profession, from law professors and practising lawyers, and from the press and even the executive branch when they dislike the substance of the decision itself. Much of this can be accepted in good grace, in the realisation, as Stone wrote, that a professor of law has greater freedom to express his personal views than a Justice. But Justices also have their pride, and criticism, if it touches upon a point of which they are peculiarly conscious, can hurt. Fred Rodell's strictures on Harold Burton hurt the genial Ohioian, but collegial friendship did something to erase the pain, when Hugo Black and William Douglas—both often on the other side of decisions—instantly contacted him to smooth ruffled feelings (Berry, 1978). It is not only outsiders who judge the Justices' output; a weak opinion will fail to hold the votes and provide for the minority an easy target to attack. The majority opinion, usually the product of much internal bargaining, will tend to be blurred at the edges. But dissenters enjoy a greater freedom.

Sometimes the minority will decide among themselves who is to write the dissenting opinion pointing out the errors of the majority's argument. More frequently, however, an individual will write his own personal dissent and hope to secure support for it from some of his colleagues. In these instances, the argument can be much sharper, for they express only the Justice's own convictions rather than the highest common factor within the majority. There is a tendency, however, to overstate the majority opinion, to set up in effect a caricature of the Court's opinion and blast away at that with fine rhetoric, but to the justified indignation of the members of the majority. The tone of dissents is often cause, and effect, of unreconciled personal conflict within the Court and to that extent affects the efficiency of the Court as a collegial institution. Some dissents are echoes of the past, as Felix Frankfurter's increasingly came to be; others, in Hughes's words, are appeals 'to the brooding spirit of the law, to the intelligence of a future day, when a later decision may possibly correct the error into which the dissenting judge believes the Court to have been betrayed' (Hughes, 1928, p. 68); such were Louis Brandeis's and Hugo Black's early dissents and often they became the basis for majority opinions. But dissents, however impassioned and articulate they may be, are to some extent signs of failure. The true test of a judge, Robert Jackson wrote as his days on the Court drew to an end, is his influence in leading, not opposing, his court (Jackson, 1955, p. 19). Chief Justices Taft and Hughes both argued that there should be no dissents unless absolutely necessary, since they weakened the impact of the decision. Indeed, Taft dissented only twenty times during his nine years on the Court and wrote only four dissenting opinions. He would have echoed Judge Learned Hand's view that 'disunity conceals the impact of monolithic solidarity on which the authority of a bench of judges so largely depends' (Hand, 1958, p. 72).

But recent decades have seen a considerable growth in the number of dissenting opinions prepared; indeed, in his last four complete years on the Court William Douglas averaged forty-two, three times the number he penned for the Court and appreciably higher than the fifteen average of the previous four Terms or the eleven of the earlier 1953-6 period. It was during Harlan Fiske Stone's Chief Justiceship that the development began to get under way. He had joined the Court in the days of Howard Taft when the norm was to remain silent except in very special cases, but he had come to chafe under the constraints imposed by this norm, which Hughes also encouraged. When he was elevated to the Chief Justiceship, he permitted, and indeed encouraged by his own actions, the proliferation of opinions. This emphasis on personal intellectual integrity was much appreciated by many Justices after the Second World War and new members joined a Court where dissents were acceptable and tolerated. As the years have passed, Justices seem to have been more and more concerned to publicise their own differences and their own ideological positions. Thomas Jefferson had opposed John Marshall's successful attempts to prevent *seriatim* opinion-writing and institute the tradition of a single Court opinion; by the 1960s, as John Harlan pointed out, the plethora of dissents and concurrences had virtually created Jefferson's ideal, though whether it increased the respect in which the Court was held is a very different matter. Yet we should remember also that the opinion of the Court may well have started out as a powerful dissent. Minds may well be changed and votes altered as opinions are circulated. Robert Jackson once admitted in oral argument to Arthur Goldberg, himself to become an Associate Justice, that he often changed his mind after the circulation of an opinion, adding with singular self-realisation, 'and I am as stubborn as most' (Westin, 1958, p. 124; see also Brennan, 1959, p. 19).

While we know which decisions and which defences of those decisions individual Justices have supported, we do not know why they have acted in that way. Since, in particular, the opinion of the Court is often a compromise between several Justices' ideals, it is not clear that the views expressed in an opinion can be categorically applied even to the writer. Perhaps the increased tendency to write concurring opinions gives greater credence to those who deduce Justices' values from their written opinions. But this tradition of analysis, which is built upon the assumption that the votes of Justices are cast entirely in accordance with a set of issue-oriented values, seems to oversimplify a very complex process (see, especially, Schubert, 1960, 1965).

To think exclusively in terms of policy-oriented Justices would be a mistake. Murphy's definition of a policy-oriented judge ('a Justice who is aware of the impact which judicial decisions can have on public policy, realizes the leeway for discretion which his office permits, and is willing to take advantage of this power and leeway to further particular policy aims') could apply to most Justices (Murphy, 1964, p. 4). It is essentially a question of degree. Although it is of course true that the Court's decisions are political in the sense that they 'authoritatively allocate values' and true that the members of the Court often hold strong subjective views about the merits of particular actions which are the subject of litigation, there is no simple correlation between a Justice's ideological stance and his vote (Becker, 1967; Howard, 1971). Some Justices clearly approximate to the policy-oriented and intensely personal position more closely than others; Wiley Rutledge, for instance, is supposed to have said that he studied the briefs and records 'to determine if possible on which side justice lay. If that was clear, he searched the law for a legitimate means of rendering justice. It was usually possible, he said, to find a route that satisfied both the requirements of the case and sound principles of law' (quoted in Danelski, 1967, p. 75). Stanley Reed and Felix Frankfurter certainly thought of Rutledge in these terms (Lash, 1975, p. 205). Frank Murphy also had tendencies in this direction for he would accept Felix Frankfurter's arguments entirely but refuse to follow his contrary vote, burying his face in his hands as he admitted his indefensible subjectivity (Lash, 1975, p. 299). Statistical evidence certainly suggests that the issue and the nature of the plaintiff were determinative of Murphy's vote (Pritchett, 1954, p. 190). But almost every Justice is aware that he is a member of a court of law and that the role of a Justice involves generally accepted norms and values (James, 1965). For some, interpretation of this role can be self-denying and primary, so that his notion of the judicial role dominates his behaviour to such an extent that he votes in Conference for a course of action which offends his own policy preferences, but matches his sense of judicial duty. Felix Frankfurter was often at pains to make this clear, as his dissent in *West Virginia* v. *Barnette* (1943) makes painfully obvious. When Harold Burton was nominated to the Court by his friend, Harry Truman, he noted in his diary that he was 'to do a thoroughly judicial job and not legislate' (Danelski, 1970,

p. 121). Most Justices would assert that such attitudes guided their behaviour, but it is quite clear that there have genuinely been very different perceptions on the critical factors involved in doing 'a thoroughly judicial job'. This differential perception may have been at the heart of the personal antagonism between Frankfurter on the one hand and Black and Douglas on the other (Grossman, 1963; Lash, 1975). As Chapter 6 indicates, the debate on this aspect of the Court is unlikely to come to a universally accepted conclusion.

Another value which can persuade a Justice to vote against his own views about the right and just solution to a controversy is his belief in the importance of consistency. The idea that the law should be stable, reliable and known, lies at the centre of much jurisprudential thought. As Cardozo put it, 'the labour of judges would be increased almost to the breaking point if every past decision could be reopened in every case, and one could not lay one's own course of bricks on the secure foundation of the courses laid by others who had gone before him' (Cardozo, 1921). Of course, one essence of law is its certainty; otherwise public behaviour would become something of a lottery. Although the Court is ready to overrule precedents much more frequently than the British courts, the presumption of precedential validity remains very strong. When the Court decided in 1944 to reverse a decision handed down nine years previously, and to deny constitutional blessing to the southern practice of denying negroes meaningful participation in the electoral process by permitting the Democratic Party to hold primary elections limited entirely to white voters, Owen Roberts wrote tartly that this reversal put the adjudic-ation of the Supreme Court 'into the same class as a restricted railroad ticket, good for this day and train only' (*Smith* v. *Allwright*, 1944). The same analogy had been used a few years earlier by Stone in a private letter to Frankfurter, in which he complained that some of Chief Justice Hughes's opinions were 'no better than an excursion ticket, good for this day and trip only' (Mason, 1956). A good example of a Justice's concern for stability and continuity is John Paul Stevens's brief concurring opinion in *Runyon* v. *McCrary* (1976) where he stressed the importance of adhering to precedents even when, as in this case, he thought the precedents had been wrongly decided.

Conflicting values certainly complicate explanation. Perhaps even more significant is the realisation derived from studying retired Justices' private papers that in many cases they are genuinely in doubt and change their minds. This is hardly unexpected. As Taft and Vinson implied, the primary role of the Supreme Court is to decide upon matters of general applicability which divide American citizens and are usually not amenable to simple solutions. If they were, the Supreme Court would not have granted full review. Although

Frankfurter's diaries indicate that, in some areas, policy-oriented values were clearly determinant for some Justices, they also indicate the doubts, hesitations and changes of mind in others (Lash, 1975). The Burton papers show many cases, a high proportion of which would normally be considered 'significant', in which even the most activist Justices changed their minds. In the 1945 and 1950 Terms, for instance, Burton changed eleven times to the majority and once away from it, Stanley Reed changed twenty times to the majority and once away, while the 'scores' for William Douglas, Felix Frankfurter and Hugo Black were, respectively, 5:1, 10:4 and 9:4 (Danelski, 1970, p. 139; see also Berry, 1978). There is, then, a 'fluidity of judicial choice' (Howard, 1968), a readiness and tendency to persuade, and be persuaded by, the written and occasionally oral arguments of colleagues. Opinions can garner extra votes, just as they can sometimes lose them, for the issues involved and the appropriate legal arguments to support the Court's decisions are not simple and amenable merely to an automatic assertion of personal policy preferences.

The fact that there is a fluidity of judicial choice suggests that there is room for leadership to be exercised. The obvious person to exercise this leadership is the Chief Justice, since he presides over the Conference and is more fully aware than any of his colleagues of the work in progress and doubts and concerns of the Associate Justices (Mason, 1968). But it is not always the case that leadership is exercised by the Chief Justice, either alone or with another. For a Court to perform its essential function of disposing of its docket efficiently, two types of leadership are probably required as a minimum: task leadership (the ability to delineate the issues facing the Court and to suggest clear solutions for them) and social leadership (the ability to defuse tension within the group and create a degree of harmonious co-operation in performing the group's substantive functions). Danelski has examined the Chief Justiceships of Taft, Hughes and Stone in this light and suggested that in Taft's day the two roles were performed by van Devanter and Taft respectively, in Hughes's day by Hughes himself, and in Stone's day neither role was adequately performed (Danelski, 1974). This is only one way of looking at the distribution of power within the Court, but it provides a focus of some importance. As the biographical studies of past Justices clearly indicate, the process of judging is more than an abstract intellectual exercise indulged in by nine independent and unreflective individuals.

John Marshall's biographer wrote of the great Chief Justice's command of his Court:

> His control . . . was made so easy for the justices that they never resented it; often, perhaps, they did not realize it. The influence

of his strong, deep, clear mind was powerfully aided by his engaging personality. To agree with him was a pleasure ... The sheer magnitude of his views was, in itself, captivating, and his supremely lucid reasoning removed the confusion which more complex and subtle minds would have created in reaching the same conclusion. The elements of his mind and character were such, and were so combined, that it was both hard and unpleasant to differ with him, and both easy and agreeable to follow his lead. (Quoted in Mason, 1974)

Perhaps this analysis is over-fulsome, but the description clearly encapsulates the image of the supreme leader, masterly in both the task and social fields. In the somewhat cloistered environment of the Court, where nine men must work alongside each other in close proximity for many years, the importance of the social aspect of leadership ought not to be underplayed. In the 1940s it was well known among Court-watching circles that personal animosities and rivalries bedevilled the Court; it did not help the smooth running of the Court that Stone made no secret of his belief that the Nuremburg Trials, to which Robert Jackson had been seconded as a judge, were nothing more than a high-grade lynching party and Jackson's unhappiness was compounded by his belief that Hugo Black had lobbied powerfully against Jackson's elevation to the Chief Justiceship when he was away in Nuremburg. The conservatives at this time tended to refer to Black, Douglas and Murphy as 'the Axis', a soubriquet conspicuously lacking in humorous overtones. By contrast, Hughes gained Hugo Black's affection by assigning to the former Klu Klux Klan member a pro-civil rights decision soon after he came on to the Court and Earl Warren, by a shrewd appreciation of the personalities and personal intellectual problems of his fellow Justices, did much to marshal a unanimous Court for both the *Brown* decisions. There can be no doubting that, except in certain classes of cases where the Justices are irrevocably and immovably divided, there is always room for the personal skills of Justices, whether social or intellectual, to gather votes for their own point of view.

Finally, then, an opinion for the Court is hammered out, except on those rare occurrences when, through lack of time for negotiation or through irreconcilable differences of opinion, no single opinion can gain the support of a majority of the Justices. When an opinion is ready, it appears on the agenda of one of the regular Conferences and it is agreed that the case should 'go down'. Until recently, Monday was the day for delivering opinions. The most junior Justice who authored an opinion would start the proceedings, announcing the name of the case, and then presenting the opinion orally; sometimes a

Justice would give a summary, sometimes he would garnish the summary with the most pithy and telling paragraphs of his opinion, sometimes he would read the opinion in its entirety; occasionally, he might extemporise, adding to the written word, a practice which once brought Frankfurter a sharp rebuke from Earl Warren. Much of the Monday could be taken up with the presentation of opinions. This, and the way in which the bunching of opinions tended to exaggerate the superficiality with which the press reported them, persuaded the Court to alter its traditional practice. Both Frankfurter and Douglas, who disagreed on many matters, were at one in their excoriation of the media which, they maintained, oversimplified and trivialised the decisions of the Court (see also Newland, 1964). Now, Monday is no longer the only day for delivering opinions and the ritual of personal presentation is virtually dead. The opinions are now published and distributed as and when they are ready. The litigation has thus run its full course. The Court has decided to consider the case, has studied the briefs and heard oral argument, has made its decision in principle and justified that decision in its opinion. Yet this is not always quite the end of the story, for, as the next chapter shows, an opinion is merely a printed paper and cannot, of itself, enforce anything.

4

Enforcement

The Court may have spoken, whether unanimously or with a divided voice, but words have no force of their own. All that a judicial decision does is to require the appropriate official, sometimes a lower judicial officer, sometimes a governmental appointee, sometimes a state judge or official, sometimes merely private parties like union leaders or company directors, to do, or refrain from doing, something. Normally people obey; but there are degrees of obedience, and it would be naïve to imagine that judgements ensure their own fulfilment. When, for example, the Court handed down its historic and unanimous decisions in *Brown* v. *the Board of Education of Topeka* (1954 and 1955), in which separate educational facilities were deemed inherently unequal and such denial of the equal protection of the laws to black children required remedial action 'with all deliberate speed', it might be imagined that two centuries of segregated schools had come to an end. The decisions, however, did not mean that single-race schools ceased to exist; it did not mean that blacks were admitted to previously all-white schools; it did not mean that integration was close at hand.

The ability of southern school boards to delay integration for fifteen years or more is a stark, and exceptional, instance of the weakness of the Court. It employs no police, no strong armed men, to ensure that its judgements are translated from paper pronouncements into positive action. Power, it has been said, grows out of the barrel of the gun. If so, then the Supreme Court is indeed the least dangerous branch of the United States' political system, for it possesses no guns, only its prestige, some moral authority, hopefully the obedience of the lower courts and, in the extreme, sometimes the goodwill of the President and *his* guns. To those adamantly refuse to comply with the judgements of the Court, there is little that it can of itself do. Outright rejection of Court edicts is rare, although by no means unknown. In most instances the response to a Court decision lies somewhere between the two extremes of instant universal obedience and extended refusal to obey. The lack of visibility as far as many of the Court's decisions are concerned, and sometimes the less than crystal clear opinion itself, will produce a partial and erratic response to the formulation of new constitutional precepts. To have decided a case, then, is not to have made the Union behave in accordance with that decision.

POWERS OF ENFORCEMENT

The simple view of the process of adjudication assumes that the judgement of a court presages immediate action, that obedience is the natural response of those involved in a case. And the simple view, as is usually the case, is not far off the truth. When the Supreme Court decided that Clarence Gideon had been unconstitutionally denied a lawyer in Florida, he was released and tried again with a lawyer paid for by the state. When the Supreme Court decided that Allan Bakke had been improperly denied entry to Davis Medical School, he was granted entry. Although the losers in both these cases had hoped for different results from the litigation, they obeyed the Supreme Court's edicts without outward sign of disapproval or resentment. This is not always the case. For example, in 1966 the Indiana supreme court, faced with an obscenity case involving Henry Miller's *Tropic of Cancer*, expressed its profound distaste for the book but deferred to the Supreme Court's ultimate authority on the constitutional issue with these words: 'Regardless of our personal opinion on this matter both as to the law and the facts, we are bound as judges of this Court, under the oath we took, to follow the Constitution of the United States, as interpreted by the Supreme Court of the United States, and that Court in our opinion has determined the issue in this case' (quoted in Levine and Becker, 1970, p. 561). For all its implied criticism, the Indiana supreme court acknowledged its inferiority in the hierarchy of courts and followed the Supreme Court's lead.

However, obedience may be the norm, but it is not the rule. The publication of an opinion does not ensure that anything occurs to make the principle of the opinion operationalised reality. Intermediaries must translate the judicial fiat into action. Since many cases on which the Court is called upon to adjudicate derive from the state courts (in those instances where a right protected by the Constitution is alleged to have been abridged), the intermediaries for enforcing a decision are often state officials. The normal procedure for the Court in creating an appropriate relief is to remand the case to the court from which it has come, to be reconsidered in a way 'not inconsistent with this opinion', as the usual phraseology puts it. Such solicitude, which may assuage to some extent the ruffled pride of the judge whose decision has been overruled and perhaps help the judicial system to keep running smoothly, clearly also has its disadvantages. If a Supreme Court decision is to effect change, it needs the co-operation of others but this co-operation is particularly hard to achieve when a federal institution reprimands or overrules a state one. The doctrine of states' rights and widespread resentment at Washingtonian influence over local matters is not a dead letter, however much the universal appeal of consumerism and the nationalising of politics may suggest to the contrary.

Two examples, drawn from the 1950s, illustrate in extreme form what can happen. A black called Virgil Hawkins had been trying for five years to get admitted to the Florida Law School when the *Brown* decision was handed down and his own case remanded back to the Florida supreme court to reconsider in the light of *Brown*. A majority of that court, while admitting that the Supreme Court's decision was holding, felt none the less that 'sound judicial discretion' required them to inquire into the effects of integration before instructing the law school to admit Hawkins. The need to maintain order, it was held, excused officials from obeying desegregation decrees issued by the Supreme Court. So Hawkins appealed again and the Supreme Court promptly stated that delay due to a consideration of consequences was constitutionally impermissible. Once again, the Florida supreme court demurred and, in the belief that any integration would foster violence, again exercised what it deemed to be a traditional power of 'the highest court of an independent sovereign state', the exclusive control of the *timing* of issuing a decree. So Hawkins returned to the Supreme Court and the Supreme Court, as part of its policy to limit its own involvement in the extremely heavy flow of desegregation litigation, remanded the case to the district *federal* court. Here Judge Dozier DeVane, a 74-year-old segregationist, presided and procrastinated; the court of appeals for the fifth circuit reprimanded him for his delaying tactics and reluctantly, in June 1958, nine years after Virgil Hawkins had begun his litigation, DeVane issued an order of the most limited kind instructing Florida Law School not to exclude qualified blacks. The bitter tailpiece must record that DeVane found Hawkins unqualified and that, in the autumn of 1958, a black did enter the law school, but he was not Virgil Hawkins (Murphy, 1959; Peltason, 1961).

A more macabre case arose in Georgia where Aubrey Lee Williams, a black sentenced to death for murder, had appealed his conviction and sentence on the grounds of an unconstitutionally impanelled jury. The Supreme Court, relying upon one of its own recent decisions, remanded Williams's appeal back to the Georgia supreme court; Felix Frankfurter authored the brief opinion and noted that the Court 'rejected the assumption that the courts of Georgia would allow this man to go to his death as the result of a conviction secured from a jury which the State admits was unconstitutionally impanelled' (*Williams* v. *Georgia*, 1955). The response from Georgia contradicted Frankfurter's assumption. 'We will not supinely surrender sovereign powers of the State,' the unanimous opinion of the Georgian supreme court thundered, and it went on to read a lecture to the Supreme Court on its reprehensible oversight of the Tenth Amendment and reaffirmed the death penalty. On 30 March 1956 Aubrey Williamns died in the electric chair (Murphy and Pritchett, 1974, pp. 336-9).

Given the United States' federal system of government and the participant culture of white America, the problems of enforcement are seen in a very stark light. Many local judges, members of school boards, electoral commissioners, and sheriffs are elected and are part of the political life of the locality and vulnerable to pressures from the party activists and their constituents at large. They thus have good political motives as well as philosophical ones for ignoring or obstructing Supreme Court decisions. This is especially true in those few, but well-publicised, cases which attract the attention of the ordinary citizenry. It is also true, however, of those judges in the *federal* system who man the district courts. Although these judges are appointed by the President with the advice and consent of the Senate and are not elected, as many state judges are, they do not always represent the political ideology of the Presidents who nominated them. For the most part they must, by law, live in the district to which they are assigned; consequently, the federal judges in the southern states are normally southerners, brought up and educated in the state, sharing in the social and political environment of the state, and subject to the social pressures—and indeed sometimes physical pressures—of the communities in which they live. In addition, the part played by the Presidents in their selection is small, since there has grown up what can loosely be termed a constitutional convention that such appointments fall fairly and squarely within the province of senatorial courtesy. Most of the southern Senators have been gentlemen and conservatives rather than bigoted segregationists, but few were likely, either out of personal predilection or electoral calculation, to offer to the President the names of liberal men eager to break down the racial barriers so long and so determinedly erected in the south. The courts of appeal, which cover a number of states, are not so much subject to the limitations of senatorial courtesy, though no President is likely to make nominations to these important courts without some calculation of political advantage. Thus, the general rule must be that the district courts in the south, and indeed in many other parts of the United States, will be manned by judges sharing the beliefs and prejudices of the articulate political leaders around them, while in the appeals courts more liberal, and nonconforming, judges are likely to be found (Richardson and Vines, 1970).

Federal judges can, and do, frustrate the intention of the Supreme Court in the same ways as state judges. Although federal judges above all judges should take cognisance of the decisions of the Supreme Court, they can on occasions simply ignore them or wilfully misconstrue their real meaning. Less unusual is a skilful use of legal procedures in order to postpone, or even nullify, the effects of the decisions with which they disagree ('Note', 1963-4). There are several techniques by which a judge can avoid reaching the conclusion consistent with Supreme Court precedent. The initial trial proceedings can be extended by various devices, of which the heavy burden of other judicial work may be as genuine as it is convenient; formal inadequacies in the complaint itself, of which the judge is naturally the sole arbiter, or judicial abstention (that is, the principle that federal courts should wait until the state supreme court has spoken authoritatively on the issue), can both be pressed into service to delay matters. There can also be a considerable lapse of time between the conclusion of the trial and the announcement of the judgement; four months is not unusual, and instances of nine or even sixteen months have occurred. At this stage, a finding against the civil right being claimed will be merely the prelude to further litigation in the appellate process. Since the courts of appeal are burdened with an ever increasing number of cases, even the circuits most favourable to civil rights will normally take some time to consider the appeal, for it is not immediately obvious why other conflicts which also affect individual hopes and aspirations should be relegated in importance to all civil rights cases. Finally, there are often opportunities either to delay the relief granted by the court of appeals or to emasculate its order, so that a further barrier is erected to curtail the exercise of declared rights.

By the early 1960s, the appeal courts were aware of the tactics of some of the district judges in their attempts to frustrate the true significance of the *Brown* decision and they began to ignore the customary courtesies by which a higher court allows a lower court to correct its own mistakes. And yet there was still resistance, even in the area of higher education where decisions declaring the unconstitutionality of segregated facilities antedated *Brown*. A classic instance of invoking most of the tactical ploys in the book comes, not altogether surprisingly, from Mississippi. On 31 May 1961 James Meredith filed a complaint against the officials of the University of Mississippi that his application for admission had been blocked solely because of his race. District Judge Mize sat on 12 June for the hearing, just four days before the first summer session began; but the hearing was suddenly adjourned on the grounds that other court business required his attention. Resuming hearings on 11 July, Mize then adjourned the case again for thirty days on the request of the defendants, the University of Mississippi, and reconvened on 10 August, already more than three weeks into the second summer session. Mize then recessed for four days and completed the hearing on 16 August. Although the last date by which students entering the autumn term had to register was 28 August, Mize took almost four months to render a decision, which surprised no one in its denial of Meredith's motion. Meredith now appealed to the court of appeals for the fifth circuit, in which Mississippi is grouped, and his case was heard on 9 January 1962. Three days later the court of appeals affirmed Mize's judgement, but only because the record was so unclear that it was 'impossible to determine whether there were valid non-discriminatory grounds for the University's refusing Meredith's admission'; they suggested that Mize proceed promptly with a trial on the merits of the case and hand down a decision by 15 February, the last day on which Meredith could register for the spring term.

Mize could perhaps have continued his delaying tactics, but pressure was being brought to bear upon him by colleagues in the federal judiciary not to be overtly recalcitrant. His judgement was accordingly ready on 5 February. This, however, dismissed Meredith's complaint that he had been excluded from the University of Mississippi on account of his race. Meredith immediately appealed, but it was not until 25 June that the court of appeals, despite having expedited the case over others of longer standing, was able to hand down its decision. It overruled Mize and drew disapproving attention to his excessively slow processing of the case. But the saga was not yet complete. The court of appeals had overruled Mize and they now had to remand the case back to Mize to dispose of consistent with their own opinion. But Circuit Judge Cameron, who was a firm believer in the propriety of segregation, four times stayed the remand order so that Justice Hugo Black, once a public prosecutor in Birmingham and Senator from Alabama and now the Justice responsible for the fifth circuit, had to invoke his statutory powers and effectuate the remand himself. Mize reluctantly granted Meredith the relief he sought and so, one whole academic year and two sessions after the filing of the initial complaint in an area where the law was well known, he was entitled to enter the University of Mississippi ('Note', 1963-4).

Long-drawn-out judicial struggles of this kind are extremely expensive and part of the southern strategy to nullify the effects of *Brown* was precisely to use the almost inexhaustible coffers of state-financed attorneys to destroy the black opposition by driving it into penury. The new constitutional right to be educated in non-segregated schools grew out of the five specific controversies decided on that famous day in May 1954 and narrow legalists, ignoring the very general arguments in which Warren clothed his specific findings, could maintain that the injunctions applied only to the five school boards involved in the litigations. At any rate, southern leaders acted as if this were possible; they could circumvent the unpalatable logic of the ruling merely by waiting until a black had the courage to run foul of a school board by attempting to enrol his child in an all-white school and then bring a case against the local board. If the district judge found in the black's favour, which was by no means always the case, an appeal would follow. Litigation takes time and money. Few blacks would have the financial support, and the NAACP coffers were by no means over-flowing. Local state judges and federal district judges largely acquiesced in this case-by-case procedure. It was not until December 1968 that the Supreme Court finally gave up its normal procedure of adjudicating cases as individual and separate disputes. It refused to hear oral argument on an appeal from an Alabaman school board against a programme of desegregation drawn up by the fifth circuit court of appeals. Instead, it issued a short, sharp, *per curiam* opinion, dismissing the Alabaman request and overruling the court of appeals as well; the principle of 'all deliberate speed' was categorically laid to rest and all school boards were mandated to desegregate at once (*Alexander* v. *Holmes County Board of Education*, 1969). So, four-teen years *after Brown* school boards had still not obeyed, and federal judges had been unwilling, or unable, to enforce the instructions implicit in the Supreme Court's historic ruling.

The Supreme Court had, of course, made it possible for the south to procrastinate by the very words of its opinion. In 1954 the Court, speaking through Earl Warren, found that 'separate educational facilities are inherently unequal' and that plaintiffs had been 'deprived of the equal protection of the laws guaranteed by the Fourteenth Amendment'. But they did no more than that at the time; on the contrary, they asked counsel for the litigants to return and argue about the appropriate relief to be declared. In May 1955, another unanimous opinion set out the constitutional requirements. The nine Justices had debated this issue at length, both informally and formally in the Conference, and they felt, all but Felix Frankfurter having been politicians of some eminence, that to declare all segregated systems unconstitutional at a stroke might paralyse the whole educational system and evoke extremely widespread hostility and violent dis-obedience (Ulmer, 1971b; Berry, 1978). Their solution was to trust the local authorities and the district judges and to soften the blow by permitting the south to put its own house in order without external interference. 'The cases are remanded to the District Courts', the 1955 opinion ran, 'to take such proceedings and enter such orders and decrees consistent with this opinion as are necessary and proper to admit to public schools on a racially non-discriminatory basis with all deliberate speed the parties to these cases.' Hugo Black, as the only deep southerner on the Court, had favoured this course but this consideration for his fellow southerners did not relieve him of widespread vilification; in later years, he came to believe in the light of history that the phrase 'with all deliberate speed' may have seemed politically tactful at the time but had eventually proved to be a serious miscalculation.

Certainly most people in public life in the south, and this includes judges, were deeply offended by the *Brown* decision. Their estimation of the Supreme Court was not improved by a series of decisions in 1957 in which state laws designed to weed 'security risks' from the public service were found unconstitutional. There were still some public figures who believed, like the judges of the Florida supreme court, that the southern states were 'sovereign states' who had voluntarily given up a small part of their sovereignty to the federal government only for the purposes of national defence and who thus felt strongly that the Supreme Court had impinged improperly on matters of exclusive state concern. In 1958 the Conference of State Chief Justices issued a sharp reprimand to the Justices of the Supreme Court accusing them of usurping state judicial power by confusing their own policy views with the demands of the Constitution. At the same time, in a well-orchestrated attempt to reverse the most distasteful rulings— and the loyalty/security decisions were as detested as was *Brown*— southern Congressmen attempted to limit the jurisdiction of the Court (Pritchett, 1961; Murphy, 1962). This particular ploy failed, partly because the composition of the Congress changed and partly because the Court itself read the storm signals and responded to them by a marginal retreat; but, failure or not, it illustrated the genuine and deeply felt political opposition in the south and conservative quarters elsewhere towards the Court's decisions.

A natural consequence of this was an unwillingness to respect the implications of *Brown*. The programme of massive resistance in Virginia, the passage of state laws making it an offence for school boards to integrate, and the political and police support for those eager to make *Brown* a dead letter, are now well known (Peltason, 1961). It is not surprising, therefore, that there was also an unwillingness to follow the spirit of *Brown* and dismantle the barriers of racial segregation in other public places. The Court extended the *Brown* ruling, which it increasingly saw not only as interring the 'separate but equal' doctrine of *Plessy* v. *Ferguson* but also as establishing a principle of incompatability between separation and equality, through a series of *per curiam* decisions, into other areas. Some southern judges could not see the logic of this, since *Brown* appeared to them to be based on psychological and sociological considerations. In South Carolina, District Judge George Timmerman—who happened to be the state governor's father—twice after 1954 insisted on applying the 'separate but equal' doctrine to segregation on buses, asserting that the school cases had only involved education and not transportation. 'One's education and personality', Timmerman wrote disdainfully, 'is not developed on a city bus.' On another occasion, a lower federal judge remarked: 'The underlying reasons for the rejection of the "separate but equal" doctrine would not appear to be applicable to toilet facilities.' The way in which *Brown* came to be the ruling decision in a wide range of non-educational matters disturbed some academics as well (Kurland, 1970); it thus added further fuel to instincts for non-compliance.

Adamant refusal and direct confrontation with the Court is rare, but not unknown. After the *Brown* decisions, the school board of Little Rock in Arkansas, all-white and all-elected, nevertheless voluntarily drew up a plan for the very gradual integration of the town's white and black schools. Although the NAACP complained that this particular scheme envisaged too slow a process of desegregation, the district court with jurisdiction in that part of Arkansas upheld the scheme as a reasonable one in the circumstances. So, on 4 September 1957, after two years of careful planning, the first nine black children showed up at Central High School, Little Rock, only to find that the Arkansas militia stood between them and the main entrance. It had been called out by Governor Faubus on the grounds that 'there is imminent danger of tumult, riot, and breach of the peace and the doing of violence to persons and property in Pulaski County, Arkansas'. On this September day, however, there were few signs of imminent tumult, merely the militia denying young black children access to the high school and a jeering group of disapproving white adults. The school board immediately petitioned the federal district court for instructions, urging it to grant a delay in the implementation of the desegregation scheme because of Governor Faubus's action. The district judge, however, maintained that the law was the law and ordered the black children to be admitted. The Arkansas militia remained to bar their entry. The district judge then issued an injunction against Faubus, General Clinger, the Adjutant-General of the State of Arkansas and Lieutenant-Colonel Marion E. Johnson of the Arkansas National Guard, their agents and subordinates, commanding them to cease their obstruction, pointing out that as a matter of fact there had been no violence. Faubus had originally denied that the district court even had jurisdiction over 'the sovereign state of Arkansas' and had walked out of the hearing which preceded the injunction. However, with the threat of being cited for contempt of court, he grudgingly obeyed the court's instructions, though still protesting they were invalid, and withdrew the militia on 20 September.

The school board planned to admit the black children three days later, but early that morning a large, noisy, disorderly and far from good-tempered crowd of whites had gathered by the main gate to Central High School. Among its leaders was a man well known to be a close friend of Faubus. The black children were sneaked into the back of the school, but by now the police were losing control of the mob and the children were sent home. That evening President Eisenhower issued a Proclamation: 'Whereas certain persons in the state of Arkansas . . . have wilfully obstructed the enforcement of orders of the United States District Court . . . I, Dwight D. Eisenhower, President of the United States . . . do command all persons engaged in such obstruction of justice to cease and desist therefrom.' On the next morning, in defiance of the President's Proclamation, a crowd reassembled in front of the school to bar the entry of the black children. The President then issued an Executive Order permitting the Secretary of Defense to use federal troops to enforce the court's decision; according to his close advisor, Sherman Adams, this represented 'a Constitutional duty which was the most repugnant to him of all his acts in his eight years in the White House' (quoted in Abraham, 1974, pp. 233-4). And so, on 24 September 1957, troops from the 101st Airborne Division went into Little Rock and integration was carried out at bayonet point. The school board was very much aware of the disruption at the high school and of the bitterness between the races caused by the events and so asked the district court for permission to suspend integration for two years until tempers cooled. This was granted, but reversed on appeal to the court of appeals. The Supreme Court then convoked a special session, for only the fifth time in thirty-eight years, and affirmed the court of appeals' judgement; in their first opinion since 1955 on the question of school integration and with an unprecedented show of solidarity, they all signed personally the unanimous opinion that 'the Constitutional rights of respondents are not to be sacrificed or yielded to the violence and disorder which have followed upon the actions of the Governor and Legislators . . . Thus law and order are not here to be preserved by depriving the negro children of their Constitutional rights' (*Cooper* v. *Aaron*, 1958).

In Little Rock, quite clearly, the Supreme Court's decision depended upon presidential muscle if it were to be effective. Article III, section 3, of the Constitution states that the President 'shall take care that the laws be faithfully executed' and it is arguable that the President is therefore obliged to see that the Supreme Court's interpretations of the Supreme Law are faithfully obeyed; yet no one can force the President to act if he chooses not to do so. One celebrated occasion when a presidential refusal did occur gave rise to the immortal, but probably apocryphal, statement of Andrew Jackson: 'Well, John Marshall has made his decision; now let him enforce it.' In 1832, the Court ordered the state of Georgia to release some missionaries it had incarcerated, on the grounds that the laws they had allegedly broken contravened the Constitution and other laws and treaties of the United States (*Worcester* v. *Georgia*, 1832). Although the details of the dispute centred on imprisoned missionaries, the real issue was the oppressive Georgian legislation directed against the Cherokee Indians, among whom the missionaries were working and whom the Georgian legislators intended to drive out, landless and uncompensated, across the Mississippi river. Georgia refused to release the missionaries and it is at this point that Andrew Jackson is supposed to have made his celebrated remark. Jackson did not necessarily approve of Georgia's discriminatory behaviour but political realities, as well as the relative strengths of Georgia's militia and the sparse federal troops, demanded that he tread warily, lest Georgia be alienated and driven into the arms of South Carolina, where there was already serious talk about secession from the Union. Georgia and the Carolinas in the 1830s were arguing in the same way as Arkansas in the 1950s that the states were 'sovereign' and not therefore subject to the edicts of the Supreme Court. In the 1850s this dispute led to civil war and the primacy of the federal union was affirmed. In the 1950s the repercussions were less drastic, but even so President Eisenhower and President Kennedy both felt obliged to employ federal troops to ensure the efficacy of Supreme Court decisions.

The issue of desegregation is a spectacular one, of course, and should not be taken as a norm; yet it emphasises in a particularly dramatic way the problems of enforcement. Less dramatic instances of non-compliance can be provided. For instance, the Court ruled in 1962 and 1963 that reading the Bible in state schools at the start of the day or singing hymns or saying special prayers was an encroachment on the First Amendment, made applicable to states through the Fourteenth, which prohibits the making of laws 'respecting an establishment of religion' (*Engle* v. *Vitale*, 1962; *Abington School District* v. *Schempp*, 1963). As Justice Black put it, 'it is no part of the business of government to compose official prayers for any group of the American people'. Attempts were made to pass a Constitutional Amendment to nullify the Court's decision banning prayer readings in public schools and the Senate in fact gave its approval to such an

Amendment. As Table 4.1 shows, the practice outlawed by the Court continued after its judgement, although there was clearly some pulling back, especially along the Atlantic coast. Similarly, *Miranda* v. *Arizona* (1966) set out specific procedures to be followed by police officers when dealing with suspects and, in effect, provided an idealised blueprint of what the proper relationship between the two

Table 4.1 *Comparative Compliance with* Engel *and* Schempp (Percentage of school boards, by region, carrying on certain classroom religious practices)

Classroom Religious Practices	South	New England	Middle West	Middle Atlantic	Rocky Mountain Far West
Bible readings before 1962	80	64	28	62	14
Bible readings 1964-5 year	57	20	12	5	6
Morning prayers before 1962	87	95	38	80	14
Morning prayers 1964-5 year	64	27	21	7	5

Source: Way (1968), p. 199.

parties should be in a civilised society. Studies have shown that this counsel of perfection has not been realised, that police officers do not always know, let alone follow, the procedures (Milner, 1970, 1971), that criminal suspects do not make good use of the rights accorded to them ('Note', 1966-7; Medalie *et al.*, 1968), and that, in any case, the procedures enunciated in *Miranda* do not of themselves limit improper police practices (Amsterdam, 1970).

THE SUPREME COURT AND PUBLIC OPINION

Since the Supreme Court cannot enforce its own decisions, it must depend upon others for its efficacy. The most satisfactory situation, from its point of view, consists of a public which grants it legitimate authority to determine the constitutionality of public actions and voluntarily obeys its every instruction. There are several reasons which can be adduced for the Court's being deemed to have this legitimate authority: to reject the view is to challenge the entire, established legal order; the mere possession of expertise often clothes the possessor with a special status; the actions of the Court in defending individuals and minorities against governments satisfies a personal need for security; the awesome setting of the Court and its mystique of being above the political strife set it apart (Petrick, 1968). Not all these reasons are persuasive, but there is little doubt that the political social-isation of American youth tends to exaggerate the apolitical role and high status of the Supreme Court and inculcates a widespread sense of reverence for the institution. This diffuse support for the Court does not necessarily translate into obedience to the Court, for notions of public opinion which accept the pollsters' assumption that the opinions of each individual are of equal weight are singularly poor indicators of likely political action (Hodder-Williams, 1970). Put simply, some people's opinions are more significant than others', since in the real world of politics power and influence are unequally distributed.

The mass public is in general favourably oriented towards the Court (Murphy and Tanenhaus, 1968; Kessel, 1966; Murphy *et al.*, 1973). This situation appears to have altered slightly in the decade spanning the last years of the Warren Court and the first years of the Burger Court, but diffuse support remained comparatively high (Sarat, 1977). Alongside this diffuse support went considerable ignorance; less than half a 1964 sample could name even one Supreme Court case (Murphy and Tanenhaus, 1968, p. 360). Nevertheless, despite this widespread lack of knowledge, politicians have tended to take account of, and to try to influence, mass opinion towards the Court, as the campaigns of many Senators throughout 1968 clearly indicated. This may well be part of candidates' common habit of exaggerating the visibility of public events, but it may also be a shrewd realisation that detailed knowledge is not a necessary prerequisite to strong views on a topic. It suggests, however, that attitudes to the Court are independ-ent of party loyalty and thus possible causes in themselves of an individual's political behaviour. It is little wonder, therefore, that politicians have taken a keen interest in what they know, or more usually guess, about mass opinion; in electoral calculations, each man, however ill-informed the basis for his opinions may be, casts one vote, neither more nor less than the best-informed and serious citizen.

The evidence, however, suggests that it is the party which provides the cues for attitudes towards the Supreme Court. The Gallup figures during the 1937 battle over President Roosevelt's attempt to reorgan-ise the Supreme Court indicate the congruence between party alleg-iance and attitudes towards the President's plans. In all the polls taken from February to April, more than 70 per cent of Democrats approved and less than 10 per cent of Republicans; where regional or occupational differences emerge, as they do most markedly, these differences merely replicate the party conflict. Recent studies have also suggested that party allegiance is probably the single most significant factor in explaining variations in general support for the Court (Kessel, 1966). It is, however, only rarely that the parties are publicly divided over an issue directly related to the Supreme Court, and the schizophrenic ideological stance of the Democrats in civil rights matters particularly clearly requires such an analysis to be treated with caution. Examining aggregate data, then, produces a picture of a mass public which instinctively supports the Supreme Court, knows precious little in the way of specific decisions of the Court, and, when the Court becomes a bone of contention between the parties, adjusts its attitude to the stance of its preferred party. But aggregate data can frequently obscure variations of significance and it is precisely these variations, these atypical small groups, who may have a marked political impact.

Some sections of society are more aware of Supreme Court actions than others. Just as the trial courts are favourably evaluated by most Americans, except by those who have direct experience of them, so also those who are aware of some Supreme Court decisions tend to be less approving of its performance than those who are in effect judging their ideal of it (Dolbeare, 1967; Murphy and Tanenhaus, 1968). The Warren Court, of course, tended to expand the rights of unpopular minorities or of the individual against the state apparatus and so it is not altogether surprising that those who in essence 'lost out' in the 1950s and 1960s, the established political majorities, should look askance at some of the things the Court did. The groups that were favoured by the Court predictably rated it comparatively highly; blacks, at all levels of education and income, evaluated the Court more highly than whites, yet at the same time expressed a lack of confidence in the courts in general (Hirsch and Donohew, 1968). The state courts and the lower federal courts have rarely been generous towards them; the Supreme Court, on the contrary, has been the forum where their rights have most consistently been defended. It is, however, only the Court's most controversial decisions which are reasonably well known so that, in general, attitudes towards the Court stem from individuals' images of the Court. Dominant among the images remains the myth of objectivity above the law, of nine distinguished jurists 'finding' the law, of a court expressing the concrete and discoverable reality of the Constitution. Those who have the most idealised picture of this mechanical jurisprudence support the Court most; yet even those who realise that this picture is idealised nevertheless retain a surprisingly high attachment to the myth (Dolbeare, 1967; Casey, 1974). The group likely to have the greatest knowledge of the Court is the legal fraternity, whose training, it may be thought, inculcates feelings of respect for the Court and a commitment to the convention of deference to it. Yet the lawyers do not always form the basis of the Court's public defence. In the regular confrontations between Congress and the Court, the lawyer members of the legislature did not provide the Court with its major support (Schmidhauser and Berg, 1972). Nor are they noticeably supportive of the actual performances of the Court (Beiser, 1972-3). Once again, therefore, · factors other than internalised, but unthinking, support for the Court become prevalent; party allegiance—lawyers are disproportionately Republican—and ideological considerations play their part.

In mapping attitudes to the Court, therefore, there is the need to acknowledge both the enduring significance of the myth of mechanical jurisprudence and also the less enthusiastic response of that small, but perhaps influential, public which is interested in and knowledgeable about the Court's actions. Yet, when the second, smaller group is examined, it turns out that its attitudes towards the Court follow precisely the same format as attitudes developed towards other institutions. A psychological mechanism seems to operate which merely reinforces attitudes already in existence. That is to say, those who have a high estimation of the Court generally approve its decisions, recall cases they favour, read material supportive of the Court, and generally filter communications to strengthen initial attitudes; opponents, in a similar vein, recollect decisions they dislike, praise writings drawing attention to Court failings, and reinforce their objections by filtering out communications favourable to it (Kessel, 1966; Dolbeare, 1967; Murphy *et al.*, 1973). Change in the attitudes of the attentive public is thus unlikely to alter rapidly.

Attitudes only become politically significant when they are in a position to affect action. Typically, the decisions of the Supreme Court affect only a portion of the public, so that the attitudes relevant to considerations of compliance are in the first instance those held by the Americans directly involved in each decision. *Schempp*, which outlawed the reading of the Bible in state schools, depended for its impact on the actions of the state commissioners of education, school boards and the teachers themselves. In Tennessee, these three relevant publics were lukewarm or antagonistic towards the decision and compliance was much less noticeable than on the eastern seaboard, for example (Birkby, 1966, with Way, 1968). The response to *Brown* depended on southern judges and southern politicians largely hostile to its philosophy. The impact of *Miranda* varied in relation to the knowledge and commitment of those ordinary policemen who are primarily concerned with the interrogation of suspects. Thus, to maintain that the Court relies for the enforcement of its decisions upon public opinion is a simplification which exaggerates the importance of the mass public and underestimates the obvious, but often unconsidered, point that some publics are more relevant than others.

The Justices of the Supreme Court are normally well aware of this. Their process of adjudication is dominated by the intellectual problems generated by specific litigation, in which past decisions and accepted interpretations of particular clauses of the Constitution provide the starting position from which to grapple with novel conflicts presented as adversary litigation. But attention is also given to the possible consequences of a decision; indeed, in some instances questions about political repercussions weigh heavily in the form of questions addressed to attorneys and the shape of relief granted. The political feel of Justices, most of whom have been involved in the hurly-burly of congressional or executive politics, is in many cases crucial to the final cast of a Court judgement and opinion. And it is just as well that this dimension of political awareness is present, for the efficacy of the Court, both in the short term and in the long run, depends upon strengthening the instinctive approval of the mythological Court with decisions acceptable, in form at least if not in content, to all parties involved in a dispute. The credit which the Supreme Court still enjoys could be dissipated if too many decisions became too visible and too unacceptable to that portion of the public from whose actions mass public opinion is ultimately formed.

FACTORS AFFECTING LEVELS OF COMPLIANCE

If all the decisions of the Supreme Court were accepted instantly and their principles put into force, the Supreme Court's impact would be extremely great. Obviously compliance is linked closely to impact, but impact is something more. For a decision of the Supreme Court does not occur as a bolt from the blue, devoid of antecedents and unrelated to the substance of society into which it falls; on the contrary, there is a tendency for an opinion to 'radiate constitutional sanctions far beyond its original boundaries' (Sorauf, 1959, p. 790), to draw its meaning from the context of the dispute and to act as a signpost for future developments. The study of the impact of Supreme Court decisions is not yet well developed, but it is essential if any serious evaluation of its role in the American political system is to be made (Becker, 1969; Wasby, 1970). What is clear is this: simple notions that the reality of impact can be deduced from the reading of opinions are manifestly absurd. A starting point, a necessary but not sufficient prologue, to the evaluation of impact must start with considerations of compliance.

For an opinion of the Court to have political consequences, it must first be communicated to those potentially affected by it. The extent to which this happens is variable. The most visible and well-publicised decisions, like *Brown*, are widely known and elicit a response, though not always, as we have seen, a favourable one; the vast majority of cases, however, is barely visible at all and even decisions of great significance, like *Miranda*, are unlikely to permeate deeply into the consciousness even of those Iowans who actually read the *Cedar Rapids Gazette*. Teachers' knowledge of the Bible-reading and prayer cases and policemen's knowledge of rulings affecting the interrogation of suspects are far from complete and thus not universally kept. Furthermore, the process of communication, from Court opinion through the media or professional bodies to the general citizenry, is liable to distort the actual holding of the Court (Newland, 1964). Certainly the press handling of the *Bakke* decision grossly over-simplified a very complex decision; the search for 'winners' and 'losers' can easily hide the important nuances contained in an opinion of the Court. This tendency to distortion means that 'the precedent in reality consists of what influential partisans and decision-makers say the Supreme Court says it is' (Sorauf, 1959, p. 791). In the United States, as in Britain, those who most need to assert their rights are normally those least acquainted with them, for the communications networks down which judicial decisions travel are rarely the networks into which the poorest, least-educated and most marginal members of society are plugged. The sum of these observations is the often over-looked truism that the impact of Supreme Court decisions is immensely variable. What is more, it draws attention yet again to the need to situate the legal opinion of the Court within the concrete political reality with which it often deals. This reality involves the readiness of those groups involved in the litigation to press on and build upon a success before the courts. The victors of *Schempp*, for instance, were satisfied by winning the specific case and they did not, like the backers of Linda Brown, continue energetically to translate the principle lying behind their victory into a universal practice.

In evaluating the likelihood of compliance, therefore, a complex set of continua is needed. One continuum would range the type of people affected by a decision in terms of their access to, and knowledge of, the Court's actions; another would range the type of issue involved in a decision from the manifestly judicial through to the clearly personal and private; another would distinguish between decisions which require individuals or political bodies to act positively rather than merely to desist from an action; and another would note a difference between constitutional interpretations and decisions focused on federal legislation. The decision of the Court is thus one input into the confused world of American politics and its effectiveness as an agency of change consequently depends on the specific political environment with which it has to interact.

The most complete compliance occurs in those instances in which both parties are genuinely seeking resolution of a legal question and neither has invested much political capital. Many parties to litigation, particularly if their claims are not representative of broad classes of the population, are perfectly prepared to accept the Court as the authoritative body establishing the law's true meaning. The nature of the issue, as much as the nature of the litigants, can also affect the rapidity of compliance. In some areas, particularly those relating to the judiciary itself, the Court has a more immediate claim to be the final arbiter between conflicting views of proper procedure than in other areas more normally the province of legislative action. In others again, the price of non-compliance may be thought too high. This was probably the case with the redistricting decisions, which were bitterly resented and which spawned a number of attempts to amend the Constitution or alter the appellate discretion of the Court, but which were, nevertheless, quickly implemented. The Supreme Court did not provide the states with precise standards for permissible variations in the population of districts—and, indeed, in its decisions immediately after *Reynolds*, could find no special circumstances to dilute the equal population principle—so that many states attempted all manner of contortions to satisfy local party requirements or to create safe seats for all sitting members. *Baker* produced a prodigious amount of subsequent litigation; seventeen volumes of between 100 and 350 pages were required to hold all the opinions. Yet the states, for all their abortive attempts to circumvent the Court's commands, rapidly complied. Within four years of *Reynolds*, thirty-five states had redistricted and more than half the intake of 1968 into the House of Representatives were elected from new constituencies. Two political fears underlay this acquiescence in an unpopular requirement. Not to redistrict might well give rise to litigation challenging every act of the ensuing legislature on the grounds of an unconstitutionally elected legislature; in the second place, an 'at large' election—that is, an election in which the whole state would become a single constituency—alarmed all politicians since it introduced an unacceptable amount of doubt into their calculations.

More problematic are those decisions which effectively require affirmative action on the part of public figures. Several decisions of the Warren and Burger Courts have required states, or their agents, to respond positively to Court initiatives. The requirement in *Gideon*, and later *Argersinger* v. *Hamlin* (1972), that states should provide lawyers for indigents, the requirement that school boards should bus children in order to integrate their schools, the requirement that police officers should inform suspects very precisely of their rights, all those impose a new obligation on public authorities in a way normally associated with legislatures. But the Court is supposed to be a judicial body and thus its readiness to take a lead not merely in suggesting ways of meeting new constitutional standards but actually in instructing state authorities which ways should be followed has inevitably produced resentment. Since the Court is usually associated in state politicians' eyes with central government, it is not helped by the federal government's increasing interference in matters once thought the prerogative of states. Opposition to the Court is thus part of a widespread feeling among many state officials that their independence and integrity are being undermined by the dual attack of congressional legislation and judicial fiat.

The areas of interference differ. Broadly speaking, those which are seen as affecting local practices rather than national ideals are those which generate the greatest antagonism. Redistricting, the provision of counsel for indigents, and reform of police procedure have a national flavour, linked as they are to notions of democracy and justice; furthermore, the consequences of non-compliance can be dire. But on the other issues, like schooling or the reading of the Bible before prayers or the control of obscene materials, the plea that local standards should prevail and the comparative safety of non-compliance ensure that ignoring the Supreme Court's mandate is more common. This is a function not only of the intensity of feeling— after all, the dominating elite felt very strongly about the iniquities of the redistricting decisions—but also of the need to comply. The fear of popular opinion is present in most politicians' minds; defending segregation in the south, keeping school prayers in the Bible belt, and discriminating against communists or all those who might be tarred with a communist brush, were thought to be congruent with popular opinion, while preserving gross inequalities in the size of electoral districts was not. The differential impact of the Supreme Court in the school desegregation and prayer-reading cases closely parallels the differential attachment to segregation and prayer-reading.

Focusing on enforcement compels a reappraisal of the power of the Supreme Court. Concentrating on those decisions which stir up antagonisms because they run counter to the strongly held values of significant sections of American society diminishes the significance of those instances where the Court upholds the actions of elected legislatures and officials. The Court does not only chart new courses; it legitimates existing ones. It was Congress which passed the 1964 Civil Rights Act and the 1965 Voting Rights Act, but in both cases it stretched the sparse words of the Constitution almost to their limit. Those who challenged the constitutionality of these Acts had reasonable grounds for doing so, even if their ulterior motives were hardly commendable. The Founding Fathers would surely have been astonished that Congress was permitted to regulate the clientèle of Ollie McClung's hamburger café and to supervise the registration of electors in the states. But the Court accepted these extensions of congressional power in *Katzenbach* v. *McClung* (1964) and *South Carolina* v. *Katzenbach* (1966), and thus legitimised that power. Not all the grumbles were foreclosed, but the new situation was hardly open to renewed public consideration. And that is an important power.

Even if it is argued that the Supreme Court cannot by itself produce radical social change, but must depend ultimately on Congress and the executive to back its powerless words with the force of statute law or federal power, it does not follow that the decision's impact is negligible. The redistricting cases are testimony enough against that. But the dismantling of segregation and access to the ballot box for blacks did require the involvement of Congress; without Title VII of the 1964 Civil Rights Act or the 1965 Voting Rights Act, the Supreme Court judgements in these fields would have taken many years more to yield their full consequences. Yet Supreme Court decisions should be seen as stones cast into a pond; they produce a ripple effect which touches upon state politics, congressional politics and executive politics. Agenda-setting is in many ways a real power (Bachrach and Baratz, 1961). The black struggle for civil rights was much advanced by the Supreme Court, although it was not won by the Court. To be successful, it required direct action in the states, a march to Washington, lobbying in Congress and executive sympathy. Yet without *Shelley* v. *Kraemer* and *Brown* v. *the Board of Education of Topeka*, that struggle would have been harder and longer. By putting items on the agenda and by injecting a shock or two into the political system, the Supreme Court remains an influential force in the nation's politics, despite its obvious and very real problems in the face of noncompliance.

The response to the Court's judgement in *Gideon* illustrates vividly how the Court can spark off immediate reforms (Lewis, 1964, pp. 193-207). The omens were not propitious; in 1938 the Court had held in *Johnson* v. *Zerbst* that federal criminal defendants had an absolute right to counsel. Yet by 1963 Congress had still not passed a law authorising federal expenditure to support the lawyers who were appointed by federal judges as counsel to indigent defendants. Randomly selected, ill-prepared, unpaid and frequently uninterested, these lawyers clearly made a travesty of the high ideals of a system where there was genuine equality under the law. The problem in the state courts, where twice as many defendants were indigent, was both larger and more difficult. Converting the ideal of *Gideon* into reality would require legislation to appropriate money, lawyers to man legal aid schemes and judges to ensure that the new principle was known. There was, however, an increasing awareness of the problem and a crescendo of voices calling for reform, so that *Gideon* fell on surprisingly fertile ground. Barely two months after the Court's decision, the Florida legislature had passed a statute creating a public defender in each of the state's sixteen circuits and other states followed suit with rapidity. 'Without the Supreme Court,' Gideon apparently told a visitor, 'it might have happened sometime, but it wouldn't have happened in this state soon' (Lewis, 1964, p. 204). This particular stone produced dynamic ripples; others die on the shore.

A careful balance, therefore, has to be maintained between overestimating and underestimating the power of the Court. In a mechanistic sense, it has no power. Yet even the cursory glance at the development of the United States' constitutional system described in the next chapter suggests that the decisions of the Supreme Court are deeply etched on American history and have played a major part in establishing the current political system, in both the formal distribution of power and the rights of individuals. The opponents of the Court, on the other hand, have often exaggerated its power and have ignored those instances when the successful translation of its fiat into action has depended upon the assistance of the other branches of government. In virtually every great case that comes before the Court there are interests ranged on both sides; whatever the judgement, therefore, the Court will be able to rely on some support, just as it will expect some opprobrium. It will move some interests to back it in the less rarified environment of congressional or state politics. Without this perspective, without the realisation that the Court is neither the supreme political power nor a toothless bulldog, without the understanding that litigation before the Court masquerades group political conflict under the guise of a suit between individual adversaries, the difficult question of the Court's proper role in a democratic political system cannot be adequately considered. This theoretical problem, which is discussed in the last chapter, should not be divorced from analysis of the Court's real power.

5

The Supreme Court and the American Polity

The politics of the Supreme Court can be examined at several levels and in many ways. A comprehensive examination would include an analysis of its decisions over time and in all the various issue areas which have dominated its efforts at one time or another, noting not only the development of the law but also the changes in society which follow, and are in part the product of, those developments. There are, in effect, no substitutes for a conventional study of American constitutional law and a detailed look at the changing treatment of specific problems. A single chapter cannot pretend to do this task adequately, but it can at least provide a large-scale map of the historical scene and also a look in somewhat greater detail at two parts of that terrain. The first section of this chapter thus summarises some of the major decisions handed down by the Court, decisions which seem, in the perspective of time, to have been a decisive influence on the structure of American political life and on the distribution of political power within the Union. The second and third sections dwell, in a much more detailed fashion, upon two areas in which the Court has played a significant role, the enunciation of the principle 'one man, one vote, one value', and the attempt to end racially segregated school systems. These are not only interesting in themselves; they illustrate two important truths about the Court's activity, the incrementalist nature of change and the complexity of issues which may seem to the enthusiastic and liberal observer to be comparatively simple. Other issue areas could have been taken, such as civil rights generally (Abraham, 1977) or the relationship between church and state (Sorauf, 1976) or the development of particular clauses such as the Fourteenth Amendment (Berger, 1977) or the Commerce Clause (Benson, 1970) or the interaction of the Court and a specific economic group (Miller, 1968), and so on. This chapter is thus consciously designed to be no more than illustration of the Court's influence on the American polity.

THE DEVELOPING CONSTITUTION

Ratification did not resolve the ambiguities of the Constitution; it did not authoritatively assert who should be the final arbiter of the meaning of the Constitution, or whether state law should take precedence over federal law, or what commerce between the states might include. The Supreme Court was soon established as that final arbiter and came, through its interpretation of the Constitution, to establish the distribution of power throughout the nation. The first step was to assert successfully the right of judicial review or, rather, judicial supremacy. This was achieved in the celebrated case of *Marbury* v. *Madison* (1803).

Marbury is historically of fundamental significance, but it in fact derived from nothing more than 'a trivial squabble over a few petty political plums' (Garraty, 1962, p. 13). The facts are simply stated. In November 1800 the Federalists were overwhelmingly defeated in the national elections, John Adams being defeated by Thomas Jefferson and an anti-Federalist Congress being elected. However, in those days the Constitution provided that both Adams and the Congress elected in 1798 should continue in office until 4 March 1801 and the Federalists took this opportunity, by legislation and executive appointment, to repair as much as possible of the damage inflicted upon them by the 1800 elections. An expanded judiciary, filled by the nominees of the outgoing President, was the result. William Marbury was one such appointee and was commissioned as a justice of the peace for the district of Columbia; or, rather, he was not actually commissioned, because the excessive haste in the last days of the Adams administration resulted in John Marshall, then Secretary of State as well as Chief Justice, failing to ensure that the commission, already signed and sealed, was actually delivered. Marbury, a staunch Federalist, immediately filed suit asking the Supreme Court to command James Madison, Jefferson's Secretary of State, to deliver the commission. The stage was set therefore for a dramatic confrontation between the elected Republican administration and the appointed, Federalist judiciary, a confrontation given added piquancy by the known antagonism between two great Virginians, John Marshall and Thomas Jefferson.

Marshall's judgement was a masterly side-step, deceptively simple and politically shrewd. He asserted, somewhat unconvincingly, that the section of the 1789 Judiciary Act permitting the Supreme Court to issue a *mandamus* was an unconstitutional grant of power; as such, the Court could not instruct Madison to deliver Marbury's commission, although it could, and did, issue a sharp but irrelevant rebuke to the Republicans. The power to invalidate an Act of Congress, which this decision for the first time asserted, was not conjured entirely from Marshall's imagination. Before independence, many of the states' highest courts had used judicial power to strike down legislation they deemed unconstitutional; and Congress itself had engineered a case to test whether their carriage tax was unconstitutional (*Hylton* v. *United States*, 1796), while the Republicans, now so hostile to the judiciary, had sought to use the federal courts to hold unconstitutional the hated Alien and Sedition Acts and the United States Bank Charter. The rights and wrongs of this thorny question may be left to the final chapter. The ability to outlaw congressional action was perhaps the least important aspect of the case (it was not until 1857 that the Court next invalidated federal legislation); most important was its assertion that the Supreme Court was the ultimate arbiter of the Constitution.

If that were so, then state action was also subject in the last resort to Supreme Court overview. The Judiciary Act of 1789, section 25, established that state court decisions that denied a claim made in the name of the federal Constitution, laws or treaties could be reviewed by the Supreme Court. In 1810, with the impeachment scare of Jay behind him, Marshall felt able to strike another blow for supremacy and strike down a state law on the grounds of unconstitutionality. In *Fletcher* v. *Peck* (1810), Marshall found that the Georgian legislature's attempt to rescind the grants of land made by its bribed predecessors was impermissible. From that moment on the Court has not felt hesitant in annulling state actions which contravened its understanding of the Constitution and its understanding of the Constitution was very much a nationalist, centralising one. Furthermore, it took it upon itself to assume the final responsibility to decide what were the constitutional limitations on state action.

The third leg of the nationalist platform was the establishment of federal law as supreme over state laws where the two conflicted. This was accomplished in *McCulloch* v. *Maryland* (1819). At the beginning of the nineteenth century, the state of Maryland, along with several others, forbade all banks not chartered by the state itself to issue bank notes except on special terms arranged by the state. A penalty of $500 was inflicted for each contravention; and this meant a vast amount for a flourishing concern like the Baltimore branch of the Second Bank of the United States. McCulloch was the cashier of this branch and he refused to pay the penalties demanded by the state of Maryland. The case was argued for nine days before the Supreme Court by some of the finest lawyers of the day and it resulted in what is commonly thought to be John Marshall's greatest opinion. He noted that the federal government had the power 'to lay and collect taxes, to borrow money, to regulate commerce, to declare and conduct war and to raise and support armies and navies'. Employing a notion first used, but little noticed, fourteen years earlier, Marshall enunciated the doctrine of implied powers, arguing that, since the Constitution granted Congress the power 'to make all laws which shall be necessary and proper for carrying into execution the foregoing powers', the federal government had the right to organise methods to fulfil its functions. 'Let the end be legitimate,' he wrote, 'let it be within the scope of the Constitution, and all means which are appropriate, which are plainly adapted to that end, which are not prohibited, but consist with the letter and spirit of the Constitution, are constitutional.' Thus far, Marshall had merely introduced an expansive interpretation of congressional power, entirely in keeping with his whole philosophy of adding to the strength and prestige of the national government. To argue, however, that Congress could incorporate a bank, even though the Constitution does not explicitly say that it may, antagonised many vocal Americans who objected strongly to the National Bank, and it left unresolved the really crucial question.

What happens when a legitimate law of Congress clashes with a legitimate law of a state? Marshall now coined the classic phrase: 'the power to tax is the power to destroy'. If, therefore, Maryland were permitted to tax an instrumentality of the federal government, it could drive it out of existence and thus nullify the purpose of central government. To Marshall this was unthinkable, for it was tantamount to giving the states a right to destroy the Union itself. Federal law must be supreme. Logic was clearly on John Marshall's side and, without the principles so adeptly formulated in *McCulloch*, the United States would surely no longer be united and certainly would not have a formidably influential central government. It demonstrates, in addition, the problems that arise from a Constitution where the enumerated powers are limited and where general phrases must be applied to actions unforeseen by its originators.

To illustrate the problems arising from a Constitution which does not provide specifically for all possible eventualities, we can go back to 1807, when the newest technological miracle was a steamboat, which travelled successfully from New York City up the river to the state capital at Albany (Garraty, 1964). In 1808, the New York legislature granted the two men who had pioneered the development of the steamboat the monopoly right to operate steamboats in New York waters, no one else being entitled to navigate New York waters without a licence from the two men. As steamboats developed, this monopoly, which was replicated in New Orleans and other navigable waters, became more and more unpopular, until a certain Gibbons, operating boats the few miles between New York City and New Jersey under a coasting licence granted by the federal government, fell foul of Ogden, who held a licence to operate in and out of New York granted him by the two monopoly pioneers. The lower courts affirmed the state of New York's right to grant a monopoly for steamboat operations within the state and instructed Gibbons to desist. Gibbons appealed against this judgement and his case, *Gibbons* v. *Ogden*, came to the Supreme Court in 1824. Now, the Constitution says nothing about steamboats; furthermore, the Tenth Amendment states that 'the powers not delegated to the United States, nor prohibited to the states, are reserved to the states or to the people'. Clearly it would need Daniel Webster's most eloquent pleading and John Marshall's most persuasive arguments to uphold the national interest against the state monopoly.

Marshall's tactics were bold in the extreme. He declared that the power of Congress to regulate foreign and interstate commerce embraces every species of commercial intercourse between the United States and foreign states and every commercial transaction that is not wholly carried on within the boundaries of a single state. Its power over interstate commerce did not stop at the boundary line of any state but is applicable within the interior of the state. Recollecting the principle of *McCulloch*, Marshall found that where, as here, a federal grant collided with a state grant, the federal grant should prevail. *Gibbons* v. *Ogden* not only put an end to steamboat monopolies, the first great anti-trust case as it has been called, and thus made John Marshall uncharacteristically popular; it also began an almost continuous process of expanding the scope of 'interstate commerce' (Benson, 1970). This singularly imprecise phrase came to include virtually anything which passed from state to state (railways, aeroplanes, radio, and so on) and beyond that to the details of the organisation of the railway, aeroplanes and radio, to minimum wages for railway gangers, safety regulations for airport employees, and so forth. Except for the first thirty-five years of the twentieth century, when a majority of the Justices, as we shall see, began to limit congressional attempts to oversee the national welfare, a combination of *McCulloch*'s principle that federal actions are supreme over state actions and *Gibbons*'s principle that interestate commerce is an elastic phrase has enabled the federal government to extend its activities into most aspects of American life—even if it sometimes needed proof that 46 per cent of Ollie McClung's meat came from outside Alabama.

When John Marshall died in 1835, he left behind him a Supreme Court with a status and potential power it had not enjoyed when he was appointed in the bitter months between Jefferson's presidential victory and Adams's relinquishing office. He managed this by a mixture of bold initiatives and cautious restraint and in opinions which owed their force not to the accumulation of precedents and legal scholarship (of which there was remarkably little) but to the confident manner of his logical argument. Marshall believed fervently, and he persuaded even those colleagues of his who might be thought to believe differently, that the role of the Supreme Court was to police the American political system and to strengthen the nationalist forces within his country. He established the principle of judicial supremacy, despite constant criticism by several Presidents to the contrary, on sufficiently firm foundations that it could survive the upheavals of Civil War and the heightened passions of the mid-nineteenth century. The second congressional statute to be invalidated was the 1820 Missouri Compromise in what is perhaps the most disastrous of all Supreme Court cases, *Dred Scott* v. *Sandford*; here a majority of the Court maintained that blacks were not, and could not be, citizens to bring suits in a federal court, that Dred Scott himself, despite his living for several years in the 'free' state of Illinois, remained a slave as he had originally been; that the Missouri Compromise which declared that part of the Louisiana purchase north of the southern boundary of Missouri 'free' was an unconstitutional exercise of congressional power. Some, at least, of the Justices thought that a firm pro-slavery judgement would resolve the deeply divided issue of slavery now dominating national politics. If anything, it exacerbated differences. And in the aftermath of that bloody Civil War, the jubilant Republicans used their control of Congress to reduce the size of the Court to prevent Andrew Johnson from nominating a new Justice and altered its appellate jurisdiction to prevent the Court from reaching the constitutionality of some of the reconstruction statutes (*Ex Parte McCardle*, 1869). Despite *Dred Scott* and despite the obviously partisan inclinations of Congress, the Court nevertheless retained its independence and most of its status.

The Civil War had effectively resolved the question of national integration. New questions now dominated political life and foremost among these was the extent to which governments could control the vibrant capitalism of the rapidly expanding American economy. The postwar Court was no more disposed than Marshall had been to leave the question of federalism alone. The Justices who now sat on the Court were every bit as political animals as the great Chief Justice and they were prepared to use judicial power to defend the interests which they saw as central to a thriving and powerful nation. But, like Marshall before them, they moved cautiously, establishing the stepping-stones by which they could reach their ultimate goal. By the 1870s it was the property-owner, or businessman (for the two were conceptually interchangeable), who was being harried by governments and being hampered in his freedom of action, the very driving force of successful capitalism. The growth of intellectual and political support for an ideology of *laissez-faire*, with its mixture of normative and empirical arguments, was mirrored in the beliefs of the Justices who were drawn, after all, from the dominant coalition of the time. The vehicle by which their notions of the ideal America were to be slowly written into the Constitution was the Fourteenth Amendment, ratified in 1868 and destined to become the centre of much of the most significant constitutional adjudication to this day. In 1873, however, the meaning of its delphic phrases was unclear and untested; the questions that were raised were many and profound. What precisely constituted 'equal protection of the law' or 'due process of law'? What were the 'privileges or immunities' of citizenship? Did the fifth section, permitting Congress to enforce by appropriate legislation the provisions of the Article, allow the national legislature to reach into private discrimination? There were no simple answers then, just as there are no simple answers now. Those who proposed the Amendment and those who ratified it left no clear indication of what exactly it was intended to achieve. McCloskey has argued that the framers must have known how the Court had shaped the vague phraseology of the commerce clause or the contract clause to meet specific requirements and, therefore, that they intended the Fourteenth Amendment to be given reality and life through judicial interpretation; that is, after all, what the Court had done with other imprecise mandates and the framers of the Fourteenth Amendment could have been much more precise had they wished to be. Maybe. Whatever their visions of the future, the truth is that 'their failure to clarify their intentions provided the Court with a golden opportunity to inaugurate a new era in the history of judicial review' (McCloskey, 1960, p. 118).

The first authoritative pronouncement came in 1873 in the so-called *Slaughter-House Cases*. In 1869 a 'carpetbag' legislature in Louisiana passed a law effectively granting a monopoly in the slaughtering of livestock to a single New Orleans company, which naturally infuriated the 1,000 or so butchers in New Orleans who were forced to discontinue their activities. Before the Fourteenth Amendment's ratification, this law would manifestly have been beyond the reach of the Supreme Court, since the states' control of such matters was recognised as being plenary. But now it was argued that the 'privileges and immunities' of citizenry were the rights set out in the Bill of Rights, that the due process and equal protection clauses limited state action, and that Louisiana's invasion on the right to occupational freedom was therefore invalid. Five Justices did not agree; the butchers had had their day in the legislative process and in the courts and had lost. This slender majority held a few years later, in *Munn* v. *Illinois* (1877), which upheld state laws setting minimum charges for the storage of grain; the warehouse-owners had recourse to the polls if they disliked the legislature's actions. Behind these two self-restrained acceptances of state regulation of the economy, however, lay two developments which were to have profound effects in the years to come and which were to nullify several attempts at congressional and state involvement in social and economic matters.

The first basic point was this: the privileges and immunities of citizenship were narrowly defined and the Fourteenth Amendment was taken to apply quite specifically to the action of states or their instrumentalities. Thus, the attempts in the Civil Rights Act of 1875 to outlaw private discrimination against blacks was deemed to be beyond the constitutional authority of Congress (*Civil Rights Cases*, 1883; Garraty, 1964, pp. 128-44). The consequence of this was to leave the plight of the blacks to the tender mercies of state governments and the only defence they had against discrimination was the due process and equal protection clauses of the Fourteenth Amendment; the rights set out in the first eight Amendments were not yet deemed in any part to be subsumed under the privileges and immunities clauses. Once the Court had interpreted the equal protection clauses to permit equal, but separate, treatment for the races, the constitutionality of Jim Crow laws became a formality (*Plessy* v. *Ferguson*, 1896; Garraty, 1964, pp. 145-58).

The other development was the gradual transference of the dissenters in the *Slaughter-House* and *Munn* cases into a majority. In these cases Swayne and Field respectively had argued that the due process clauses implied the constitutional defence of special interests, essentially property rights. The due process clause, which is to be found in the Fifth Amendment and has its roots as far back as Magna Carta, had always been thought of not as a check on what a government could do but on the process it had to follow in order to do it. But, in the last decade and a half of the nineteenth century, the position of Field, strengthened by appointments steeped in the new emotions of the burgeoning and conflict-ridden American capitalism, came to dominate the Court's decisions. The idea of natural rights, which has a long history in American jurisprudence, was allied to an understandable fear that popular majorities and labour unions would limit the freedom with which individual Americans could use their property. In short, the principles of *laissez-faire* and social Darwinist philosophy came to be written into the Constitution through the due process clause. As always, the change was a gradual one, growing on *obiter dicta* (such as Chief Justice Waite's comment in *Munn* that 'under some circumstances' a regulatory statute might be so arbitrary as to be unconstitutional), and on incremental growth, until the Court was prepared to declare that it had the last word on the reasonableness of rates. By moving in a somewhat ambiguous way to a position where the precise criteria for substantive due process remained unclear, the Court could now help shape social policy as it wished, yet at the same time respect the boundaries imposed by economic necessity and political possibility.

The first third of the twentieth century is thus marked by a mixture of judicial control of, and acquiescence in, governmental intervention in the economy. The Court could use an array of tools to strike down legislation of which it disapproved; taxes, following *McCulloch*, could be interpreted not as money-raising techniques but as devices to destroy particular practices, as they were in the 1922 Child Labor Tax case when the Court found unconstitutional Congress's 10 per cent tax on the profits of production industries that employed children (*Bailey* v. *Drexel Furniture Co.*, 1922); the commerce clause could be narrowly defined and thus used to prevent congressional control of matters which were not 'directly' affected by interstate commerce (*United States* v. *E. C. Knight & Co.*, 1895) or which did not have a harmful effect as a result of moving in interstate commerce (*Hammer* v. *Dagenhart*, 1918). The most regularly employed method of limiting regulation was, however, the due process clause and between 1900 and 1937 184 decisions were handed down which invalidated state laws on this basis (McCloskey, 1960, p. 151). In *Lochner* v. *New York* (1905), a majority of the Court attempted to stop the regulatory movement in its tracks by outlawing a minimum hours law as a grave infringement on an individual's contractual freedom, a 'meddlesome interference with the rights of the individual', and thus violating due process.

Yet, beside these attempts to check the regulatory movement were many cases where regulation was upheld, essentially because a majority of the Justices approved the purport of that regulation. The veto power inherent in judicial supremacy was in fact more a threat than an instrument of continuous control. It surfaced dramatically from time to time, but remained unused at others. It was Franklin Roosevelt's New Deal which galvanised a narrow majority of the Court into a final daemonic attempt to preserve the *laissez-faire* capitalist system it idealised. In 1935 and 1936, central planks in Roosevelt's programme to combat the Depression were deemed to be unconstitutional extensions of Congress's legitimate powers. In 1937, however, the majority changed and, with a number of ardent New Dealers being appointed to the Court, economic regulation became an unexceptionable feature of the American political system. For nigh on forty years, the Court had used a number of discrete parts of the Constitution from time to time to prevent legislatures encroaching on areas its members believed should be immune from interference. Although the direct consequence of this action may not have been as great as the bland assertion of unconstitutionality suggests, the indirect ramifications of the Court's preferences surely dissuaded several legislatures from embarking on imaginative attempts at regulation. The years immediately following the 1937 turnabout were marked primarily by a readiness once again to grant to the national government virtually unfettered powers, so long as the means chosen were rational. However, the economic liberals were in some cases also liberals in other fields, and the impact of Justices like Hugo Black, William Douglas, Frank Murphy and Wiley Rutledge was felt in the field of civil rights. To some extent the liberal expansion of individual rights and the advancement of black rights, with which the Warren Court became closely connected, had their origins in the 1940s.

The Warren Court itself actually passed through these stages—an early phase when it tended to balance individual rights against governmental requirements, a middle phase when it boldly struck out in favour of the individual against governmental action, and a final phase when it consolidated its earlier innovations in constitutional law (see, generally, Levy, 1972). The central thread was the Bill of Rights and its proper position in America's political system (Cox, 1968). Both Warren and Black saw it as the centrepiece of the Constitution and peculiarly the province of the Court to uphold and oversee. The Fourteenth Amendment, either by itself or by partially incorporating the first eight Amendments into it, was the chief vehicle for its striking enlargement of individual rights. The *Brown* decision in Warren's first Term was an indication of what was to come, though the cautious action in formulating a remedy and the hesitancy to give full support to black attempts to turn new rights into concrete gains in the lower courts also suggest the less than radical thrust of its early period. It was not really until the 1960s that the Court established its major novel constitutional principles and was prepared to get itself embroiled in a wide range of social and political questions. Racial discrimination was one theme which runs throughout the three periods and which provides a good litmus test of current jurisprudence. The early years saw some clear advance for blacks, though the approach was generally low-key and often unhelpful; the middle years witness the major determination to use judicial power to put an end to the obnoxious, and now unconstitutional, practice of racial discrimination; in the final years, grateful to Congress and conscious of the limitations on judicial power, it moved more carefully.

But there were other areas in which the Court was creative (Funston, 1974). It gave real substance to First Amendment rights and became involved in the constitutionality of censoring pornographic material; it set stricter requirements on law enforcement officials in the matters of seizing material and electronic eavesdropping as it also enlarged the rights of suspects and the convicted; it created a right to privacy; it kept church and state rigorously apart. The weapons forged by Marshall were there to be employed as the Court felt appropriate. Judicial supremacy, the elastic commerce clause, the notion of inherent power, all were well suited to the needs of America in the 1960s and enabled both the Court and Congress to legislate in the social field in a way probably unforeseen by the Founding Fathers. In addition, the Fourteenth Amendment came close to embracing all the rights, themselves expanded by judicial evolution, set out in the Bill of Rights. But the Warren Court was by no means a unanimous Court, as Table 5.1 indicates. Consequently it was not at all clear whether the constitutional revolution over which Earl Warren had presided would survive through the 1970s, especially since Nixon had the extraordinary good fortune to be able to appoint four Justices and thus potentially alter the balance within the Court.

Table 5.1   *Dissent in the Warren Court*

Term	Total Opinions	Total Dissenting Votes	Dissenting Index
1953	65	132	50.8
1954	78	117	43.0
1955	82	147	44.8
1956	100	203	50.7
1957	104	244	58.6
1958	98	190	48.5
1959	96	223	58.1
1960	109	232	53.2
1961	84	130	38.7
1962	110	177	40.2
1963	111	162	36.5
1964	91	125	34.3
1965	97	138	35.6
1966	100	213	53.3
1967	110	141	32.0
1968	99	181	45.7

Note: The dissenting index expresses the number of actual dissenting votes as a percentage of the possible maximum dissenting vote (i.e. assuming *all* cases were decided 5:4); 0.0 would therefore represent consistent unanimity and 100.0 consistent 5:4 divisions.

While some observers have seen massive and major cutbacks on the Warren Court's pathbreaking road, the broad consensus is somewhat different (Wasby, 1976; Funston, 1978; Hodder-Williams, 1979). As the former Justice Arthur Goldberg has put it, 'there is an enormous difference between not opening frontiers of human liberty and closing ones formerly open, between declining to move forward and legitimizing oppression' (Goldberg, 1973, p. 93). There have, it is true, been some cutbacks, marginally over suspect rights, over access to the courts, over the principle of equality in local elections, over censorship, but there have also been major advances. The very strict limitations now set on the constitutional use of the death penalty and the variable rights to abortion provide classic examples of what is, in effect, legislation by judiciary (*Furman* v. *Georgia*, 1972; *Roe* v. *Wade*, 1973; *Doe* v. *Bolton*, 1973; *Coker* v. *Georgia*, 1977). Although the unanimity noticeable in the later Warren Court on racial discrimination and school desegregation cases is no longer present and the burden of proof of discrimination has been somewhat altered, there has been no reversal of the determination to grant blacks the same constitutional rights as other Americans. Women have largely found the Court a hospitable place (Getman, 1973; Cook, 1977) and minority groups, though no longer enjoying so great a benefit of the doubt, continue to gain satisfaction in the Court. Two things seem to be happening. In the first place, a consolidation and refinement of the fundamentalist positions of the Warren Court is taking place; perhaps Burger is to Warren what Taney was to Marshall. In the second place, the Court is faced with many more problems at the margin, with shades of discrimination and subtle conflicts of competing rights. Just as the Supreme Court in the first part of the twentieth century found it impossible to fit the new principles it had created neatly to the particular disputes before it, so the current Court has to balance and calculate in as subjective a way as any of its predecessors. Some cases provide excellent vehicles for the assertion of fresh constitutional principles, but normally American life is so rich and varied that the application of such principles to the diverse reality of its society is hard indeed. This is the problem facing the Burger Court.

ONE MAN, ONE VOTE, ONE VALUE

In 1963 William Douglas wrote the Court's opinion in a case which outlawed the system of state elections in Georgia whereby each county of the state, regardless of its population, carried the same weight for electoral purposes (*Gray* v. *Sanders*, 1963). 'Once the geographical unit for which a representative is to be chosen is designated,' he wrote, 'all who participate in the election are to have an equal vote—whatever their race, whatever their sex, whatever their occupation, whatever their income, and wherever their home may be in that geographical unit . . . The conception of political equality from the Declaration of Independence, to Lincoln's Gettysburg Address, to the Fifteenth, Seventeenth, and Nineteenth Amendments, can mean only one thing—one man, one vote.' In the following year Hugo Black wrote for a divided Court in asserting that 'the command of Article I, Section 2, that Representatives be chosen "by the people of the several States" means that as nearly as is practicable one man's vote in a congressional election is to be worth as much as another's' (*Wesberry* v. *Sanders*, 1964).A few weeks later Earl Warren, once again over John Harlan's dissent, authored the Court's opinion which extended the principle to state elections (*Reynolds* v. *Sims*, 1964): 'The Equal Protection Clause demands no less than substantially equal state legislative representation for all citizens, of all places as well as of all races.' These three opinions, each of which typifies in its eloquent advocacy the non-legalistic and profoundly moral outlook of its author, brought to the United States at last the principle of one man, one vote, one value (see, generally, Dixon, 1968; Claude, 1972).

The route had been a long one and not a unanimous one. The Constitution itself is self-denying on the question of voting qualifications, mainly because the Founding Fathers themselves were not in agreement. Consequently a compromise was reached which conveniently blurred the issue. Section 2(1) of Article I states that in elections to the House of Representatives 'the electors in each State shall have the qualifications requisite for electors of the most numerous branch of the State legislature' and thus appears to ensure that states decide the criteria by which electors qualify for federal elections. Section 4(1) of the same Article permits Congress at least an overseeing role in *how* elections are carried out. 'The times, places and manner of holding elections,' it runs, 'shall be prescribed in each State by the legislatures thereof; but the Congress may at any time by law make or alter such regulations.' Corrupt practices, such as ballot irregularities, are therefore within congressional reach (*United States* v. *Classic*, 1941) as are methods of financing campaigns, provided always, of course, Congress does not itself impinge on rights protected elsewhere in the Constitution (*Buckley* v. *Valeo*, 1976). But the qualification to vote in federal elections has been determined by state governments, tempered over time by Constitutional Amendments, such as the Fifteenth in 1870 which was intended to enfranchise blacks, the Nineteenth in 1920 which ended the diversity by which women were entitled to vote in only a select few of the Union's states, the Twenty-Fourth in 1964 which outlawed the requirement to have paid all taxes to qualify for the vote, and the Twenty-Sixth in 1971 which made 18 the age at which all citizens are entitled to vote. The notion of a qualified franchise is very much part of American constitutional philosophy and, historically, education, property ownership, length of residence in a state, tax payments have all been employed to limit the principle of universal adult suffrage; some qualifications apply in some states to this day.

The idea of universal adult suffrage, applicable to women and slaves as well as to free-born American men, was no part of the Founding Fathers' beliefs, any more than it was to all but a handful of progressive, and normally scorned, political thinkers living at the same time. Those who have endeavoured in recent years to put a brake on the extension of the franchise have found it comparatively simple to show that the Constitution did not give its seal of approval to the principle of universal equal franchise. If the first ten Amendments are considered in effect as part of the framers' original intention, nothing further was said. When the Seventeenth Amendment in 1913 introduced the principle of direct elections to senatorial contests, it retained the clause which set the qualifications for electors in terms of state requirements. Nevertheless, the Court has played a significant part in giving life to the Fifteenth Amendment's command that the vote cannot constitutionally be denied solely on the grounds of a person's race and has, in recent years, employed the equal protection clause of the Fourteenth Amendment to ensure that each vote, once granted, carried equal weight.

For the first 100 years of the Union, the Supreme Court was not involved in the struggle for voting rights. It was not until the immediate aftermath of the Civil War in any case that suffrage became a matter of major national controversy. Two easily identifiable groups of Americans were primarily concerned, women and blacks. While several states in the west began to grant the franchise to women, more because the politicians in office hoped for political gains than because they held any fundamental beliefs about sexual equality, many states remained obstinately opposed to the dilution of male supremacy (Flexnor, 1959). Frances Minor was president of the Missouri Woman Suffrage Association and a keen disciple of the feminist Susan Anthony; she read the newly confirmed Fourteenth Amendment as an entitlement to all citizens, male and female, to enjoy 'the privileges and immunities' inherent in citizenship, amongst which, she claimed, was the right to vote for a Congressman. But the vote was limited by state law in Missouri to male citizens only and Happersteth, the election registrar, thus refused to list Mrs Minor as a lawful voter. She thereupon sued Happersteth on the ground that she was denied by a state official the privileges and immunities of citizenship granted by the Fourteenth Amendment. Five years later, the Supreme Court announced its decision (*Minor* v. *Happersteth*, 1875) and found in favour of Happersteth. Forty-five years later the Nineteenth Amendment outlawed such sexually discriminatory laws as that which had existed in Missouri.

The principle behind the decision was simple: the right to vote 'comes from the state'. But it was not yet clear how much, if at all, state action could be limited by Congress or the Constitution. In 1884, a part answer was given; the right to vote, once it was granted, could be protected by Congress acting under the 'times, places, and manner' clause. Thus, when some Georgian members of the Klu Klux Klan fell foul of an 1870 statute by preventing a duly qualified black from voting, the Court found that Congress was perfectly entitled to extend its powers to safeguard the rights of black voters enshrined in the Fifteenth Amendment (*Ex Parte Yarborough*, 1884). But it was precisely to prevent blacks from voting that much energy in the south was spent. Violence and intimidation, however, provided no permanent solution to the problem of disfranchising the black, so southern politicians studied the findings in *Happersteth* (that the right to vote comes from the state) and *Ex Parte Yarborough* (that the vote, once granted, could be protected by federal legislation) to devise a legal way of excluding blacks from the ballot box. All that was required was a system of qualifications which excluded blacks from the voters' registers (and thus put them beyond the reach of congressional action), without actually falling foul of the Fifteenth Amendment. The imagination of white politicians in the south was almost equal to this ingenious challenge.

One general approach was to establish qualifications which, although not openly making race the criterion for denying the vote, could be administered to produce an equivalent result. Towards the end of the nineteenth century Mississippi statutes required intending voters to be able to read any portion of the United States' Constitution or to give a 'reasonable interpretation' of any constitutional provision to the registrar. In 1898, the Court found that this statute did not offend the equal protection clause (*Williams* v. *Mississippi*, 1898) and, in a similar case five years later, Alabama's mandatory literacy tests passed unconstitutional muster (*Giles* v. *Harris*, 1903). In both cases, however, there was a hint that defence lawyers might well have achieved a different result if they had presented their cases more competently; already, the Court was looking beyond the colour-blind letter of statutes to their potentially colour-conscious administration. This remained the touchstone. In 1959, for instance, William Douglas accepted as constitutional North Carolina's requirement that qualified voters should be able to read and write any section of the state constitution; there was, he asserted, a rational purpose behind the requirement and the blacks who had refused to take the test because they had believed it to be discriminatory had properly been denied the vote (*Lassiter* v. *Northampton County Board of Elections*, 1959). Douglas had a sharp eye for discrimination, but where there was none there was no breach of the Constitution.

Discriminatory administration was, however, the purpose of most qualificatory schemes. For example, Oklahoma instituted a rigorous, but fairly administered, educational qualification which few blacks could hope to meet; but many whites also failed it. An exclusionary provision was therefore inserted, freeing from the test those who were legal voters in 1866 or the linear descendants of such legal voters. This 'grandfather clause' gave back the franchise to most of the whites, but the Supreme Court maintained that it violated the Fifteenth Amendment (*Guinn* v. *United States*, 1915). There may have been no mention of race, but the choice of 1 January 1866 as the basic classificatory date was clearly designed to exclude blacks. Alabama, by contrast, merely administered a colour-blind qualification to discriminate against blacks. The Boswell Amendment required aspiring electors to convince electoral registrars that they could 'understand and explain' any article of the United States' Constitution. This vague standard effectively allowed registrars, who were very much part of the Democratic Party machine, to accept or reject whomever they wished. In one Alabaman county, where blacks made up 36 per cent of the population, they made up 3.7 per cent of the qualified voters and even blacks with higher degrees were failing to satisfy the registrar. Once the discriminatory *effect* had been shown, the Court agreed that the statute, although it made no mention of race or colour, was nevertheless unconstitutional (*Davis* v. *Schnell*, 1949).

A second standard practice was the 'white primary'. In the south, nomination by the Democratic Party was, and mostly still is, tantamount to election; to deny blacks access at the primary stage would ensure that their vote in the election proper was valueless, since the crucial choice of candidates would already have been made. In 1921, the Court issued a confused judgement which seemed to assert that primary elections (which find no mention in the Constitution) were beyond regulation by Congress (*Newberry* v. *United States*, 1921). Two years later the Texas legislature passed a law which bluntly stated that 'in no event shall a Negro be eligible to participate in a Democratic party primary election held in the State of Texas'. Dr Nixon, a leading black, challenged the statute and the Court found it unconstitutional on its face (*Nixon* v. *Herndon*, 1927). The Texas legislature promptly passed a new statute permitting the executive committee of the political parties in Texas to determine by themselves who was eligible to vote. Promptly the Democratic Party's executive committee passed a rule excluding blacks from the 1928 Democratic primary. Dr Nixon, denied a ballot paper again, sued the election official, lost in the district court, lost again in the court of appeals, and, four years later, somewhat late in the day, won a victory before the Supreme Court (*Nixon* v. *Condon*, 1932). Benjamin Cardozo,

writing for the five-man majority, found that the executive committee's action was not analogous to the private acts of a golf club or a
Masonic lodge, but was an extension of the state's action, under
whose authority it had made its discriminatory policy. The committee's action was as if the state itself had denied to Dr Nixon the equal
protection of the laws guaranteed by the Fourteenth Amendment. The
Texas legislature thereupon did nothing. But the state's Democratic
Party Convention immediately adopted a resolution declaring that 'all
white citizens of the State of Texas . . . shall be eligible for membership'. On the strength of this resolution, a black called Grovey was
denied a ballot paper at the 1932 Democratic primary elections. He
sued, lost in the lower courts, and finally appealed to the Supreme
Court. A unanimous Court found against him; the Texas legislature's
careful silence meant that no state action was involved and thus the
Fourteenth Amendment was inapplicable (*Grovey* v. *Townsend*,
1935). Blessing had been given to the white primary and the exclusion
of blacks from the crucial elections of the one-party south seemed to
have been legitimised.

But the history of constitutional interpretation is replete with
examples of the Supreme Court surmounting, in time, the apparently
insurmountable. In 1939 the Department of Justice, under the liberal
Frank Murphy, established a Civil Rights Section to take action and
give life to those Acts of Congress and Articles of the Constitution
which guaranteed civil rights to individuals. One of its earliest
prosecutions was against Patrick Classic and others who, in the
overkeen but perhaps laudable attempts to thwart the political
machine of Huey Long, had in some cases altered and in others failed
to count ballots in a congressional primary. The outlook was bleak.
The two comparatively recent decisions in *Grovey*, emphasising the
essentially private nature of political parties, and *Newberry*, seem-
ingly finding the 1910 Federal Corrupt Practices Act inapplicable to
primary elections, suggested that it would be difficult to reach the
ballot irregularities indulged in by Patrick Classic.

However, precedents are often ambiguous, the Constitution is a
flexible instrument, and Justices are not without policy goals or
awareness of new and evolving standards. Harlan Fiske Stone's
opinion owed much to definitional dexterity, for he broadened the
scope of Article I's implied right to elect legislators first into a right to
choose and then into a right to participate meaningfully (*United States*
v. *Classic*, 1941). Substance once more had come into play. 'The
primary in Louisiana', he wrote, 'is an integral part of the procedure
for the popular choice of Congressmen. The right of qualified voters
to vote at the congressional primary in Louisiana and to have their
ballots counted is thus the right to participate in that choice.'

Consequently, far from accepting Classic's plea that primaries were not elections for Senators or Representatives, as set out in Article I, section 4(1), of the Constitution, but for candidates, Stone found that they were, by state law, an integral part of the process and thus within the grasp of congressional overview and the 1870 Reconstruction Act forbidding conspiracies to prevent qualified voters from effective participation. *Newberry* was quietly interred; *Grovey* was ignored.

But *Grovey* could not be ignored for ever. The conflict between that decision, that parties are private institutions beyond the reach of the Fourteenth Amendment or congressional action, and the new *Classic* finding had to be resolved. The case which did this came, appropriately enough, from Texas. Lonnie Smith, a black, sued a Texas election official for refusing to give him a ballot paper in a primary election for nomination of House and Senate Democratic candidates. The importance attached to the case may be measured by the list of organisations filing *amicus curiae* briefs on Smith's behalf—the NAACP, the American Civil Liberties Union, the Committee on Constitutional Liberties, the National Lawyers' Guild and the Workers' Defence League. They were successful (*Smith* v. *Allwright*, 1944). Stanley Reed wrote the Court's opinion and he immediately tested Smith's plea against the first principle enunciated in *Classic* and found that the primary was an integral part of the electoral process required by the Texan constitution. 'The privilege of membership in a party', he stated, 'may be . . . no concern of the state' [here he bowed stiffly towards the *Grovey* ruling], 'but when, as here, that privilege is also the essential qualification for voting in a primary to select nominees for a general election, the state makes the action of the party the action of the state.' That action denied Lonnie Smith a ballot paper because of his race and thus, because primaries were still on the Texas statute book, violated the Fifteenth Amendment. Despite Owen Roberts's impassioned defence of the *Grovey* decision which he had penned, it was explicitly overruled.

For internal political reasons, Texan Democrats accepted the decision. It was left to South Carolina to attempt an outflanking manoeuvre to bypass the consequences of *Smith* v. *Allwright*. The state legislature repealed nearly 150 statutory provisions in which primaries were authorised, regulated or just mentioned, and passed a special constitutional amendment deleting all mention of primaries in the state's constitution. In this way, it was argued, the action of the party could not be the action of the state. The federal courts thought otherwise. They looked closely at what actually happened, at the crucial importance of the Democratic Party's pre-election process, and at the denial of access to that process to blacks; even the local district court maintained that the Fifteenth Amendment had been violated and the Supreme Court acquiesced in this decision by refusing to grant *certiorari* (*Rice* v. *Elmore*, 1948). The white primary thus ultimately died, a belated attempt by some Texans to devise a private system not integral to the Democratic Party being its last vestige (*Terry* v. *Adams*, 1953). Nevertheless, blacks did not manage to register in large numbers in the southern states, for the power of the Supreme Court is itself limited and is not present at the sharp end of political action. Fear among blacks was a powerful force against registering in the 1950s and there were genuinely colour-blind qualifications which kept many blacks off the electoral rolls. It should be remembered that an individual must act positively to claim a vote in the United States and this, as elsewhere, deters a sizeable proportion of the least educated, least affluent, members of society. Many of this group were blacks and, until the Court outlawed the payment of poll tax as a constitutionally permissible qualification in 1966 (*Harper* v. *Virginia Board of Elections*), they suffered as much from educational and economic disadvantages as from racial discrimination. What was needed was positive action from Congress, administered enthusiastically by the executive branch, to seek out non-registered citizens, to assist them to register and to protect them from the often intangible, but none the less real, deterrents inherent in the public offices of the white-dominated south.

Table 5.2   *Percentage of Voters Registered in the South, by Race*

	1960		1964	1968	
	Blacks	*Whites*	*Blacks*	*Blacks*	*Whites*
Alabama	13.7	63.6	23.0	51.6	89.6
Arkansas	37.7	60.9	54.4	62.8	72.4
Florida	39.0	69.5	63.7	63.6	81.4
Georgia	n.a.		44.0	52.6	80.3
Louisiana	30.9	77.0	32.0	58.9	93.1
Mississippi	6.1	n.a.	6.7	59.8	91.5
North Carolina	38.2	92.8	46.8	51.3	83.0
South Carolina	n.a.		38.8	51.2	81.7
Tennessee	64.1*	83.5*	69.4	71.7	80.6
Texas	33.7*	50.9*	57.7	61.6	53.3
Virginia	23.0	46.2	45.7	55.6	63.4

*calculated for only two-thirds of the counties
Source: Congressional Quarterly, 1968.

Table 5.2 provides an estimate of the percentage of blacks and whites of voting age in certain states, who were registered voters in

1960, 1964 and 1968. The marked increase between 1964 and 1968 followed the executive action provided for in the 1964 Civil Rights Act and 1965 Voting Rights Act and is not confined only to blacks. Indeed, 70 per cent of those enfranchised by the revolution in participation that followed the 1965 Voting Rights Act were whites, most of whom were themselves poor and ill-educated; as Charles Morgan of the southern American Confederation of Labor Unions so aptly exclaimed, 'My God! the galoots are loose' (Bartley and Graham, 1975). The history of the extension of the franchise merely stresses the comparative impotence of the Court, for it was not able to translate the clear commandments of the Fifteenth Amendment into reality without considerable assistance from the legislature and executive. It could, and did, chip away at attempts to disfranchise blacks, but the statistics tell only too clearly that constitutional rights are essentially paper rights and that the labour of the Court, excoriated as it was by some sections of the great American public, often produced little more than a mouse. Where the Court has been much more instantly successful has been in the succeeding stage, in establishing an equal value for each individual vote.

We are familiar in the United Kingdom with constituencies of unequal-sized electorates which appear to devalue the votes of those in the largest ones in comparison to the voters in the smaller ones (Bromhead and Bromhead, 1976-7). This practice is different from, but just as discriminatory as, the more widely acknowledged activity called gerrymandering, which ensures that a careful delineation of constituency boundaries will provide maximum benefit to the drawers at the expense of more aesthetic or egalitarian considerations. The term owes its origin to the United States, where Governor Gerry of Illinois once managed to encompass the vast majority of his opponents into a single legislative district shaped like a salamander, but its practice is not alien to British politics, as Richard Crossman admitted (Crossman, 1975, p. 65). While gerrymandering requires positive human action, electorates of very different sizes can develop without any human agency other than neglect. Throughout the United States, states had failed to redraw the boundaries both of their congressional constituencies and also of their own legislatures, in many cases despite provisions in their constitutions to do so.

The twentieth century had witnessed in the United States a rapid process of urbanisation and a concentration of population into cities and towns. Whereas in 1900 over 60 per cent of the American people did not live in centres of 2,500 people or more, by 1940 that percentage had dropped to 43.5 and by 1960 to 30. What should have happened in these years was an increase in the representation of urban dwellers, often poor and ununionised and increasingly black in

composition, and a decrease in the representation of the more conservative rural areas. In Illinois, although half the population was
concentrated in the metropolitan area of Chicago, the state legislators,
overwhelmingly drawn from the southern rural districts, refused to
yield their political advantage and had obstinately refrained from
reapportioning the state. This was still the position after the 1940
census, when the state legislature once again refused to alter the
boundaries of the state's congressional seats which had remained
untouched since 1901. One district encompassing most of Chicago had
a population of 914,053, while another in the southern part of the
state had only 112,116. Professor Colegrove went to court claiming
that his right to the equal protection of the law under the Fourteenth
Amendment had been abridged and asking the federal district court to
prevent state officials from holding congressional elections in
November 1946 on these boundaries. If the court had granted the
injunction sought, Illinois would have been forced to elect its
Congressmen in a single state-wide multi-member election, in which
the inhabitants of Chicago would have been able to cast a vote of
precisely the same value as the most reactionary member of a southern
rural county.

When *Colegrove* v. *Green* reached the Court in 1946, only seven
Justices took part in the decision; Chief Justice Stone had just died
and Robert Jackson was absent at Nuremburg. Frankfurter was
supported by Stanley Reed and Harold Burton in holding that the
issue was a 'political question', not amenable to judicial review, and
warned his brethren against entering the 'political thicket' of reapportionment. Hugo Black, William Douglas and Frank Murphy disagreed, maintained that the Court did have jurisdiction, and were
themselves prepared to do something about it. All thus depended
upon Wiley Rutledge, whose view on the issue vacillated. Like Black,
his initial reaction was against intervention; like Black he later
changed his mind. But ultimately he lent the crucial vote to refusing
Colegrove's request not, as Frankfurter wanted, for the philosophical
reason that he believed it improper for the Court to get embroiled in
the issue of Fourteenth Amendment rights and apportionment, but
for the pragmatic reason that fashioning a suitable remedy so near to
the election was not practicable (Howard, 1968). This decision, with
its divided and truncated majority, became accepted as the definitive
position on whether districting decisions were open to judicial involvement. For the next fifteen years courts merely cited this *Colegrove*
decision as the precedent for their refusal to hear, or rule on, the
merits of apportionment contests appealed to them. By 1961, however, many courts in the country had been faced with a series of suits
financed and organised on the whole by minority groups like the

NAACP or the Civil Liberties Union, but also in some instances by the Justice Department itself. Some of the courts had accepted jurisdiction. In these circumstances it was not surprising that the Supreme Court decided to grant *certiorari* to one such case so that a definitive answer could be given to the new and burgeoning demand, supported by articles in prestigious law journals and other aspects of informed opinion, to bring apportionment within the reach of the Fourteenth Amendment and judicial resolution.

Baker v. *Carr*, decided on 26 March 1962, was the case which forged a new principle. It involved a complaint from eleven Tennessee voters and taxpayers that the unequal size of legislative districts in the state effectively debased the value of their votes and thus denied them the equal protection of the law guaranteed in the Fourteenth Amendment. The facts were not in dispute. It was clear that a voter in Moore County, with its population of only 2,340, had twenty-three times as much influence in choosing a state representative as a fellow Tennessee voter living in Shelby County, the seat of the city of Memphis, with its population of 312,345. Furthermore, the existing apportionment operated so that 60 per cent of the state's voters could elect only thirty-six of the ninety-nine members of the lower house and no Reapportionment Bill since 1901 had received more than thirty-six votes. A similar imbalance, and the same reluctance to reapportion, happened with respect to the state's senate. As one judge in the federal district court observed when the case first came to him in 1958, the 'situation is such that if there is no judicial remedy there would appear to be no practicable remedy at all'. But *Colegrove* v. *Green* appeared to deny the possibility of judicial remedy.

The Court was acutely divided. The case had been on the Court's docket for two years, had been reargued, and occupied six hours of oral argument. Ultimately only two members of the Court did not file some sort of individual opinion with their name attached. William Brennan wrote the opinion of the Court, which did not go to the merits of the particular case and decide whether the legislative apportionment of Tennessee was unconstitutional but contented itself with establishing clearly that federal courts could properly become involved in cases of malapportionment. Briefly, he suggested that the principle of *Colegrove* had in fact been misunderstood; a majority of the Justices had actually disagreed with Frankfurter's argument that the Supreme Court lacked the authority to exercise its judicial power and Brennan elaborated on the doctrine of 'political questions' to support his view. He was also responsive to a 1960 decision of the Court which had been prepared to enter the thicket of boundary-drawing by finding unconstitutional an Alabaman law redrawing the boundaries of the city of Tuskegee in such a way that the normal transatlantic quadrilateral was altered into 'a strangely irregular twenty-eight sided figure', thus excluding all but four or five blacks; this was no 'ordinary geographic redistricting measure even within familiar abuses of gerrymandering', as Frankfurter nicely put it, and fell foul of the Fifteenth Amendment (*Gomillion* v. *Lightfoot*, 1960). Noting the lower court judge's comment already mentioned and the Solicitor-General's brief that the Fourteenth Amendment and the courts themselves had already been involved in matters of voting rights, he pronounced the case justiciable. But he forebore to say what the remedies might be.

This was where the dissents of Felix Frankfurter and John Harlan and the doubts of Potter Stewart were clearly most telling. Frankfurter had always been nervous of entering the political thicket, or the 'mathematical quagmire', as he now called it. In reapportionment cases, there were no clear constitutional guidelines to defend judges from accusations of subjecting the people of the United States to their own private views about standards of representation. The question remained, despite Brennan's assertion that 'judicial standards under the Equal Protection clause are well developed and familiar' and Douglas's acknowledgement that 'universal equality is not the test; there is room for weighting': to what extent precisely does the Fourteenth Amendment permit a state to weight one person's vote more heavily than it does another's?

The answers to this came in 1963 and 1964 in the decisions mentioned at the beginning of this section, of which *Reynolds* v. *Sims* was the most significant. Earl Warren announced that population had to be the starting point and the controlling criterion for judgement in legislative apportionment cases. The opinion carefully avoided enunciating an absolute principle of constituency equality, but the implication was there. The five other cases decided together with *Reynolds* in fact covered a wide variety of practices and Warren struck them all down as deviations lacking sufficient justification to overcome the primary requirement of constituencies of equal size. Neither heterogeneous characteristics, nor sparse settlement, nor difficulty of access, nor attempts to ensure the representation of separate interests were permissible. Indeed, in the Colorado case, even the approval of every county in a referendum to a Senate apportionment which over-represented certain parts of the state was insufficient to override the necessity of numerical equality (*Lucas* v. *Colorado General Assembly*, 1964). For a majority of the Court, then, representation was to be defined in terms of an individual's access to an intermediary; representing interests, or geographical regions, or particular social or ethnic groups was repudiated. As Warren, in his typically blunt and unlegalistic way put it, 'legislators represent people, not trees or acres.

Legislators are elected by voters, not farms or cities or economic interests.' John Harlan, in forty-five pages of dissent, challenged Warren's interpretation at every stage from theories of representation to the historical background to the Fourteenth Amendment. But in the Supreme Court a majority, however small, carries the day.

But, as so often happens with the Supreme Court, *Reynolds* had not in fact finalised the issue. First, the question arose whether the dictates of the Fourteenth Amendment enjoined the same principle on smaller and more parochial units of government. In 1968, an affirmative answer was delivered in *Avery* v. *Midland County*. It was an ideal case by which to extend the principle established in *Reynolds*, since the four districts involved had, respectively, populations of 414, 828, 852 and 67,906. In 1970, the Court expressed with the utmost clarity its fundamental principle in these words: 'whenever a state or local government decides to select persons by popular election to perform governmental functions, the Equal Protection Clause of the Fourteenth Amendment requires that each qualified voter must be given an equal opportunity to participate in that election, and when members of an elected body are chosen from separate districts, each district must be established on a basis that will ensure, as far as is practicable, that equal numbers of voters can vote for proportionally equal numbers of officials' (*Hadley* v. *Junior College District*, 1970). The extent of the reach of *Reynolds* became clear, though the requirements of *Reynolds*, that states must 'make an honest and good faith effort to construct districts . . . as nearly of equal population as is practicable', remained less clear.

A careful reading of the *Reynolds'* opinion, and of Douglas's concurring opinion, implied that some rational considerations might permit constituencies of unequal size to pass constitutional muster. A series of cases then tested this possibility, but none succeeded (for example, *Swann* v. *Adams*, 1967). When Missouri agreed that its 1967 reapportionment, which limited the variances in size to 1.6 per cent from the ideal, could have produced constituencies of yet more equal population, the Court instructed it to do so (*Kirkpatrick* v. *Preisler*, 1969). The emphasis on a state's good faith effort did to some extent move the argument away from defining the minimum permissible deviation from absolute equality, but it did not ultimately rescue the Court from the mathematical quagmire about which Frankfurter had warned. As far as congressional districts are concerned, the Burger Court's majority has kept strictly to the principle of exact equality. With state and local government districting, the implication latent in *Reynolds* has not lain dormant. In 1971, the Court admitted that mathematical 'exactness or precision is hardly a workable constitutional requirement . . . but deviations from population equality must be justified by legitimate state considerations' (*Abate* v. *Mundt*, 1971). And in 1973 the Court, speaking through William Rehnquist, permitted a 16.4 per cent discrepancy in a state's districting plan; the scheme's aim to respect the boundaries of existing political subdivisions, although it was approaching 'tolerable limits', had a rational justification (*Mahan* v. *Howell*, 1973). The Warren Court tended, though without unanimity, to suspect all deviations; the Burger Court, also divided but still keeping to the language of *Reynolds*, has had a more generous notion of 'good faith' and a greater readiness to accept factors contravening the exact equality principle, at least where state apportionment is concerned. The changing emphasis can be seen in the number of cases in which the Burger Court has overruled lower federal court decisions imposing the exacting standards of the late Warren Court upon the states. But the principle of equality in congressional districts remains undiluted, if not enthusiastically endorsed. In 1973, variance of less than 1 per cent was not permitted since the differences were not unavoidable (*White* v. *Weiser*, 1973).

One man, one vote, one value is a fine slogan and the Supreme Court has played a major part in ensuring that it is largely translated into practice. But the issues are not settled. The Court is being asked to deduce from the Constitution whether residence requirements infringe on individuals' right to vote or whether there can be differential access to the ballot box for a referendum on a specialised topic. More problematic is the question of gerrymandering, which was raised before the Court in 1964 (*Wright* v. *Rockefeller*), but which elicited no judicial intervention, though some legal scholars have argued that the equal protection clause is relevant here too (Edwards, 1970). A majority of the Court, however, has remained wedded to the notion that the vote is an individual right and districting schemes which have as their consequences the underrepresentation of particular groups are not unconstitutional unless, of course, the scheme is designed to destroy the intent of the Fifteenth Amendment (*Whitcomb* v. *Chavis*, 1971). This, however, is an open invitation to gerrymandering and, given the information available to legislators through computers, the temptation to draw district boundaries to suit the personal predilection of legislatures becomes very powerful and the possibility for extensive partisan gerrymandering is thereby enhanced (O'Rourke, 1972). When Wells succeeded in persuading the Court in 1969 that New York's legislature had been unconstitutionally districted (*Wells* v. *Rockefeller*, 1969), he soon became alarmed at the extremely partisan nature of the ensuing state gerrymandered apportionment schemes; he returned to the federal court in February 1970 to plead that, if the Court did nothing else, it should at least restore the plan he had successfully contested the year before! He lost.

With regular decennial censuses demanding reapportionment, the Court will continue to struggle in the political thicket and wallow in the mathematical quagmire. To that extent Frankfurter and Harlan have been proved correct. Yet Tom Clark's concurring opinion in *Baker* remains unanswered, for the only practical way equal representation could be won was through judicial action. 'If men were angels,' Madison wrote in the *Federalist*, 'no government would be necessary', and Clark knew only too well that politicians in America were no angels. Judicial involvement *was* the only practical remedy, but was it *constitutionally* required? This represents well the enduring conflict in the American system of government between the precise and limited imperatives of the Constitution and the need to adapt to new situations and new values. It is difficult to see, realistically, how the Court could have avoided being drawn into the mathematical quagmire of reapportionment at some stage in the egalitarian mood of the 1960s; and it is difficult to see how it can extricate itself.

SCHOOL INTEGRATION

The Supreme Court has become involved in a wide array of matters affecting the schools of America. Reading the Bible or reciting a specially written prayer at the beginning of the day were deemed to contravene the First Amendment's separation of church and state; on First Amendment grounds, too, the loyalty oaths required of teachers came under judicial scrutiny, as did Arkansas's law which forbade the teaching of Darwin's evolutionary theories. The right of children to wear armbands as a political protest against the Vietnam War was argued before the Court, as was the proposition that caning fell foul of the new 'fundamental respect for humanity' principle now written into the 'cruel and unusual punishment' clause of the Eighth Amendment. However, the most famous and perhaps most contentious area of involvement has been the Court's attempts to resolve questions arising out of racially segregated patterns of schooling. The landmark decision here was, of course, *Brown* v. *the Board of Education of Topeka* (1954).

The overruling of the 'separate but equal' doctrine set out in *Plessy* v. *Ferguson* (1896) followed, as is usually the case, a set of stepping-stones which prepared the ground for the Court's historic break with the past. A series of decisions concerned with higher education foreshadowed the ultimate demise of the 'separate but equal' doctrine in the nation's schooling. In 1938, the Court had taken a much tougher look than before at the reality of the separate provisions for blacks and whites and did not allow Missouri, in order to retain its law school as a Caucasian preserve, to pay for the graduate training of a black in a university outside the state (*Missouri ex rel. Gaines* v. *Canada*, 1938). Then, in 1950, the Court found that the state of Texas, although it provided a law school for blacks as well as others for whites, did not meet the requirements of equality; significantly, its reasons for so doing stressed the intangible factors making for greatness in a law school and implied that no exclusively black law school could ever meet the new tests for equal provisions (*Sweatt* v. *Painter*, 1950). In an accompanying case, the Court found that Oklahoma's admission of a black to its state law school was vitiated by the treatment meted out to the student; he was obliged to work and eat in segregated portions of the university and to be tutored separately (*McLaurin* v. *Oklahoma State Regents*, 1950). The 'separate but equal' principle had not been overruled, but the possibility of doing this was that much closer. In the 1950 cases, Chief Justice Vinson had cast the cases as tests of the equal protection clause and had gone some way, if only by studied implication, to suggest that segregated establishments could never provide equal protection. This was a trend not only to be observed in the educational field, for the Court had, over the years, found the separate facilities on which it was called to pass judgement consistently unequal.

When no attempts were made by southern politicians to respond to the 1950 decisions and to improve the facilities of negro schools and colleges, the NAACP's lawyers, led by Thurgood Marshall, prepared five desegregation suits in carefully selected parts of the country. The lawyers did not argue the familiar point that the educational facilities were unequal, but the revolutionary point that the 'separate but equal' rule, the Court-sanctioned principle which had legitimised and perhaps encouraged the Jim Crow laws of the south, was itself a violation of the equal protection clause of the Fourteenth Amendment. The cases, it need hardly be said, failed in the lower courts. However, the Supreme Court decided, narrowly, to grant *certiorari* and extensive oral argument took place in December 1952. In June 1953, however, the Court set the cases down for re-argument, asking the lawyers of both sides to address themselves to some specific questions, of which the intention of the framers and ratifiers of the Fourteenth Amendment was only one. In December oral argument took place again and on 17 May 1954 Earl Warren announced the unanimous decision. 'In the field of public education the doctrine of "separate but equal" has no place. Separate educational facilities are inherently unequal ... the plaintiffs and others similarly situated for whom the actions have been brought are, by reason of the segregation complained of, deprived of the equal protection of the laws guaranteed by the Fourteenth Amendment.' The care and assistance which went into Thurgood Marshall's efforts on behalf of the blacks and Earl Warren's contribution to the unanimity of the ultimate disposition of the cases have been told elsewhere (see Garraty, 1964, pp. 243-68; Ulmer, 1971b; Berry, 1978, pp. 154-61). How this principle was to be translated into remedial action is our present concern.

The first consequence was further argument and a second opinion dealing with implementation. The May 1955 decision, *Brown II*, recognised the political realities of the day and forbore to outlaw segregation immediately. As Chapter 4 has already described, the phrases used by Earl Warren ('good faith compliance', 'practical flexibility in shaping remedies', 'prompt and reasonable start', 'all deliberate speed') permitted a speed of implementation which was deliberately slow. For nearly ten years, the Supreme Court, except for the incursion into Little Rock's affairs, kept out of the fray and left the task of giving concrete effect to its edict to the lower courts. The southern states followed the March 1956 Southern Manifesto, which pledged its signatories to use all legal means to maintain legislation. Prince Edward County, Virginia, provided one of the companion cases to *Brown* and one of the most extreme examples of procrastination. The Virginian legislature enacted a programme of 'massive resistance', which included closing all integrated schools, cutting off all their funds, paying tuition grants to students in private schools, and providing state and local financial aid, including retirement benefits for teachers, to those schools. When Virginia's own supreme court found that this programme contravened the state constitution, the legislature enacted instead a law which made school attendance a matter of local option and thus, it thought, beyond the reach of the Fourteenth Amendment's limitations on state actions. Prince Edward County promptly closed its own schools and provided various kinds of financial support for privately operated segregated schools. It was not until 1964 that a sharp and wide-ranging rebuke came from a unanimous Supreme Court (*Griffin* v. *School Board of Prince Edward County*), and the board of supervisers reopened its schools on an integrated basis. Yet even then they paid out $180,000 in tuition grants to white pupils in private, segregated schools, an action which the court of appeals found to be a contempt of court, and in the summer of 1967 the board finally returned the money to the county treasury.

Until the Court was prepared to involve itself in establishing new, and more precise, rules to guide the overseeing of the desegregatory process, the southern school boards could, and did, procrastinate almost indefinitely. The 1955 ruling was held by lower courts to forbid segregation, but not to require integration, and thus permitted plans which involved choice or neighbourhood schools or other ostensibly non-racial criteria. The vagueness of *Brown II* clearly assisted recalcitrant authorities, as this description of a single New Orleans case so vividly illustrates:

> Over a relatively short span of time between 1952 and 1962, the one case consumed thousands of hours of lawyers' and judges' time: it required 41 separate judicial decisions involving ultimately the energies of every Fifth Circuit judge, two district court judges, and the consideration of the United States' Supreme Court on eleven separate decisions. By the end of the decade, backed by the Fifth Circuit and in the face of attacks from all flanks, Federal District Judges J. Skelly Wright and Herbert Christenberry had invalidated a total of forty-four statutes enacted by the Louisiana legislature; had cited and convicted two state officials for contempt of court; and had issued injunctions forbidding the continued flouting of their orders against a state court, all state executives, and the entire membership of the Louisiana legislature. (Read, 1975-6, pp. 14-15)

Yet, even after all that, only token desegregation actually took place.

Two developments in the early 1960s helped to accelerate the process of desegregation, which had got under way with only limited procrastination in the border states. In the general political field, direct action by blacks brought to the whole nation's attention the treatment they were receiving at the hands of southern politicians. Although Eisenhower's Attorney-General had filed an *amicus* brief in *Brown II*, the Republican administration had been conspicuous for its unconcern with the difficulties of court-ordered desegregation and the President, apart from that single Little Rock incident, had studiously refrained from lending his authority and prestige to the desegregatory movement. A new President in 1961 and mounting pressure on Congress produced a different climate of opinion and, following Kennedy's assassination and a determined push from Lyndon Johnson, the 1964 Civil Rights Act was signed into law on 2 July. This statute was the most far-reaching and comprehensive civil rights legislation since the Reconstruction era and only passed after the longest filibuster in senatorial history. Title IV ('Desegregation in Public Education') provided for technical assistance, funds for training, and grants to schools and educational systems to aid their desegregation plans and processes. Title VI ('Non-Discrimination in Federally Assisted Programs') provided for the withholding of federal funds from institutions which discriminated on grounds of race. The Act thus provided the Department of Health, Education, and Welfare

(HEW) with sticks and carrots to bully or cajole school boards into accepting the letter and spirit of *Brown*.

The second development took place within the judiciary. The appeals judges of the fifth circuit, which was deeply involved in desegregation suits, devised a new tactic to cope with their acute problems. *Brown II* was a general opinion and the Supreme Court refrained for more than a decade from enunciating new principles which would be less easy to circumvent. The appeals court was thus faced with an apparently endless process of case-by-case adjudication, remanding disputes back to district courts but without uniform standards laid down by the highest court. In 1965 and 1966, the appeals court, speaking through Judge John Minor Wisdom, broke with the past and established new uniform standards to be binding throughout its circuit. These minimum standards were the guidelines established by the Department of Health, Education, and Welfare which school boards had to meet if they were to qualify for federal funds. In *United States* v. *Jefferson County Board of Education* (1966), the appeals court, or rather nine of its twelve members, consolidated seven cases from Alabama and Louisiana, where not a single school district involved had made a start to desegregation in the decade following *Brown II*, and announced that the new standard which school boards had to meet was this simple one: would the plan actually produce integrated schools?

The Supreme Court finally entered the fray in 1968, when it heard oral argument in the case of *Green* v. *County School Board*, and addressed itself for the first time since 1955 to the means of desegregation. *Green* was an ideal case. There was little residential segregation in New Kent County and there were only two schools. The school board operated a freedom of choice plan, the consequence of which was a dual system; not a single white had chosen to go to the formerly black school, while the enrolment of blacks in the formerly white school was limited to 15 per cent. Brennan, who authored the Court's unanimous opinion, used much of the language Wisdom had employed in *Jefferson*, and asserted that school boards now had an affirmative duty to integrate the state schools. Yet he still forbore to set out precise criteria by which courts could recognise when a school was in fact sufficiently integrated to pass constitutional muster. The percentage of each race in the schools, staff as well as pupils, was one criterion, but *what* percentage would suffice was never spelled out. 'Delays are no longer tolerable', the Court thundered, but such an assertion of high principle did not resolve the legal question of what exactly was, and what was not, the equal protection of the law.

Richard Nixon's arrival in the White House threatened to put a further brake on desegregation. The *Green* decision had angered many southern politicians and they attempted to outflank the Court in two ways. One tactic was to move from a state system of education to an entirely private system of education. In September 1968, 6,000 Mississippi children went to private schools; in September 1969, the number was over 20,000 and more than 300,000 children in the eleven states of the old Confederacy were enrolled in 'private academies'. Ultimately, financial pressures and the Court's refusal to permit public money or facilities to be used in any way to help private, segregated educational institutions chipped away at that tactic. The second approach was to bring pressure to bear on the executive department. Senators like Stennis and Thurmond, conscious of Nixon's debt to them on the electoral front and well aware of the tenor of Nixon's campaign speeches, encouraged the new President to slow down the enthusiastic attempts of HEW officials to desegregate the southern schools. This the administration attempted to do, and Chief Judge John R. Brown was actually written to and asked to delay desegregation orders. For the first time, then, the executive and the NAACP found themselves on opposing sides; the NAACP appealed a judgement from the fifth circuit court of appeals which had fashioned a two-stage remedy to avoid too much disruption in the middle of a school year (*Alexander* v. *Holmes County Board of Education*, 1969).

Earl Warren had begun his Chief Justiceship with *Brown*; Warren Burger was to begin his with a school desegregation case as well. *Alexander* was a brief *per curiam* opinion which buried for ever notions of 'all deliberate speed' and announced that the rule in the United States was 'desegregate schools now, litigate later'. At last, genuine integration began in earnest. The fifth circuit decided that all that could be said about school cases had been said and that there was no further purpose in writing opinions; between 2 December 1969 and 24 December 1970, the circuit handed down 109 orders involving eighty-nine separate school districts. In addition, a standing panel of three judges issued fifty-seven further orders in the Hinds, Alexander and Holmes county districts of Mississippi alone. This new toughness paid dividends. By the beginning of the 1972-3 academic year, only 8.7 per cent of blacks in the deep south were still attending all minority schools, as opposed to more than 90 per cent only three years earlier, and half of all black children were in schools which were predominantly white. In the north, this last figure was only just over a quarter (Smith, 1975, p. 323). Although the Court's firmer action contributed greatly to the massive changes in the south, much of the credit must go to the federal judges of the lower courts. In the 1950s and early 1960s, they had been in part responsible for the deliberately snail-like pace of desegregation; but in the late 1960s and 1970s they were more liberal than the Nixon administration in many instances and managed to distance themselves from the social pressures which inhibited their predecessors. Only when their court was located within a district which was litigating did judges permit high levels of segregation to occur (Giles and Walker, 1975); otherwise they gave concrete reality to the Supreme Court's far from precise edicts.

One of the difficulties which remained concerned the appropriate methods by which integration should be achieved. In areas where the races are divided geographically, only busing can remedy the segregation in the local school system. But busing is not a popular policy because it is manifestly an instance of positive integration and grates on many Americans' instinctive belief in the virtue of neighbourhood schools. A district judge ordered the busing of children in the large school district of Charlotte-Mecklenburg in North Carolina and this order was appealed. A unanimous Supreme Court upheld the lower court's decision in an important, but again ambiguous, decision (*Swann* v. *Charlotte-Mecklenburg Board of Education*, 1971). Burger's opinion stressed a number of permissible considerations a judge could take into account and also a variety of practices he could order as relief. Mathematical ratios of students and staff, for instance, were good starting points rather than an inflexible requirement; busing, which has a long history in the educational systems of the American states, was an appropriate relief in certain circumstances, as here (where most children would actually spend *less* time on a bus than in segregated days), but was not the only one. Perhaps it is too much to ask a Court of law to define what equal educational facilities are and to lay down a policy for ensuring their existence; this certainly emphasises how inappropriate in many ways it is to expect the Supreme Court to resolve major questions of educational policy. *Swann* did not solve the problems of the circuit court of appeals because it did not define the law. On the contrary, the 'long-awaited decree from Mount Olympus was instead an ambiguous, two-sided Delphic pronouncement raising crucial issues which have yet to be decided' (Read, 1975, p. 38).

One issue which *Swann* consciously left unresolved was the constitutionality of all minority schools in those cities, in the north and west, where minorities lived in minority ghettos not as a result of state-authorised segregatory practices. Does the Fourteenth Amendment reach *de facto* segregation? By 1972, the worst examples of dual systems were in the north and cases from cities there began to appear on the Supreme Court's docket. On 21 June 1973, a divided Court looked as though it might reach the heart of this extraordinarily difficult matter. In *Keyes* v. *School District No. 1*, it found that the segregated pattern of schools in Denver flowing from segregation of housing was unconstitutional. But the Court achieved this result by extending the concept of *de jure* segregation considerably and arguing that certain laws and practices had in fact produced the racially segregated pattern of housing reflected in the unintegrated schools. One year later, the Court divided by five votes to four on the fundamental question of the constitutionality of one-race schools in areas dominated by a single race. The case came from Detroit, where the plaintiffs claimed that the imposition of school attendance zones over the existing segregated residential pattern had produced a dual system. Intra-district relief could not desegregate, because the school district was itself overwhelmingly black. The blacks' lawyer argued that school district lines were simply matters of political convenience and could not be used to deny constitutional rights. The district judge agreed and ordered cross-district relief, integrating the overwhelmingly white suburbs with the overwhelmingly black inner city area into a single school district. The Supreme Court reversed (*Milliken* v. *Bradley*, 1974). For Burger and the three other Nixon appointees, political boundaries, unless consciously drawn with the intention of creating racially specific populations, were beyond the reach of the Court; Potter Stewart joined them 'on the facts', implying that a different set of facts might persuade him that cross-district relief was permissible. As a consequence, the black children of Detroit's inner city, just as the children of many such cities, are locked into an increasingly black, segregated school district, with no real hope of escape into the better-financed, predominantly white schools of the affluent suburbs. This may be tragic; but it may also be an issue which the politicians rather than the courts should resolve. Since, however, the dominant coalition has little intention of redrawing school district boundaries to produce an integrated educational system, the unfortunate blacks almost inevitably take their plight to the courts in the hope that the majority's will may be circumvented.

This is the fundamental truth behind so much litigation before the Court. The first attempts at integration came from individuals who were denied, by duly passed laws, the opportunity of going to the law schools of their choice. History has come, ironically, almost full circle. The higher education cases and the *Brown* cases were based on three factors: the importance of education, the intangible qualities of education and the blacks' historical deprivation of education. This thread runs wide as well as long. In 1969, for instance, John Harlan found that unequal educational facilities in the past so discriminated against blacks that literacy tests, even if impartially administered, unconstitutionally deprived blacks of the franchise (*Gaston County* v. *United States*, 1969). In recent years, many law schools and medical schools have made positive attempts to attract and encourage students from minority groups and have, as it were, positively discriminated in their favour, setting aside a quota of places for them in their annual intake. Allan Bakke is a white man, who was twice refused entry to the University of California Medical School at Davis, even though his test scores were higher than some blacks who were admitted under the Davis special programme intended to undo some of the damage created in the past by the nation's discriminatory treatment of minorities. The supreme court of California, in an opinion clearly designed to ensure that the Supreme Court spoke authoritatively on the matter, found that Bakke had been unconstitutionally refused entry. The University of California appealed (*Regents of the University of California* v. *Bakke*, 1978).

The case brought into question the whole principle of affirmative action. Ever since the 1964 Civil Rights Act, and more especially since the first government programmes in 1967, public and private institutions have tried to improve the educational and job opportunities for minorities and women. Comprehensive plans are designed with the conscious purpose of increasing the number and percentage of minorities and women at all levels and this can only be achieved, as at Davis, by favouring minorities (or women) over others. Allan Bakke contended that the special admissions programme at Davis, which set a fixed quota for minority students, operated to exclude him on the basis of race in violation of the equal protection clause of the Fourteenth Amendment and Title VI of the Civil Rights Act. The Supreme Court provided in its response another studied show of ambiguity. A majority of five ruled that Allan Bakke should be admitted; quotas, it was held, contradict equal protection for all individuals. Yet, a different majority ruled that race was a legitimate consideration in educational admission and thus gave renewed legitimacy to the principle at least of affirmative action. This five-man majority accepted that individuals at a disadvantage to compete because of past discrimination do need special assistance in obtaining and improving opportunities.

The issue of integration in the United States' educational system is not yet ended. The right to equal education, like the right to vote, is a fine slogan, but it lacks precision. It just is not possible to divine from the Fourteenth Amendment what does, and what does not, meet the requirements of equal protection. Once the Court entered the uncharted seas of substantive equal protection, it created for itself a set of questions for which there are no clear answers, let alone judicial ones. By asserting what did not meet the equal protection requirements, it was bound to be drawn into the much more difficult problem of deciding what did. The readiness of American citizens to have recourse to the judicial branch when they have lost the day in the electoral political arena puts an extraordinary burden on the Justices of the Supreme Court. For they are called upon to resolve disputes as a Court of Law when the issues are manifestly often non-legal in substance. They could avoid this impossible task if they chose not to arbitrate on much of their docket; but what, then, would be left of the Bill of Rights and the Fourteenth Amendment if the Court refused to specify what behaviour fell foul of them? Yet, having once become immersed in the detail of concrete disputes, where are the lines to be drawn? As these case studies indicate, a Supreme Court Justice's life is in many ways made much easier if the legislatures will address themselves to the major social issues of the day. If they do not, by default, the social issues will be resolved, for better or worse, temporarily or permanently, by the Supreme Court.

6

The Supreme Court and American Democracy

If the Supreme Court were merely a mechanism which 'discovered' the law according to objective, impartial and universally accepted principles, its role in the American political system would be an unexceptionable one. It would still remain a political institution, because it would authoritatively allocate values, but it would perform its allocative task in such an antiseptic and immutable manner as to give rise to no controversy. But the simple fact is that the Supreme Court is not, and never has been, a mechanism, beyond the reach of human passion and frailty, by which particular legal disputes may be satisfactorily resolved. The power inherent in judicial review is exercised by nine men, who frequently disagree and whose ultimate decisions manifestly affect the social and economic fabric of American life. In a country which prides itself on its democratic political culture, the existence of a Court which is composed of nine unelected and unaccountable men, and which has the potentiality for considerable impact on society, is clearly something of a contradiction.

Judicial review appears in many guises and is practised to varying degrees in a large number of the world's independent states. Three distinct meanings can be attached to the phrase. First, members of a judiciary review the actions of the executive to ensure that they are not beyond what the statutes of the land permit; in short, they interpret the statutes of a country. This statutory interpretation may assert, for instance, that a British minister has exceeded his authority in prohibiting Freddie Laker from inaugurating a cheap air service to the United States or in forcing the Tameside Education Authority to implement a comprehensive system of education in its schools. Such exercises of judicial review are common throughout the world; if, however, the legislature finds fault with the judges' interpretation of a statute, it can, and frequently does, amend existing legislation to circumvent the limitations set down by the court. Secondly, in federal systems of government judges are constantly adjudicating between the rival claims of the central and unit governments. Indeed, it is difficult to envisage a truly federal system of government where there is no institution performing this function, because no form of words in a Constitution can quite manage to encompass every eventuality so that no disputes arise over the proper area of competence and authority allocated to the different levels of government. Finally, and to a large extent an extension of the previous distinction, courts measure the actions of legislatures and executives against the grants of power specified in a national Constitution and against the limitations enjoined on governments by, for example, constitutionally entrenched individual and group rights. The courts' decisions in both these last two instances can only be reversed by constitutional amendment. To the extent that this process may be extremely difficult, it is possible to speak of judicial supremacy. This is the phrase most appropriate for the United States, since neither the President and the executive branch nor the Congress nor the states can of themselves rescind a Supreme Court judgement. The cumbersome process of constitutional amendment must be followed if there is widespread antagonism towards the Court's decision on the current meaning of the Constitution.

Judicial supremacy is necessarily an uneasy bedfellow of representative democracy. It is, as Felix Frankfurter once proclaimed, 'a limitation on popular government' (*Minersville School District* v. *Gobitis*, 1940) and therefore inherently suspect. Five Justices of the Supreme Court, after all, may invalidate legislation passed by a duly elected Congress or state legislature and thus, unelected and unaccountable though they are, elevate their own preferences over those of a body whose authority flows from the very wellsprings of democratic participation. This may be an extreme presentation of the conflict between judicial review and representative democracy, but it underlies, often more implicitly than explicitly, much of the debate over the most appropriate behaviour of Supreme Court Justices. In this simple juxtaposition, the Court becomes a third legislative chamber, but a superordinate one subject to no constraint but its own sense of self-restraint; it usurps, in decisions like *Brown* and *Roe*, the law-making function which can only properly be performed by elected bodies and it does this without being accountable to any elected political master or any electorate. Judicial supremacy is thus profoundly undemocratic.

This argument, however, cannot pass without some initial general observations. The political system of the United States is not, never has been, and was not intended to be, marked by an undiluted principle of majority rule. The composition of the Senate, the processes by which the President is elected, the acceptance that states establish the qualifications for voting, all these indicate a certain distrust of unbridled egalitarianism. Furthermore, the first eight Amendments, themselves to some extent the price necessary for several states actually joining the Union, are categorical statements of limitations on the power of elected officials and were expressly designed to deny politicians the full fruits of their electoral victories. Thus, the Supreme Court's authority to frustrate legislative majorities is not, in itself, opposed to the traditions of the American political system, but represents, on the contrary, one fundamental theme constantly recurring in American political thought and consciously written into the Constitution. Alexander Bickel is surely wrong to state so categorically that 'judicial review is a deviant institution in American democracy' (Bickel, 1962, p. 18), for the fear of popular majorities, which lies at the heart of doctrines about judicial review as well as providing a central pillar of the constitutional edifice itself, is implicitly part of the mainstream of American political philosophy.

Yet, having said this, it is by no means clear that the Supreme Court has a legitimate right to be the final arbiter of the constitutional thresholds to the exercise of political power. Few people have seriously argued for long that the Constitution is so unambiguous that unconstitutional action is instantly recognisable. No, the ambiguities of the Constitution require constant examination and resolution and there are no specific skills unique to judges which enable this function to be performed in an objective way entirely separate from the individual judge's own notions of the judicial role and the relative importance of competing claims and rights. To some extent—and this is the crucial caveat to which we will return—constitutional adjudication is necessarily a subjective exercise, except in those rare instances where express provisions of the Constitution have been manifestly ignored. (These, in any case, do not bother the Supreme Court, because the decisions of the lower courts are promptly affirmed.) However, there are no *prima facie* reasons why Congress or the President, both of whom swear to uphold the Constitution, could not do the job just as well, or badly, as the Supreme Court. Surely, the argument runs, Senator Hugo Black or Attorney-General Frank Murphy were the same people as Justice Black and Justice Murphy. Nowhere in the Constitution itself does it lay down that the final arbiter of the meaning of the Constitution, supreme law of the land though it is, shall be the Supreme Court.

Historians, unfortunately, cannot resolve decisively questions about the role intended for the Supreme Court by the Founding Fathers. Each side in the argument can find scraps of evidence to buttress their points of view. What is clear is that in their deliberations the Founding Fathers were well aware of the potential role of the

Supreme Court and some foresaw clearly the developments that actually took place, though this prescience produced disquiet as well as satisfaction. Hamilton's essays on the Constitution, designed to persuade New Yorkers to ratify it, give an indication of what one faction within the Constitution's framers envisaged. Although he noted that the judiciary would be 'the least dangerous branch', he also clearly envisaged judicial review of legislative acts and observed that the limitations built into the Constitution could only be ensured in practice through the courts, 'whose duty it must be to declare all acts contrary to the manifest tenor of the Constitution void', for 'the interpretation of the laws is the proper and peculiar province of the courts' (Hamilton, 1971, pp. 395-7). After all the Constitution established three branches of government, each of which exercises some control over the other and each of which is thus also to a certain extent controlled by the others. The Bill of Rights, if it were to be an effective bulwark against overweening national power, required the courts to defend the protected rights against any attacks on them by the federal government. 'If the Bill of Rights is incorporated in the Constitution,' James Madison said at the time echoing Thomas Jefferson's earlier reservations on the 1789 document, 'independent tribunals of justice will consider themselves in a peculiar manner the guardians of those rights.' Judicial supremacy is thus not necessarily antipathetic to the general principles of the Constitution. Yet it is also true that the Constitution does not contain, as it could easily have done, any categorical grant to the Supreme Court of the power to exercise final judgement on the meaning and reach of the Constitution's clauses. To those who assert with unrepentant certitude that the Constitution did not grant the Court the power of judicial review, and ultimately judicial supremacy, there can be no riposte.

Yet such an absolutist position is singularly unhelpful, for that particular argument has long since ceased to carry weight. The facts are indisputable; the Supreme Court *does* exercise the power of judicial review and *is* the ultimate arbiter of constitutionality. This was John Marshall's legacy and it is a legacy which has been eagerly inherited by succeeding Justices as well as accepted by successive generations of politicians. The requirement in a federal system for a supreme body to arbitrate between the competing claims of national and state governments, as well as the need for an authoritative voice to guard the rights entrenched in several Amendments, give the Supreme Court's role a logic and defence of its own. It may be that the Court is not an ideal vehicle to perform the tasks it is now called on to carry out, in that the adversary system of justice knows only rights and wrongs and lacks the capacity to adjust competing claims in the pluralistic tradition of congressional politics. It may be that the

Court's exercise of its power weakens the proper distinctions between national government and state autonomy just as it detracts from the principle of three branches of government, separate and equal. And it is certainly true that in moments of its history its members have acted, not as Platonic guardians, but as partisan politicians, that rights have not been safeguarded against the passions of a discriminatory majority, that the role of umpire has merged suspiciously into the role of player. But those lapses from grace do not detract either from the philosophical point that the Supreme Court is the least inappropriate institution to state authoritatively the meaning of the Constitution or from the empirical point that it is now expected to do so and cannot escape what has become its duty. The haste with which the 1964 Civil Rights Act, the 1965 Voting Rights Act and 1971 Voters' Qualifications Act were brought to the Court to test their constitutionality testifies to that.

The argument, then, is not *whether* the Supreme Court should exercise its powers, but *how* and *in what instances* it should do so. As has been repeatedly stressed, the meaning of the Constitution is not self-evident and problems arise when rights conflict. Doubt entails choice. And, as Oliver Wendell Holmes once wrote, '[w]here there is doubt, the simple tool of logic does not suffice, and even if it is disguised and unconscious, the judges are called on to exercise the sovereign prerogative of choice' (Holmes, 1920). In order to minimise the subjectivity of a Justice's action, it is necessary to minimise the areas where doubts are legitimately raised. Learned Hand, for instance, took as a basic, unargued assumption that the words of the Constitution should be understood within the historical context in which they were written. Like Roger Taney's judgement in *Dred Scott*, then, he assumed that the Constitution spoke with the same words and the same meaning to all generations. Even on his own terms, this view presents problems, since the historical context does not always ensure a clear and perfect understanding of the precise implications intended by the Founding Fathers in the general phrases of the Constitution. Besides, it is, as John Marshall said, a Constitution to be interpreted, a blueprint requiring detailed infilling in the interstices and grey areas left by its generalities. The notion of what constitutes 'equal protection', for example, does change over time both in meaning and application. Indeed, one of the strongest defences of the Supreme Court has been that, despite momentary and sometimes not so momentary aberrations, it has adapted and reformulated the Constitution to meet the exigencies of the time. This has been crucial; for only by a gradual process of reformulation and redefinition could the Constitution retain its reverence, its legitimacy and its effectiveness.

The label 'self-restrained' is commonly appended to those who minimise their 'sovereign prerogative of choice' and abstain from exercising the Court's potential power to outlaw the legislative and executive actions of national and state politicians. Justices of this school tend, therefore, to presume the constitutionality of legislation, to give legislators the benefit of the doubt and accept claims of benign intention unless the evidence is manifestly to the contrary. It was the actions of the Supreme Court in the first third of the twentieth century, reaching their culmination in the wholesale invalidating of Roosevelt's New Deal, which were mainly responsible for encouraging the notion of self-restraint. The tendency, and until 1934 it was only a tendency, to read into the 'due process' clause of the Fourteenth Amendment what a majority of the Justices believed to be wise policy was to extend beyond proper bounds the undeniable power of judicial review. As Harlan Fiske Stone wrote in his powerful dissent to *United States* v. *Butler* (1936), the decision which declared the Agricultural Adjustment Act unconstitutional, 'Courts are not the only agency of government that must be assumed to have capacity to govern'. The philosophy of self-restraint, which grants to politicians' actions the presumption of constitutionality, was in the 1930s and 1940s very much associated with liberal causes and liberal public men. But there is no necessary correlation between the two. A self-restrained Court is merely one that is in step with the legislative and executive branches of government; it will thus be liberal or conservative depending upon which role the other branches have adopted. In the 1960s and 1970s, the apostle of self-restraint, John Harlan, was often thought of as a conservative, which in many ways perhaps he was, but his words echo those of Stone. In *Harper* v. *Virginia Board of Elections* (1966), he wrote in dissent:

> Property and poll tax qualifications, very simply, are not in accord with current egalitarian notions of how a modern democracy ought to be organised. It is of course entirely fitting that legislatures should modify the law to reflect such changes in popular attitudes. However, it is all wrong, in my view, for the Court to adopt the political doctrines popularly accepted at a particular moment in our history and to declare all others to be irrational and invidious . . . The due process [clause] of the Fourteenth Amendment does not enact the laissez-faire theory of society . . . The equal protection clause of that Amendment does not rigidly impose upon Americans an ideology of unrestrained egalitarianism.

A line, nevertheless, still has to be drawn between what is, and what is not, permissible; a self-restrained Justice would tend to choose a position near the non-interventionist end of the continuum. Yet this act of choice remains a matter of subjective judgement.

To avoid this element of subjectivity and to escape from the charges of imposing personal value preferences on to the function of judging, attempts have been made to establish firm principles which would avoid, or at least drastically diminish, the need for choice. For the most part, these have been unsuccessful attempts at creating an ordered universe out of the confusion of reality; there are no neutral principles, apart from the complete abdication of judicial review itself, which could alleviate a Justice's duty to make choices (Wechsler, 1959, argues that there are; Miller and Howell, 1960, dispute). But there are clearly certain principles which limit the extent to which justices are free to give full rein to their personal predilections. Harlan Stone, who preached the virtues of self-restraint, was associated with one such set of principles, but it was a set of principles which actually permitted him, and those who followed him, to dilute the presumption of constitutionality with a clear conscience. In a case of scant intrinsic importance, *United States* v. *Carolene Products Company* (1938), Stone observed that even in the absence of specific legislative findings, the existence of facts to support a legislature's judgement of appropriate policy must be presumed. He then inserted a footnote, the celebrated Footnote 4, which runs in part as follows:

There may be narrower scope for operation of the presumption of constitutionality when legislation appears on its face to be within a specific prohibition of the Constitution, such as those of the first ten amendments, which are deemed equally specific when held to be embraced within the fourteenth . . . It is unnecessary to consider now whether legislation which restricts those political processes which can ordinarily be expected to bring about repeal of undesirable legislation is to be subjected to more exacting judicial scrutiny under the general prohibitions of the Fourteenth Amendment than are most other types of legislation . . . Nor need we inquire whether similar considerations enter into the review of statutes directed at particular religions . . . whether prejudice against discrete and insular majorities may be a special condition, which tends seriously to curtail the operation of those political processes ordinarily to be relied upon to protect minorities, and which may call for a correspondingly more searching judicial inquiry.

In this way Stone introduced the notion of preferred freedoms, of particular rights which demand special scrutiny from the Court. In

fact, Stone's clerk, Louis Lusky, drafted the second and third paragraphs and the first was added by Charles Evans Hughes, but Stone
took the credit for it.

The notion of preferred freedoms set out here has much to
commend it. The assumption that the will of immediate majorities
should prevail is not by any means the only cornerstone of the
American political system. The Constitution is entirely explicit in its
concern for individual rights and the Court is sometimes thought of as
the bastion of those rights. Nobody has championed this view more
strongly than Hugo Black, whose public reputation for activist
defence of civil rights against discriminatory legislative and executive
action disguised his essentially restraintist political philosophy. Black
was a New Dealer, one of those Roosevelt nominations to the Court
who validated with alacrity congressional attempts to control and
regulate the national economy; but he was also a firm believer in
constitutionalism, in the theory that good government, the ideal
American government indeed, depended upon a dispersal of power,
limitations on governmental officers, and an assured place for
individual liberties (Sartori, 1962). Black consequently saw the first
eight Amendments as a central pillar of his country's constitutional
system and he extended the rights adumbrated there, through the
'privilege and immunities' clause of the Fourteenth Amendment, to
the states themselves (Black, 1960, 1968). Perhaps this did violence to
history as it did violence to the strict notions of dual federalism; but,
on the other hand, it enabled Black to strike out actively against many
state actions without exercising much personal evaluation. At least,
the incorporation of the Bill of Rights into the Fourteenth Amendment served him well in the 1940s and 1950s when the challenges in the
courts to state action were still at a very fundamental level. In the
1960s, his liberal friends began to get dismayed at what they thought
of as a sharp turn towards conservatism in his decisions, but Black's
answer was simply that the rights claimed in the later Warren period
were not covered by the incorporation doctrine for they were not
included in the Bill of Rights itself. And where the Constitution,
which he carried with him wherever he went, well annotated and much
used, gave no guidance, Black would normally hold back. Absolut-
ism, however, was the easiest course, for it denied him the opportunity
of choice; thus, the First Amendment protected nearly all speech, and
communication, obscene though it may be, for assuredly the Court is
'about the most inappropriate Supreme Board of Censors that could
be found' (*Jacobellis* v. *Ohio*, 1964). Yet even Black's absolutes had
their relativities; for a man could not be permitted to shout 'Fire' in a
crowded theatre and claim First Amendment defence after the ensuing
pandemonium and injuries. Here, then, was another principle which,

itself the product of an initial leap of faith, nevertheless could prescribe in an objective fashion a large part of a Justice's action. To men like Frankfurter and Harlan, however, Stone's notion of preferred freedoms and Black's belief in incorporation were anathema; they chose rather to adjudicate case by case, discovering by some form of osmosis what the consensus of society might be for the purpose of due process or what particular rights were *really* fundamental and thus selectively incorporated into the Fourteenth Amendment.

The problem is not, in fact, amenable to simple solutions. A Stone or a Black may, in certain cases, feel more confident about exercising the power of judicial review since his initial principles, rather than his current estimations of good policy, demand that it be exercised. But there are many instances where his principles are inapplicable or where preferred freedoms or fundamental rights collide. Similarly, the upholders of a philosophy of self-restraint find, in the last analysis, that they are every bit as active in exercising their judgement and distinguishing cases as the activist colleagues they often inveigh against. It has been argued, indeed, that John Harlan was in many ways more activist than Hugo Black, if activism is taken to mean a preparedness to trust personal judgement rather than follow immutable principles which deny the opportunity for judgement (Redlich, 1975). Furthermore, the Court cannot abnegate its duty, which is well-nigh universally accepted, to use its judgement. The political process, for good or ill, has expanded into the judicial field; governments who find Congress intractable will use the courts to advance their political designs; interest groups who, in a similar way, have lost out in the congressional labyrinth, turn to the court; the pluralism that is American politics spills over into the courts and ultimately the Supreme Court must adjudicate. There are no simple rules to help the Justices. They cannot be 'strict constructionists', because the Constitution is not precise and construing its meaning is not an exercise in neat logic and exposition. The phrase 'strict constructionist', like 'self-restraint', has become a code phrase designed to lend respectability to those who would hesitate to set limits on the actions of governments, largely because they approve of what the governments do and dislike the way the Court in recent years has enormously expanded the reach of the Bill of Rights and the Fourteenth Amendment. Popular and elite judgements of the Court have always depended on *what* it did rather than *how* it reached its decisions; those who excoriated the activism of the Hughes Court now praise the activism of the Warren Court, while those who defended the activism of the 'Four Horsemen' in the 1930s now call for a Court exercising the virtues of self-restraint. Two things, however, have occurred which make these dichotomies neat debating points but which hide two marked differences between the 1930s and the 1960s.

One issue well encapsulates the first of the major differences. Felix Frankfurter, although he claimed to agree with the spirit of Stone's Carolene Products footnote, could not bring himself to admit the notion of preferred freedoms and retained his primary belief that legislatures' wishes should be upheld by the Court except in extreme cases, of which he was of course the ultimate arbiter. In *Minersville* v. *Gobitis* (1940), the Court found that there was nothing unconstitutional in a school board requiring the children in its care to salute the American flag at the beginning of each school day. Harlan Stone was the only member of the Court to dissent, and Frankfurter wrote to him in an attempt to justify his own opinion still further. 'My intention', he wrote, 'was to use this opinion as a vehicle for preaching the true democratic faith of not relying on the Court for the impossible task of assuring a vigorous, mature, self-protecting and tolerant democracy by bringing the responsibility for a combination of firmness and toleration directly home where it belongs—to the people and their representatives themselves' (Mason, 1956). This concept has echoes elsewhere; the constitutional historian, Commager, once observed that the real battles of liberalism were not won in the Supreme Court; they were won in the legislatures and in the arena of public opinion. The scholar James Thayer once claimed that by adhering rigidly to its own non-interventionist duty, the Court would help, as nothing else could, 'to fix the spot where responsibility lies, and to bring down on that precise locality the thunderbolt of popular condemnation' (quoted in Forte, 1972, p. 85). The dissents of Hugo Black and John Harlan in the late 1960s, while not preaching so touching a faith in the educative powers of democracy, certainly accepted that people should live with the fruits of their efforts at making a democracy work, however unwise the Justices actually reckoned those fruits to be.

Only three years after the *Gobitis* decision, an almost identical case involving Jehovah's Witnesses was granted *certiorari*. In that brief intermission, there had been alterations to the personnel on the Court and three members of the *Gobitis* majority—Black, Douglas and Murphy—had publicly recorded in another case their belief that *Gobitis* had been wrongly decided. The three-judge district federal court anticipated a change of view and granted an injunction against the West Virginia State Board of Education. The state officials appealed and the Supreme Court affirmed the lower court's judgement. Robert Jackson, who had in the 1930s been one of the foremost critics of the Court's tendency to overrule legislative decisions, attacked Frankfurter's reliance on the principle of legislative supremacy in this telling passage:

The very purpose of a Bill of Rights was to withdraw certain subjects from the vicissitudes of political controversy, to place them beyond the reach of majorities and officials and to establish them as legal principles to be applied by the Courts. One's right to life, liberty, and property, to free speech, a free press, freedom of worship and assembly, and other fundamental rights may not be submitted to the vote; they depend on the outcome of no elections. (*West Virginia State Board of Education* v. *Barnette*, 1943)

Here, then, is the authentic voice of preferred freedoms, firmly based upon one particular conception of the comparative significance of different sections of the Constitution. Frankfurter's opinion in *Gobitis* had also alluded, in a strikingly normative fashion, to the moral and empirical virtues of democracy. On the empirical level, his hope in the ameliorating consequences of non-involvement does not seem to have much historical credibility. The sad truth is that majorities were strengthened in their illiberal behaviour by the failure of the Courts to check their excesses. *Plessy* v. *Ferguson* provided the green light for many southern and border states to enact statutes authorising, and requiring, racial segregation.

Reconstruction gave way to the Compromise of 1877, or Redemption, as it is more properly known in the south. Democracy there worked in ways manifestly opposed to the spirit of the Civil War Amendments and the aspirations of Jefferson's ringing Declaration of Independence, not to mention the Constitution itself and the congressional statutes passed immediately after the Civil War. In oral argument before the Court in the *Brown* case, Robert Jackson began by observing to Thurgood Marshall, then representing the NAACP, that the basic question was whether the Court was entitled to outlaw segregation. The Constitution clearly gave Congress authority under the Fourteenth Amendment to make laws to enforce 'the equal protection of the laws'; but it had chosen not to do so. A few moments later, he added: 'I suppose, realistically, the reason the case is here is that action couldn't be obtained from Congress.' This appreciation of political realities dominated the Warren Court's judgements. The acceptance that justice cannot be even-handed unless each adversary has committed legal help, the acknowledgement that southern courtrooms were often too much an extension of the dominant segregationist culture and power structure to be suitable venues for blacks to receive a fair trial, or the realisation that redistricting would never occur without judicial involvement, all testify to this concern with the detailed facts of the case. Tom Clark's frontal attack on Frankfurter's warnings against entering the political thicket and mathematical quagmire is typical: 'the majority of the people of Tennessee have no practical opportunities for exercising their political weight at the polls'. Perhaps this determination to place the abstract legal arguments presented to them in the reality of specific human situations is a function of the cloistered life Justices have to live; whether that is the case or not, the consequences became clear. The Court grew more interested in righting wrongs and then establishing new constitutional principles than in applying time-honoured principles to a specific, but intrinsically insignificant, set of facts. Much of the legal profession disapproved.

The activism of the Warren Court, then, was clearly different in quality from that of the Hughes Court. It is only since the end of the Second World War that the Court has lived up to its calling as the protector of individual rights and 'insular minorities'. In doing so, it has excellent intellectual justifications, though disappointingly slender historical precedents (Dahl, 1957). Indeed, it is hard to imagine how a Justice could be as self-restrained as Frankfurter before the Warren revolution breathed some reality into the high principles of American democracy. Stone was surely correct to argue that the presumption of constitutionality is only tenable if citizens all have access to the polls and if there is a free flow of ideas and alternative political programmes. Where free speech and publications are censored or where the vote is denied to some or devalued to others, legislative and executive acts lack a substantial part of their legitimacy. Thus, the very principle on which the self-restraintists stand depends upon an active Court curbing the tendencies of majorities to devise rules that enhance their own chances of retaining power. The Warren Court did not, of course, strike out at all it believed to be wrong like a latter-day St George in search of every nefarious dragon, nor did it ground its doctrines always in the solidest of foundations. In this respect, too, the quality of the Warren Court differed from that of the Hughes Court (Kurland, 1970; Maidment, 1976). In any case, the problems it faced were considerable. Frankfurter could assert the constitutional requirement to defer to the legislative body, but there was no specific constitutional provision requiring that; on the contrary, the notion of three co-equal branches of government suggests that the Court could legitimately be an equal to the Congress and to the executive. Since self-restraintist philosophies tend to leave things alone, they stir up fewer hornets' nests than activist philosophies, and thus, necessarily, have a smaller impact on the nation's political action. But to be self-restrained is not to be impartial and devoid of all personal preferences. A Frankfurter opinion, carefully drawn and fulsomely cited, cannot escape giving off a bouquet of subjectivity; Earl Warren's opinions emit more than a bouquet and are thus more easily criticised by the legal fraternity. Style *is* important, for the Supreme Court is a court of law and its role within the American political system necessitates a careful cultivation of the illusion of objectivity and of the renewal of the myth of mechanical jurisprudence. No activist court, whether its Chief Justice be Hughes or Warren or Burger, finds this easy.

The Warren Court's activism differs from that of the Hughes Court in a further way. Many of its decisions were not prohibitions so much as commands. *Brown* required a radical alteration in the organisation of state education; *Reynolds* required immediate redistricting in many states where redistricting was no more than a distant historical memory; *Gideon* required states to establish means by which the accused could be provided with lawyers; *Miranda* required police officers to follow a detailed set of procedures when interrogating suspects; and so on. The demand for affirmative action to this degree was a novel development. What is more, it seemed to smack of legislative action rather than judicial action, whose normal remedies are usually the negative ones of injunctions, reversals and denials. Naturally enough, the Court's decisions seemed as political as those of an elected legislature and they drew criticism precisely because of this. While it is true that the Court did, in the 1950s and the 1960s, take a strong line in attempting to ensure that those great principles of the Constitution which its members valued highly were translated into action, its opponents seemed suspiciously overloaded with those who disapproved of the substance of the Court's work. Not for the first time, nor yet for the last time, the pre-eminence of the Court as the symbol of the majesty of the law has meant that basic political disagreements tend to get couched in attacks on its judicial competence. Yet the revolutionary nature of the Warren Court is precisely the precedents it has created for judicial law-making of a positive kind; the Burger Court may draw back somewhat from continuing the extensions pioneered by the Warren Court, but it and its successors will not forget what its predecessor managed to do (Glazer, 1975). After all, it was the Burger Court which authorised busings as a permissible requirement to integrate schools.

The final comparison between the modern era and the Hughes Court draws attention to the extent to which courts can continue to obstruct the law-makers. Robert Dahl has argued that the Court's power has been much exaggerated (Dahl, 1958). In the first place, the Supreme Court, as Robert Jackson put it, is 'a substantially passive instrument, to be moved only by the initiative of litigants' (Jackson, 1955, p. 2). To this extent, therefore, it is manifestly less influential than the executive and legislative branches from which the initiation of legislation originates and the vast majority of statutes and executive orders controlling American life emanate. No one can any longer deny that the Court has *some* impact, independent of the other branches of government, on the economy and society of the United States, but it is very much the junior partner in the tripartite division of governmental power. In the second place, as Chapter 4 has illustrated, the Supreme Court lacks the physical power to enforce its decisions and must depend on its own continuing good standing for voluntary obedience to give life to its dicta. This is forthcoming because the Court rarely allows itself to get out of step with the dominant political forces of the day. The need to ensure support for its decisions and the constant change of personnel, nominated by an elected President and confirmed by an elected Senate, is normally sufficient to keep the Court acting in tandem with the elected branches of the national government (Funston, 1975). It is in periods of national realignment that the Court may, for a while, lag behind the new political coalition that has come to dominate the central government. This was certainly true of the 1930s, which witnessed the end of Republican hegemony and *laissez-faire* dominance; the Court changed too slowly to avoid conflict, but once death and resignation came to its members congruence was reasserted. What sets the Warren Court apart is that it anticipated the new coalition and as a rule consciously served the minorities rather than the majority. In the perspective of history, however, the tendency for the Court to sanctify and legitimise the government's actions is its most obvious inheritance; only in rare moments of major political upheavals does the Court find itself without powerful friends in Congress and the White House. Mr Dooley was not far wrong when he noted that the Supreme Court follows the election returns.

Election returns, of course, do not always produce governments which are representative of popular majorities in all their policy outputs. The literature on American politics is replete with examples of special interest groups prevailing over the 'national interest', of differential power in Congress producing an imperfect match between the gross inputs and the net outputs of the system, in short, of the democratic process producing policies which are probably not in tune with the people's desires. Another school of political scientists has argued that American politics is distinguished by its pluralist nature, by the existence of overlapping minority groups, by the need to build coalitions. Advocates of a more responsible party system, common among political scientists in the 1950s, lamented the lack of a disciplined majority in Washington. If these analyses are valid—and they are not mutually exclusive—then it is difficult to know what individual policy orientations a committed democrat should espouse, for the laws themselves may well reflect minority desires.

It is, however, too simple a conception of the American political system to portray the Court as 'inherently undemocratic' and the law-makers as the repository of democratic virtues. The latter caricature has already been briefly examined. The former also needs a short inspection. The Justices are nominated by an elected President and they are confirmed in office by an elected Senate. While this does not provide for future control and accountability, it certainly tends to produce Courts very much in tune with the dominant Washington coalition. The party and ideology which prevail in Washington, it need hardly be said, do not automatically prevail in all the states of the Union and the conflict between elected politicians and non-elected Court nearly always mirrors the conflict between some regions of the United States and the current Washington majority. 'Although the federal judiciary has escaped the effects of popular election and Jacksonian direct democracy which swept through the state judiciary,' Richardson and Vines have written, 'it nevertheless contains impor-tant elements of the democratic culture. Judicial recruitment reflects and helps institutionalize partisan changes; it serves the needs and demands of a diverse federal system; it links the Senate to local party structures; and it helps soften the impact of the extension of national power to the states' (Richardson and Vines, 1970, p. 78). Although this analysis relates primarily to lower court federal judges, it serves to bring into focus two points: first, that judges are expected to be above the partisan battle (judicial culture) yet also in tune with popular demands (democratic culture) and, second, that the process of appointment is very much a political operation subject to the normal bargaining and conventions of patronage politics generally.

The political role of the Court is further illustrated if the American political system is envisaged as a complex of power centres, none of which can, or ought to, dominate. Since institutional power in the United States is so widely dispersed, between the President and Congress, between the Senate and House of Representatives, between the federal and state governments, between regulatory agencies and executive departments, and so on, the Supreme Court can be thought of as another part of the whole complex web of power centres through which group demands are mediated. This, of course, does not resolve the complaint that a Court is inherently an inappropriate form for mediating demands, since the adversary system precludes adjustments and compromise. Nor does it assuage the complaints of those who wish the law to be neutral and visibly untainted by any signs of bias or partiality. Inevitably, if the Court is seen as the repository of unloved minority rights, it ceases to appear as the guardian of an absolute, immutable and universal system of law. As so often happens, the normative argument is carried on in an arena where empiricists hardly tread and on a plane equally devoid of empiricist presence. The normative argument constantly examines for an ideal; the empiricist largely accepts what happens to exist before his eyes. The year 1979 is too late for the Court to change its fundamental role in the American political system. As the Supreme Court, it tends to nationalise the disparate parochial views of the lower courts and, by a careful selection of the cases to be considered, tends to disrupt the consensus of lower courts; given the huge case-load before it, its energies must be harnessed to those conflicts with whose disposition below it disagrees. It *is* a continual Constitutional Convention, chiefly because that is the role Americans have forced it into. It must antagonise significant sectors of society precisely because of its role as guardian of minority interests and amender of the Constitution. There is thus no escaping the reality that the Court is deeply enmeshed in the political process.

The passion in the debate stems, of course, from the assumption that the Supreme Court in actual fact exercises power without responsibility—'the prerogative', as Stanley Baldwin once described the British press, 'of the harlot through the ages'. This involves two separate questions. First, to what extent has the Court superimposed its ideological views on those of the legislature? And, second, in so far as it has, has this dominant role been persistent over time or does it occur only under very special circumstances? At one level, the power of the Court is open for all to see: it has found unconstitutional, and declared void, parts at least of over ninety congressional statutes and more than 750 state laws. Impressive though these statistics may appear, they reveal, under scrutiny, a less *prima facie* case of judicial usurpation of the legislative function. As a proportion of the total output of the federal legislature, for instance, the Court's interference is infinitesimal and, apart from the celebrated years of the New Deal, seldom focused on major Bills and never consistently antagonistic to a programme. As Philip Kurland, a devoted but sharp academic critic of the Court, has written: 'the fact of the matter is— whatever the romance may be—that so far as relations between Court and Congress are concerned, the invalidation of national legislation has proved historically to be neither so important nor so exacerbating of the differences between the two branches as law professors would make it' (Kurland, 1970, p. 22). The states have more to complain about. For the Court has tended, from the moment John Marshall began to mould its decisions, to favour national government over state government and to ensure that the national Constitution is not flouted in the states. But, as far as the federal authorities are concerned, the Court has been a more ardent legitimator than controller. This argument, of course, does not invalidate the blanket objection to any usurpation of the legislative prerogative, as it might be put, nor the objections to certain specific decisions of the Court. Quite clearly, the

Court has varied over time in its readiness to strike down state and federal legislation and quite clearly, too, its rationale for these actions depends upon subjective perceptions of the judicial role and the Constitution's meaning. But to act politically in this way is not necessarily to act partisanly in any narrow sense. Of course, some examples of activism do seem to be prime instances of partisan action, but it should be remembered that such cases are the exception and a power ill-used is not necessarily an inappropriate power. And it is clear to me, at any rate, that the power is a most appropriate one.

The Supreme Court is very much part of the American political system, but it is 'the least dangerous branch'. This does not mean that it packs no punch at all; nor does it deny that government by judiciary is a poor substitute for government by the people. Logic and convention have given the nine Justices a task to perform, a task of remarkable difficulty, as the American people insist on carrying on their partisan political activities within the judicial system. The importance of the Court has thus increased from its very insignificant origins. In 1790, for instance, Jay and his colleagues, meeting above a market in New York City, could not initially obtain a quorum; Rutledge and Blair were delayed by impassably muddy roads and Harrison, although confirmed by the Senate, never did arrive, for he felt it more important to be a Maryland state judge! Until 1935, the Court occupied four rooms the Senate no longer needed. Only since then has the majesty of its location matched the significance of its tasks. And these have increased in volume and complexity so that no simple rules have been devised by which the Justices can manage to sift through the applications for review before them and decide on the merits of those cases thought to be significant. At every stage in the process there is room for judgement so that it is hardly surprising that the Court is rarely unanimous. Yet it is this very lack of unanimity, the obvious divisions within the Court, and the varied interpretations that are given of the Constitution, which weaken its role as a legitimating agency and alert people to the subjectivity of its actions. Judgement, after all, is seen quite clearly not to be a mechanical exercise. However much one may wish otherwise, there is no practical way by which the Court could respond to the demands now made on it without recourse to personal evaluations.

The discussion of judicial review and of judicial supremacy has continued throughout the history of the United States and no doubt will continue to do so. There is a basic inconsistency between popular government and judicial supremacy; conflict between the two is inherently insoluble in a political system which espouses limited government, a Bill of Rights and the dangers of a majority tyrannising minorities. In such a system, some body other than the current majority coalition's spokesmen has a good claim to adjudicate between rival claims. The Supreme Court has become that body and it must perform its difficult task knowing full well that it will always be open to attack from individuals claiming to represent the majority, at whatever level of political organisation seems convenient for them. The crucial theoretical question so far as the Supreme Court is concerned has not been whether an act does, or does not, conform to the Constitution, but who shall judge regarding its conformity. The answer which history and wisdom has provided is the Supreme Court. That cannot evade the problem of accountability; nothing can. The Romans used to say 'quis custodiet ipsos custodes?': who will guard the guards themselves? And there is not, and cannot be, a simple answer to that.

Appendix 1

27 John McKinley (Alabama), Van Buren, 1838 (57), 1852 (72), 14
28 Peter Daniel (Virginia), Van Buren, 1842 (57), 1860 (76), 18
29 Samuel Nelson (New York), Tyler, 1845 (52), 1872 (80), 27
30 Levi Woodbury (New Hampshire), Polk, 1845 (55), 1851 (61), 5
31 Robert Grier (Pennsylvania), Polk, 1846 (52), 1870 (75), 23
32 Benjamin Curtis (Massachusetts), Fillmore, 1851 (41), 1857 (47), 5
33 John Campbell (Alabama), Pierce, 1853 (41), 1861 (49), 8
34 Nathan Clifford (Maine), Buchanan, 1858 (54), 1881 (77), 23
35 Noah Swayne (Ohio), Lincoln, 1862 (57), 1881 (76), 18
36 Samuel Miller (Iowa), Lincoln, 1862 (46), 1890 (74), 28
37 David Davis (Illinois), Lincoln, 1862 (47), 1877 (61), 14
38 Stephen Field (California), Lincoln, 1863 (46), 1897 (81), 34
39 Salmon Chase (Ohio), Lincoln, 1864 (56), 1873 (65), 8 Chief Justice
40 William Strong (Pennsylvania), Grant, 1870 (61), 1880 (72), 10
41 Joseph Bradley (New Jersey), Grant, 1870 (57), 1892 (78), 21
42 Ward Hunt (New York), Grant, 1873 (62), 1882 (71), 9
43 Morrison Waite (Ohio), Grant, 1874 (57), 1888 (71), 14 Chief Justice
44 John Harlan (Kentucky), Hayes, 1877 (44), 1911 (78), 33
45 William Woods (Georgia), Hayes, 1881 (56), 1887 (62), 6
46 Stanley Matthews (Ohio), Garfield, 1881 (56), 1889 (64), 7
47 Horace Gray (Massachusetts), Arthur, 1882 (53), 1902 (74), 20
48 Samuel Blatchford (New York), Arthur, 1882 (62), 1893 (73), 11
49 Lucius Lamar (Mississippi), Cleveland, 1888 (62), 1893 (67), 5
50 Melville Fuller (Illinois), Cleveland, 1888 (55), 1910 (77), 21 Chief Justice
51 David Brewer (Kansas), Harrison, 1890 (52), 1910 (72), 20
52 Henry Brown (Michigan), Harrison, 1891 (54), 1906 (70), 15
53 George Shiras (Pennsylvania), Harrison, 1892 (60), 1903 (71), 10
54 Howell Jackson (Tennessee), Harrison, 1893 (60), 1895 (63), 2
55 Edward White (Louisiana), Cleveland, 1894 (48), 1921 (75), 27
56 Rufus Peckham (New York), Cleveland, 1896 (57), 1909 (70), 13
57 Joseph McKenna (California), McKinley, 1898 (54), 1925 (81), 26
58 Oliver Wendell Holmes (Massachusetts), Theodore Roosevelt, 1902 (61), 1932 (90), 29
59 William Day (Ohio), Theodore Roosevelt, 1903 (53), 1922 (73), 19
60 William Moody (Massachusetts), Theodore Roosevelt, 1906 (52), 1910 (56), 3
61 Horace Lurton (Tennessee), Taft, 1910 (65), 1914 (70), 4
62 Charles Evans Hughes (New York), Taft, 1910 (48), 1916 (54), 5
   Edward White (Louisiana), Taft, 1910 (65), 1921 (75), 10 Chief Justice
63 Willis Van Devanter (Wyoming), Taft, 1911 (51), 1937 (78), 26
64 Joseph Lamar (Georgia), Taft, 1911 (53), 1916 (58), 4
65 Mahlon Pitney (New Jersey), Taft, 1912 (54), 1922 (64), 10
66 James Macreynolds (Tennessee), Wilson, 1914 (52), 1941 (78), 26
67 Louis Brandeis (Massachusetts), Wilson, 1916 (59), 1939 (82), 22
68 John Clarke (Ohio), Wilson, 1916 (59), 1922 (65), 5
69 William Howard Raft (Connecticut), Harding, 1921 (63), 1930 (72), 8 Chief Justice

Appendix 1   185

70 George Sutherland (Utah), Harding, 1922 (60), 1938 (75), 15
71 Pierce Butler (Minnesota), Harding, 1923 (56), 1939 (73), 16
72 Edward Sanford (Tennessee), Harding, 1923 (57), 1930 (64), 7
73 Harlan Fiske Stone (New York), Coolidge, 1925 (52), 1946 (73), 21
    Charles Evans Hughes (New York), Hoover, 1930 (67), 1941 (79), 11
    Chief Justice
74 Owen Roberts (Pennsylvania), Hoover, 1930 (55), 1945 (70), 15
75 Benjamin Cardozo (New York), Hoover, 1932 (61), 1938 (68), 6
76 Hugo Black (Alabama), F. D. Roosevelt, 1937 (51), 1971 (85), 34
77 Stanley Reed (Kentucky), F. D. Roosevelt, 1938 (53), 1957 (72), 19
78 Felix Frankfurter (Massachusetts), F. D. Roosevelt, 1939 (56), 1962 (79), 23
79 William Douglas (Connecticut), F. D. Roosevelt, 1939 (40), 1975 (77), 36
80 Frank Murphy (Michigan), F. D. Roosevelt, 1940 (49), 1949 (59), 9
    Harlan Fiske Stone (New York), F. D. Roosevelt, 1941 (68), 1946 (73), 4 Chief Justice
81 James Burnes (South Carolina), F. D. Roosevelt, 1941 (62), 1942 (63), 1
82 Robert Jackson (New York), F. D. Roosevelt, 1941 (49), 1954 (62), 13
83 Wiley Rutledge (Iowa), F. D. Roosevelt, 1943 (48), 1949 (55), 6
84 Harold Burton (Ohio), Truman, 1945 (57), 1958 (70), 13
85 Frederick Vinson (Kentucky), Truman, 1946 (56), 1953 (63), 7 Chief Justice
86 Thomas Clark (Texas), Truman, 1949 (49), 1967 (67), 17
87 Sherman Minton (Indiana), Truman, 1949 (58), 1956 (65), 7
88 Earl Warren (California), Eisenhower, 1953 (62), 1969 (78), 15 Chief Justice
89 John Harlan (New York), Eisenhower, 1955 (55), 1971 (72), 16
90 William Brennan (New Jersey), Eisenhower, 1956 (50)
91 Charles Whittaker (Missouri), Eisenhower, 1957 (56), 1962 (61), 5
92 Potter Stewart (Ohio), Eisenhower, 1958 (43)
93 Byron White (Colorado), Kennedy, 1962 (44)
94 Arthur Goldberg (Illinois), Kennedy, 1962 (54), 1965 (56), 2
95 Abe Fortas (Tennessee), Johnson, 1966 (55), 1969 (58), 3
96 Thurgood Marshall (New York), Johnson, 1967 (59)
97 Warren Burger (Virginia), Nixon, 1969 (61) Chief Justice
98 Harry Blackmun (Minnesota), Nixon, 1970 (61)
99 Lewis Powell (Virginia), Nixon, 1972 (64)
100 William Rehnquist (Arizona), Nixon, 1972 (47)
101 John Paul Stevens (Michigan), Ford, 1975 (55)

(b) AGGREGATE STATISTICS

		All	Appointed in eighteenth century	nineteenth century	twentieth century
1	Average age taking up appointment	53.1	49.6	51.7	55.4

	All	Appointed in eighteenth century	Appointed in nineteenth century	Appointed in twentieth century
2 Average age at end of service	68.2	59.3	69.8	69.0
3 Average number of completed years	15.2	10.0	17.6	13.7
4 Percentage of justices dying in office		54.5	68.9	30.6
5 Percentage of justices resigning or disabled		45.5	13.3	25.0
6 Percentage of justices retiring			17.7	44.4

Notes: (1) includes Rutledge, Waite, Hughes and Stone twice, since they each took an oath both as an Associate Justice and as Chief Justice
   (2) includes Rutledge and Hughes twice, since they left the Court on two distinct occasions
   (3) does not include Rutledge as Chief Justice, because he was never confirmed by the Senate
   (6) reflects the increasing attraction of retiring, for it was only in 1869 that a Justice who was 70 and had served ten years could retire and receive a pension

(c) THE SUPREME COURT, 1 JANUARY 1979

	Year of taking up appointment	Age on taking up appointment	Age at January 1979	Completed years of service
Warren Burger (Nixon)	1969	61	71	9
William Brennan (Eisenhower)	1956	50	72	22
Potter Stewart (Eisenhower)	1958	43	63	20
Byron White (Kennedy)	1962	44	61	16
Thurgood Marshall (Johnson)	1967	59	70	11
Harry Blackmun (Nixon)	1970	61	70	8
Lewis Powell (Nixon)	1972	64	71	6
William Rehnquist (Nixon)	1972	47	54	6
John Paul Stevens (Ford)	1975	55	58	3
Average		53.7	65.5	11.2

Appendix 2

LIST OF CASES CITED

The Official Reporter's edition, published in Washington, is the edition most commonly cited. References to cases begin with the volume number of the Reports, continue with the letters US (except for the period up to 1878 when the name of the Court Reporter is used), and end with the page on which the Court's opinion or decision begins and the year of that decision. A second source, which includes very useful commentaries and some of the briefs presented to the Court, is published by the Lawyers' Co-operative Publishing Company and its citations follow the pattern of the Official Reports except that L Ed (for the first 100 volumes) and L Ed 2d for the ensuing volumes replaces US. Finally, the West Publishing House brings out, most promptly of all, an edition of the Court's opinions which is cited with the initials S. Ct (and which has been used in this book for those cases not yet published in the other editions).

Abate v. *Mundt*, 403 US 182 (1971) 154
Abington School District v. *Schempp*, 374 US 203 (1963) 119
Adams v. *Tanner*, 244 US 590 (1917) 91
Alexander v. *Holmes County Board of Education*, 396 US 19 (1969)
Argersinger v. *Hamlin*, 407 US 25 (1972) 126
Avery v. *Midland County*, 390 US 474 (1968)
Bailey v. *Drexel Furniture Co.*, 359 US 20 (1922) 138
Baker v. *Carr*, 369 US 186 (1962)
Barenblatt v. *United States*, 360 US 109 (1959) 55
Bell v. *Maryland*, 378 US 226 (1964) 13
Bell v. *Ohio*, 98 S.Ct 2977 (1978)
Betts v. *Brady*, 316 US 455 (1942)
Brown v. *Allen*, 344 US 443 (1953) 76
Brown v. *Board of Education of Topeka*, 347 US 483 (1954)
Brown v. *Board of Education of Topeka*, 349 US 294 (1955)
Burrell v. *McCray*, 426 US 471 (1976) 75
Buckley v. *Valeo*, 424 US 1 (1976) 142
Butz v. *Economou*, 98 S.Ct 2894 (1978) 2
Chisholm v. *Georgion*, 2 Dall. 419 (1793) 62
Civil Rights Cases, 109 US 3 (1883) 137
Coker v. *Georgia*, 433 US 584 (1977)
Colegrove v. *Green*, 328 US 549 (1946)
Cooper v. *Aaron*, 358 US 1 (1958)
Davis v. *Schnell*, 336 US 933 (1949) 45

Doe v. *Bolton*, 410 US 113 (1973)
Donaldson v. *California*, 441 US 968 (1971) 75
Dred Scott v. *Sandford*, 19 How. 393 (1857)
Engel v. *Vitale*, 370 US 421 (1962) 119
Flast v. *Cohen*, 392 US 83 (1968) 70
Fletcher v. *Peck*, 6 Cr. 87 (1810) 132
Frothingham v. *Mellon*, 262 US 447 (1923) 70
Furman v. *Georgia*, 408 US 238 (1972)
Gaston County v. *United States*, 395 US 285 (1969) 162
Gibbons v. *Ogden*, 9 Wheat. 1 (1824) 134
Gideon v. *Wainwright*, 372 US 335 (1963)
Giles v. *Harris*, 189 US 475 (1903) 144
Gomillion v. *Lightfoot*, 364 US 339 (1960) 152
Gray v. *Sanders*, 372 US 368 (1963) 141
Green v. *County School Board of New Kent*, 391 US 430 (1968) 159
Griffin v. *School Board of Prince Edward County*, 377 US 218 (1964) 157
Griswold v. *Connecticut*, 381 US 479 (1965) 4
Grovey v. *Townsend*, 295 US 145 (1935)
Guinn v. *United States*, 238 US 347 (1915) 145
Hadley v. *Junior College District*, 397 US 50 (1970) 153
Hammer v. *Dagenhart*
Harper v. *Virginia Board of Elections*, 383 US 663 (1966)
Hepburn v. *Griswold*, 8 Wall. 603 (1870) 48
Hicklin v. *Orbeck*, 98 S.Ct 2482 (1978) 2
Hutto v. *Finney*, 98 S.Ct 2565 (1978) 2
Hylton v. *United States*, 3 Dall. 171 (1796) 132
Jacobellis v. *Ohio*, 378 US 184 (1964) 10
Johnson v. *Zerbst*, 304 US 458 (1938) 128
Katzenbach v. *McClung*, 379 US 294 (1964)
Keyes v. *School District No. 1*, 413 US 189 (1973) 161
Kirkpatrick v. *Preisler*, 394 US 526 (1969) 153
Knox v. *Lee*, 12 Wall. 457 (1871) 48
Lassiter v. *Northampton County Board of Elections*, 360 US 45 (1959) 144
Lochner v. *New York*, 198 US 45 (1905) 138
Lockett v. *Ohio*, 98 S.Ct 2954 (1978) 2
Lombard v. *Louisiana*, 373 US 267 (1963) 12
Loving v. *Virginia*, 388 US 1 (1967) 79
Lucas v. *Colorado General Assembly*, 377 US 713 (1964) 152
Ex Parte McCardle, 7 Wall. 506 (1869) 135
McCulloch v. *Maryland*, 4 Wheat. 316 (1819)
McLaurin v. *Oklahoma State Regents*, 339 US 637 (1950)
Mahan v. *Howell*, 410 US 315 (1973) 154
Mallory v. *United States*, 354 US 449 (1957), 35
Marbury v. *Madison*, 1 Cr. 137 (1803) 131
Minor v. *Happersteth*, 21 Wall. 162 (1875)
Marshall v. *Barlow's Inc.*, 98 S.Ct 1816 (1978) 2
Massachusetts v. *Laird*, 400 US 886 (1970), 68
Milliken v. *Bradley*, 418 US 717 (1974) 162

Mincey v. *Arizona*, 98 S.Ct 2408 (1978) 2
Minersville School District v. *Gobitis*, 310 US 586 (1940)
Miranda v. *Arizona*, 384 US 436 (1966)
Missouri ex rel. Gaines v. *Canada*, 305 US 337 (1938) 156
Mora v. *McNamara*, 389 US 934 (1967) 68
Morehead v. *New York ex rel. Tipaldo*, 298 US 587 (1936) 16
Munn v. *Illinois*, 94 US 113 (1877)
NAACP v. *Button*, 371 US 415 (1963) 89
National Mutual Insurance Co. v. *Tidewater Transfer Co. Inc.*, 337 US 582
  (1949) 96
New York Times v. *United States*, 403 US 713 (1971) 96
Newberry v. *United States*, 256 US 232 (1921)
Nixon v. *Condon*, 286 US 145 (1935) 145
Nixon v. *Herndon*, 273 US 536 (1927) 145
Oregon v. *Mitchell*, 400 US 112 (1970)
Peterson v. *Greenville*, 373 US 244 (1963) 12
Philadelphia v. *New Jersey*, 98 S.Ct 2531 (1978) 2
Plessy v. *Ferguson*, 163 US 537 (1896)
Poe v. *Ullman*, 367 US 497 (1961) 69
Pollock v. *Farmers' Loan and Trust Co.*, 158 US 601 (1895) 62
Powell v. *McCormack*, 395 US 486 (1969) 69
Pendergast v. *United States*, 317 US 412 (1943) 59
Regents of the University of California v. *Bakke*, 98 S.Ct 2733 (1978)
Reynolds v. *Sims*, 377 US 533 (1964)
Rice v. *Elmore*, 333 US 875 (1948) 148
Roe v. *Wade*, 410 US 113 (1973)
Roth v. *United States*, 354 US 476 (1957) 10
Runyon v. *McCrary*, 427 US 160 (1976) 105
Shelley v. *Kraemer*, 334 US 1 (1948) 128
Sierra Club v. *Morton*, 405 US 727 (1972)
Slaughter-House Cases, 16 Wall. 36 (1973)
Smith v. *Allwright*, 321 US 649 (1944)
South Carolina v. *Katzenbach*, 383 US 301 (1966) 128
Swann v. *Adams*, 385 US 440 (1967) 153
Swann v. *Charlotte-Micklenberg Board of Education*, 402 US 1 (1971)
Sweatt v. *Painter*, 339 US 629 (1950)
Sweezy v. *New Hampshire*, 354 US 234 (1957) 84
Tennessee Valley Authority v. *Hill*, 98 S.Ct 2279 (1978) 2
Terry v. *Adams*, 345 US 461 (1953)
Thompson v. *Louisville*, 362 US 199 (1960) 65
Tidewater Oil Co. v. *United States et al.*, 409 US 151 (1972) 51
United States v. *Butler*, 297 US 1 (1936) 170
United States v. *Carolene Products Co.*, 304 US 144 (1938) 171
United States v. *Classic*, 313 US 299 (1941)
United States v. *Jefferson County Board of Education*, 380 F.2d 385 (5th
  Circuit, 1967) 159
United States v. *E. C. Knight & Co.*, 156 US 1 (1895) 138
United States v. *Nixon*, 418 US 683 (1974)

190   *The Politics of the US Supreme Court*

Watkins v. *United States*, 354 US 178 (1957) 84
Wells v. *Rockefeller*, 394 US 542 (1969) 154
Wesberry v. *Sanders*, 376 US 1 (1964) 142
West Coast Hotel v. *Parrish*, 300 US 379 (1937) 16
West Virginia State Board of Education v. *Barnette*, 319 US 624 (1943)
Whitcomb v. *Chavis*, 403 US 124 (1971) 154
White v. *Weiser*, 412 US 783 (1973) 154
Williams v. *Georgia*, 349 US 375 (1955) 111-2
Williams v. *Mississippi*, 170 US 213 (1898) 144
Worcester v. *Georgia*, 6 Pet. 515 (1832) 119
Wright v. *Rockefeller*, 376 US 52 (1964) 154
Ex Parte Yarborough, 110 US 651 (1884) 144
Yates v. *United States*, 354 US 298 (1957) 84
Youngstown Sheet & Tube Co. v. *Sawyer*, 343 US 579 (1952) 4

Bibliography

(a) BOOKS AND ARTICLES REFERRED TO IN THE TEXT

Abraham, Henry (1974), *Justices and Presidents: A political history of appointments to the Supreme Court* (Oxford University Press).

Abraham, Henry J. (1977), *Freedom and the Court: Civil rights and liberties in the United States* (Oxford University Press, 3rd ed).

Alsop, Joseph, and Catledge, Turner (1938), *The 168 Days* (Doubleday).

Amsterdam, Anthony (1970), 'The Supreme Court and the rights of suspects in criminal cases', *New York University Law Review*, vol. 45, pp. 785-815.

Arnold, Thurman (1959-60), 'Professor Hart's theology', *Harvard Law Review*, vol. 73, pp. 1298-317.

Bachrach, P., and Baratz, Morton S. (1962), 'Two faces of power', *American Political Science Review*, vol. 56, pp. 947-52.

Barker, Lucius J. (1967), 'Third parties in litigation: a system's view of the judicial function', *Journal of Politics*, vol. 29, pp. 41-69.

Bartley, N. V., and Graham, H. D. (1975), *Southern Politics and the Second Reconstruction* (Johns Hopkins University Press).

Becker, Theodore L. (1967), 'Judicial structure and its political functioning in society: new approaches to teaching and research in public law', *Journal of Politics*, vol. 29, pp. 302-33.

Becker, Theodore L. (1969), *The Impact of Supreme Court Decisions: Empirical studies* (Oxford University Press).

Beiser, Edward N. (1972-3), 'Lawyers and the Warren Court', *Law & Society Review*, vol. 7, pp. 139-49.

Benson, Paul R. (1970), *The Supreme Court and the Commerce Clause, 1937-1970* (Dunellen).

Berger, Raoul (1977), *Government by Judiciary: The transformation of the Fourteenth Amendment* (Harvard University Press).

Berry, Mary Frances (1978), *Stability, Security, and Continuity: Mr. Justice Burton and decision-making in the Supreme Court 1945-1958* (Greenwood Press).

Bickel, Alexander M. (1962), *The Least Dangerous Branch: The Supreme Court at the bar of politics* (Bobbs-Merrill).

Bickel, Alexander M. (1973), 'The overworked Court', *New Republic*, 17 February.

Birkby, Robert H. (1966), 'The Supreme Court and the Bible belt: Tennessee reaction to the "Schempp" decision', *Mid-West Journal of Political Science*, vol. 10, pp. 304-19.

Black, Hugo L. (1960), 'The Bill of Rights', *New York University Law Review*, vol. 35, pp. 865-81.

Black, Hugo L. (1968), *A Constitutional Faith* (Alfred Knopf).

Brennan, William J. (1959), 'Supreme Court review of state court decisions', *Michigan State Bar Journal*, vol. 38, November, pp. 14-22.

Brennan, William J. (1973), 'The National Court of Appeals: another dissent', *University of Chicago Law Review*, vol. 40, pp. 473-85.

Bromhead, Peter A., and Bromhead, Marjory-Ann (1976-7), 'Malrepresentation of the people: 1974 model', *Parliamentary Affairs*, vol. 29, pp. 7-26.

Cardozo, Benjamin (1921), *The Nature of the Judicial Process* (Yale University Press).

Casey, Gregory (1973-4), 'The Supreme Court and myth', *Law & Society Review*, vol. 8, pp. 384-419.

Casper, John D. (1976), 'The Supreme Court and national policy making', *American Political Science Review*, vol. 70, pp. 50-63.

Casper, Gerhard, and Posner, Richard A. (1974), 'A study of the Supreme Court's workload', *Journal of Legal Studies*, vol. 3, pp. 339-76.

Claude, Richard (1970), *The Supreme Court and the Electoral Process* (Johns Hopkins Press).

Clark, Tom C. (1957), 'The Supreme Court Conference', *Federal Rules Decisions*, vol. 19, pp. 303-10.

Cook, Beverley Blair (1977), 'Sex roles and the Burger Court', *American Politics Quarterly*, vol. 5, pp. 353-94.

Cohen, William (1958-9), 'Justice Douglas: a law clerk's view', *University of Chicago Law Review*, vol. 26, pp. 6-8.

Congressional Quarterly (1968), *Revolution in Civil Rights 1945-1968* (Congressional Quarterly).

Cox, Archibald (1968), *The Warren Court: Constitutional decision as an instrument of reform* (Harvard University Press).

Cox, Archibald (1976), *The Role of the Supreme Court in American Government* (Oxford University Press).

Crossman, Richard (1975), *The Diaries of a Cabinet Minister*, vol. I (Hamish Hamilton and Jonathan Cape).

Dahl, Robert A. (1957), 'Decision-making in a democracy: the role of the Supreme Court as a national policy maker', *Journal of Public Law*, vol. 6, pp. 279-95.

Danelski, David J. (1964), *A Supreme Court Justice Is Appointed* (Random House).

Danelski, David J. (1967), 'Conflict and its resolution in the Supreme Court', *Journal of Conflict Resolution*, vol. 11, pp. 71-86.

Danelski, David J. (1970), 'Legislative and judicial decision-making: the case of Harold H. Burton', in S. S. Ulmer (ed.), *Conference on Political Decision-making* (Van Nostrand, Reinhard), pp. 121-46.

Danelski, David J. (1974), 'The influence of the Chief Justice in the decisional process', in Walter H. Murphy and C. Herman Pritchett (eds), *Courts, Judges and Politics* (Random House, 2nd edn), pp. 525-34.

Dixon, Robert G. (1968), *Democratic Representation: Reapportionment in law and politics* (Oxford University Press).

Dolbeare, Kenneth (1967), 'The public views the Supreme Court', in Herbert Jacob (ed.), *Law, Politics and the Federal Courts* (Little, Brown), pp. 194-212.

Douglas, William O. (1960), 'The Supreme Court and its caseload', *Cornell Law Quarterly*, vol. 45, pp. 401-14.

Douglas, William O. (1970a), 'Managing the docket of the Supreme Court of the United States', *Record of the Association of the Bar, New York City*, vol. 25, pp. 279-98.

Douglas, William O. (1970b), *Points of Rebellion* (Random House).

Edwards, James M. (1970), 'The gerrymander and "one man, one vote"', *New York University Law Review*, vol. 46, pp. 879-99.

Eisenhower, Dwight D. (1965), *The White House Years: Mandate for change* (New American Library).

Evans, Rowland, and Novak, Robert D. (1971), *Nixon in the White House: The frustration of power* (Random House).

Federal Bar Association (1965), *Equal Justice under the Law: The Supreme Court in American life* (Foundation of the Federal Bar Association).

Fish, Peter G. (1973), *The Politics of Federal Judicial Administration* (Princeton University Press).

Flexnor, Eleanor (1959), *Century of Struggle* (Harvard University Press).

Forte, David F. (ed.) (1972), *The Supreme Court in American Politics: judicial activism vs. judicial restraint* (D. C. Heath).

Frank, John P. (1958), *Marble Palace: The Supreme Court in American life* (Alfred Knopf).

Frankfurter, Felix (1951-2), 'The Supreme Court in the mirror of Justices', *University of Pennsylvania Law Review*, vol. 100, pp. 149-205.

Frankfurter, Felix (1955-6), 'Mr. Justice Roberts', *University of Pennsylvania Law Review*, vol. 104, pp. 313-17.

Frankfurter, Felix, and Landis, James M. (1928), *The Business of the Supreme Court: A study in the federal judicial system* (Macmillan).

Freund, Paul A. (ed.) (1972), *Report of the Study Group on the caseload of the Supreme Court* (Federal Judicial Center).

Funston, Richard (ed.) (1974), *Judicial Crises: The Supreme Court in a changing America* (Shenkman).

Funston, Richard (1975), 'The Supreme Court and critical elections', *American Political Science Review*, vol. 69, pp. 795-811.

Funston, Richard (1977), *Constitutional Counter-revolution? The Warren Court and the Burger Court: Judicial policy-making in modern America* (Shenkman).

Garraty, John A. (ed.) (1964), *Quarrels That Have Shaped the Constitution* (Harper, Row).

Getman, Julius G. (1973), 'The emerging constitutional principle of sexual equality', in Philip B. Kurland (ed.), *The Supreme Court Review 1972* (University of Chicago Press), pp. 157-80.

Glazer, Nathan (1975), 'Towards an imperial judiciary', *The Public Interest*, no. 41, Fall, pp. 104-23.

Giles, M. W., and Walker, T. G. (1975), 'Judicial policy-making and southern school segregation', *Journal of Politics*, vol. 37, pp. 917-36.

Goldberg, Arthur (1971), *Equal Justice: The Supreme Court in the Warren era* (Northwestern University Press).

Goldberg, Arthur (1973), 'One Supreme Court', *New Republic*, 10 February.

Gordon, Rosalie M. (1958), *Nine Men against America: The Supreme Court and its attack on American liberties* (Devin-Adair).

Gressman, Eugene (1973), 'The National Court of Appeals: a dissent', *American Bar Association Journal*, vol. 59, pp. 253-8.

Griffith, J. A. G. (1977), *The Politics of the Judiciary* (Manchester University Press).

Grossman, Joel B. (1962), 'Role-playing and the analysis of judicial behavior: the case of Mr. Justice Frankfurter', *Journal of Public Law*, vol. 11, pp. 285-309.

Grossman, Joel B. (1975), *Lawyers and Judges: The ABA and the politics of judicial selection* (Wiley).

Grossman, Joel B., and Sarat, Austin (1975), 'Litigation in the federal courts: a comparative perspective', *Law & Society Review*, vol. 9, pp. 321-46.

Hand, Learned (1958), *The Bill of Rights* (Harvard University Press).

Hanus, Jerome J. (1961-2), 'The denial of *certiorari* and Supreme Court policy making', *American University Law Review*, vol. 17, pp. 41-56.

Harper, Fowler V., and Rosenthal, Alan S. (1950-1), 'What the Supreme Court did not do in the 1949 Term—an appraisal of *certiorari*', *University of Pennsylvania Law Review*, vol. 99, pp. 292-325.

Harper, Fowler V., and Etherington, Edwin D. (1951-2), 'What the Supreme Court did not do in the 1950 Term', *University of Pennsylvania Law Review*, vol. 100, pp. 354-409.

Harris, Richard (1971), *Decision* (Dutton).

Hart, Henry M. (1959-60), 'The time chart of the Justices', *Harvard Law Review*, vol. 73, pp. 84-125.

Hirsch, Herbert, and Donohew, Lewis (1968), 'A note on negro-white differences in attitudes toward the Supreme Court', *Social Science Quarterly*, vol. 49, pp. 557-62.

Hodder-Williams, Richard (1970), *Public Opinion Polls and British Politics* (Routledge & Kegan Paul).

Hodder-Williams, Richard (1976), 'The workload of the Supreme Court: a comment on the Freund Report', *Journal of American Studies*, vol. 10, pp. 215-39.

Hodder-Williams, Richard (1979), 'Is there a Burger Court?', *British Journal of Political Science*, vol. 10, pp. 173-200.

Howard, J. Woodford (1968), *Mr. Justice Murphy: A political biography* (Princeton University Press).

Howard, J. Woodford (1968), 'On the fluidity of judicial choice', *American Political Science Review*, vol. 62, pp. 43-56.

Howard, J. Woodford (1971), 'Judicial biography and the behavioral persuasion', *American Political Science Review*, vol. 65, pp. 704-15.

Hughes, Charles Evans (1928), *The Supreme Court of the United States* (Columbia University Press).

Jackson, Robert H. (1955), *The Supreme Court in the American System of Government* (Harvard University Press).

James, Dorothy B. (1968), 'Role theory and the Supreme Court', *Journal of Politics*, vol. 30, pp. 160-86.

Johnston, John J., and Knapp, Charles L. (1971), 'Sex discrimination by law: a study in judicial perspective', *New York University Law Review*, vol. 46, pp. 675-747.

Keeffe, A. J. (1973), 'The lawyer's Washington', *American Bar Association Journal*, vol. 59, pp. 182-4.

Kessel, John (1966), 'Public perceptions of the Supreme Court', *Mid-west Journal of Political Science*, vol. 10, pp. 167-91.

Kohlmeier, Louis (1972), *This Honourable Court* (Scribners).

Kopkind, A. (1966), 'Brennan v. Tigar', *New Republic*, 27 April.

Krislov, Samuel (1962-3), 'The *amicus curiae* brief: from friendship to advocacy', *Yale Law Journal*, vol. 72, pp. 694-721.

Kurland, Philip B. (1970), *Politics, the Constitution, and the Warren Court* (Chicago University Press).

Lamb, Charles M. (1976), 'Judicial policy-making and information flow to the Supreme Court', *Vanderbilt Law Review*, vol. 29, pp. 46-124.

Landever, Arthur R. (1971), 'Chief Justice Burger and extra-case activism', *Journal of Public Law*, vol. 20, pp. 523-41.

Lash, Joseph P. (ed.) (1975), *From the Diaries of Felix Frankfurter* (Norton).

Levine, James P., and Becker, Theodore L. (1970), 'Toward and beyond a theory of Supreme Court impact', *American Behavioral Scientist*, vol. 13, pp. 561-73.

Levy, Leonard W. (ed.) (1967), *Judicial Review and the Supreme Court: Selected essays* (Harper, Row).

Levy, Leonard W. (ed.) (1972), *The Supreme Court under Earl Warren* (Quadrangle).

Lewis, Anthony (1964), *Gideon's Trumpet* (Random House).

McCloskey, Robert G. (1960), *The American Supreme Court* (University of Chicago Press).

McElwain, E. (1949-50), 'The business of the Supreme Court as conducted by Chief Justice Hughes', *Harvard Law Review*, vol. 63, pp. 5-26.

Mackenzie, J. P. (1969), 'Warren E. Burger', in L. Friedman and F. L. Israel (eds), *The Justices of the United States Supreme Court 1789-1969*, Vol. IV (Chelsea House), pp. 3114-21.

McLauchlan, William P. (1972), 'Research note: ideology and conflict in Supreme Court assignments, 1946-1962', *Western Political Quarterly*, vol. 25, pp. 16-27.

Maidment, Richard (1975), 'Policy in search of law', *Journal of American Studies*, vol. 9, pp. 301-20.

Mason, Thomas Alpheus (1956), *Harlan Fiske Stone: Pillar of the law* (Viking).

Mason, Thomas Alpheus (1968), 'The Chief Justice of the United States: *primus inter pares*', *Journal of Public Law*, vol. 17, pp. 20-60.

Mason, Thomas Alpheus (1974), 'The Burger Court in historical perspective', *Political Science Quarterly*, vol. 91, pp. 27-45.

Medalie, Richard J., Zeitz, Leonard, and Alexander, Paul (1968), 'Custodial police interrogation in our nation's capital: the attempt to implement *Miranda*', *Michigan Law Review*, vol. 66, pp. 1347-422.

Miller, Arthur S. (1973), 'Lord Chancellor Warren Earl Burger', *Society*, vol. 10, March/April, pp. 18-27.

Miller, Arthur S., and Howell, Ronald F. (1960), 'The myth of neutrality in constitutional adjudication', *University of Chicago Law Review*, vol. 27, pp. 661-91.

Miller, Merle (1976), *Plain Speaking: An oral biography of Harry S. Truman* (Hodder Fawcett).

Miller, Selwyn T. (1968), *The Supreme Court and American Capitalism* (Free Press).

Milner, Neal (1970-1), 'Comparative analysis of patterns of compliance with Supreme Court decisions', *Law & Society Review*, vol. 5, pp. 119-34.

Milner, Neal (1971), 'Supreme Court effectiveness and the police organization', *Law & Contemporary Problems*, vol. 36, pp. 467-87.

Murphy, Walter F. (1959), 'Lower court checks on Supreme Court power', *American Political Science Review*, vol. 53, pp. 1017-31.

Murphy, Walter F. (1961), 'In his own image: Mr. Chief Justice Taft and Supreme Court appointments', in Philip Kurland (ed.), *The Supreme Court Review 1960* (Chicago University Press), pp. 159-93.

Murphy, Walter F. (1962), *Congress and the Court: A case study in the American political process* (Chicago University Press).

Murphy, Walter F. (1964), *Elements of Judicial Strategy* (Chicago University Press).

Murphy, Walter F., and Pritchett, C. Herman (1961, 1974), *Courts, Judges, and Politics* (Random House, 1st and 2nd edns).

Murphy, Walter F., and Tanenhaus, Joseph (1967-8), 'Public Opinion and the United States Supreme Court', *Law & Society Review*, vol. 2, pp. 357-84.

Nagel, Stuart (1965), 'Court-curbing periods in American history', *Vanderbilt Law Review*, vol. 18, pp. 925-44.

Newland, Chester A. (1959-60), 'The Supreme Court and legal writing: learned journals as vehicles of an anti-antitrust lobby', *Georgetown Law Review*, vol. 48, pp. 105-43.

Newland, Chester A. (1960-1), 'Personal assistants to Supreme Court Justices', *Oregan Law Review*, vol. 40, pp. 299-317.

Newland, Chester A. (1964), 'Press coverage of the United States Supreme Court', *Western Political Quarterly*, vol. 17, pp. 15-36.

'Note' (1963-4), 'Judicial performance in the fifth circuit', *Yale Law Journal*, vol. 73, pp. 90-133.

'Note' (1966-7), 'Interrogations in New Haven: the impact of *Miranda*', *Yale Law Journal*, vol. 76, pp. 1519-648.

O'Rourke, Terry B. (1972), *Reapportionment: Law, politics, computers* (American Enterprise Institute for Public Policy Research).

Peltason, Jack W. (1961), *Fifty-Eight Lonely Men: Southern federal judges and school desegregation* (Harcourt, Brace).

Petrick, Michael (1968), 'The Supreme Court and authority acceptance', *Western Political Quarterly*, vol. 21, pp. 5-19.

Pritchett, C. Herman (1954), *Civil Liberties and the Vinson Court* (University of Chicago Press).

Pritchett, C. Herman (1961), *Congress versus the Supreme Court, 1957-1960* (University of Minneapolis Press).

Rathjan, Gregory J. (1974), 'Policy goals, strategic choice, and majority opinion assignment in the United States Supreme Court: a replication', *American Journal of Political Science*, vol. 18, pp. 713-24.

Ratner, Sidney (1935), 'Was the Supreme Court packed by President Grant?', *Political Science Quarterly*, vol. 50, pp. 343-58.

Read, F. T. (1975-6), 'Judicial evolution of the law of school integration since *Brown*', *Law & Contemporary Problems*, vol. 39, pp. 7-49.

Redlich, Norman (1975), 'A Black-Harlan dialogue on due process and equal protection: overheard in Heaven and dedicated to Robert B. McKay', *New York University Law Review*, vol. 50, pp. 20-46.

Rehnquist, William H. (1957), 'Who writes the decisions of the Supreme Court?', *US News & World Report*, 13 December.

Rehnquist, William H. (1958), 'Another view: clerks might "influence" some actions', *US News & World Report*, 21 February.

Rehnquist, William H. (1973), 'The Supreme Court: past and present', *American Bar Association Journal*, vol. 59, pp. 361-4.

Richardson, R. J., and Vines, Kenneth N. (1970), *The Politics of Federal Courts: Lower courts in the United States* (Little, Brown).

Roche, John P. (1955), 'Judicial self-restraint', *American Political Science Review*, vol. 49, pp. 762-72.

Rogers, William D. (1958), 'Clerks' work is "not decisive of ultimate results"', *US News & World Report*, 21 February.

Rohde, David W., and Spaeth, Harold J. (1976), *Supreme Court Decision Making* (Freeman).

Rosenzweig, S. (1951-2), 'The opinions of Judge Edgerton: a study in the judicial process', *Cornell Law Quarterly*, vol. 37, pp. 149-205.

Sarat, Austin (1977), 'Studying American legal culture: an assessment of survey evidence', *Law & Society Review*, vol. 11, pp. 427-88.

Sarshik, S. (1972), 'The Supreme Court and its clerks: bullets or blanks for the hired guns?', *Juris Doctor*, vol. 2, pp. 40-3.

Sartori, Giovanni (1962), 'Constitutionalism: a preliminary discussion', *American Political Science Review*, vol. 56, pp. 853-64.

Scharpf, Fritz W. (1965-6), 'Judicial review and the political question: a functional analysis', *Yale Law Journal*, vol. 75, pp. 517-97.

Schmidhauser, John R. (1959), 'The Justices of the Supreme Court: a collective portrait', *Midwest Journal of Political Science*, vol. 1, pp. 1-57.

Schmidhauser, John R. (1960), *The Supreme Court: Its politics, personalities and procedures* (Holt, Rinehart).

Schmidhauser, John R., and Berg, Larry R. (1972), *The Supreme Court and Congress: Conflict and interaction, 1945-1968* (Free Press).

Schubert, Glendon (1960), *Quantitative Analysis of Judicial Behavior* (Free Press).

Schubert, Glendon (1961-2), 'Policy without law: an extension of the *certiorari* game', *Stanford Law Review*, vol. 14, pp. 284-327.

Schubert, Glendon (1965), *The Judicial Mind* (Northwestern University Press).

Schwartz, Bernard (1957), *The Supreme Court* (Ronald Press).

Scigliano, Robert (1971), *The Supreme Court and the Presidency* (Free Press).

Shapiro, Martin (1968), *The Supreme Court and Administrative Agencies* (Macmillan).

Shogan, Robert (1972), *A Question of Judgement* (Bobbs-Merrill).

Smith, C. U. (1975), 'Public school desegregation and the law', *Social Forces*, vol. 54, pp. 317-27.

Sorauf, Frank J. (1959), '*Zorach* v. *Clauson*: the impact of a Supreme Court decision', *American Political Science Review*, vol. 53, pp. 777-91.

Sorauf, Frank J. (1976), *The Wall of Separation: The constitutional politics of church and state* (Princeton University Press).

Slotnick, Elliot E. (1978), 'The Chief Justices and self-assignment of majority opinions: a research note', *Western Political Quarterly*, vol. 31, pp. 219-25.

Spaeth, Harold J. (1964), 'The judicial restraint of Mr. Justice Frankfurter: myth or reality?', *Midwest Journal of Political Science*, vol. 8, pp. 22-38.

Strum, Philippa (1974), *The Supreme Court and 'Political Questions': A study in judicial evasion* (University of Alabama Press).

Swindler, William F. (1970), 'The politics of "advise and consent"', *American Bar Association Journal*, vol. 56, pp. 533-42.

Swindler, William F. (1972), 'The Chief Justice and law reform, 1921-1971', in Philip B. Kurland (ed.), *Supreme Court Review 1971* (Chicago University Press), pp. 241-64.

Tanenhaus, Joseph, Schnick, Marvin, Muraskin, Matthew, and Rosen, David (1963), 'The Supreme Court's *certiorari* jurisdiction: cue theory', in Glendon A. Schubert (ed.), *Judicial Decision-Making* (Free Press), pp. 111-32.

Thorpe, James A. (1969), 'The appearance of Supreme Court nominees before the Senate Judiciary Committee', *Journal of Public Law*, vol. 18, pp. 371-402.

Ulmer, S. Sidney (1970), 'The use of power in the Supreme Court: the opinion assignments of Earl Warren, 1953-1960', *Journal of Public Law*, vol. 19, pp. 49-67.

Ulmer, S. Sidney (1971a), 'The decision to grant *certiorari* as an indicator to decision "on the merits"', *Polity*, vol. 6, pp. 429-47.

Ulmer, S. Sidney (1971b), 'Earl Warren and the *Brown* decision', *Journal of Politics*, vol. 33, pp. 689-702.

Ulmer, S. Sidney, Hintze, William, and Kirklosky, Louise (1972), 'The decision to grant or deny *certiorari*: further consideration of cue theory', *Law & Society Review*, vol. 6, pp. 637-43.

Ulmer, S. Sidney (1973), 'Revising the Supreme Court jurisdiction: mere administrative reform or substantive policy change', *Minnesota Law Review*, vol. 58, pp. 121-55.

Vose, Clement E. (1958), 'Litigation as a form of pressure group activity', *Annals of the American Academy of Political and Social Science*, no. 319, September, pp. 20-31.

Vose, Clement E. (1972), *Constitutional Change: Amendment politics and Supreme Court litigation since 1900* (Lexington Books).

Walsh, Lawrence E. (1970), 'Selection of Supreme Court Justices', *American Bar Association Journal*, vol. 56, pp. 555-60.

Warren, Charles (1923), 'New light on the history of the Federal Judiciary Act of 1789', *Harvard Law Review*, vol. 37, pp. 49-132.

Warren, Earl (1973), 'The proposed new "National Court of Appeals"', *Record of the Association of the Bar of New York*, vol. 28, pp. 627-45.

Wasby, Stephen (1970), *The Impact of the United States Supreme Court: Some perspectives* (Dorsey).

Wasby, Stephen (1976), *Continuity and Change: From the Warren Court to the Burger Court* (Goodyear).

Way, H. Frank (1968), 'Survey research on judicial decisions: the prayer and Bible reading cases', *Western Political Quarterly*, vol. 21, pp. 189-205.

Wechsler, Herbert (1959-60), 'Towards neutral principles of constitutional law', *Harvard Law Review*, vol. 73, pp. 1-35.

Weeks, Kent M. (1971), *Adam Clayton Powell and the Supreme Court* (Dunellen).

Westin, Alan F. (1958), *The Anatomy of a Constitutional Law Case* (Macmillan).

Wheeler, Russell (1978), *Extrajudicial Activity of Supreme Court Justices* (General Learning Press).

Yarborough, Tinsley E. (1978), 'Litigant access doctrine and the Burger Court', *Vanderbilt Law Review*, vol. 21, pp. 33-70.

(b) A SELECTION OF EIGHT BOOKS FOR A DESERT ISLAND

A bibliography of over 100 items cannot discriminate between the most useful and the less useful sources, so it seemed sensible, and salutory, to imagine myself before an academic Roy Plomley and select eight books to take to a desert island (articles were not permitted). My starting point was a book which excited and yet also provided an excellent overview of the subject; there was little difficulty in selecting Anthony Lewis's *Gideon's Trumpet* (1964), for it is beautifully written, has a happy ending, and teaches a great deal *en route*. But there should also be something weightier and clearly instructive; to my mind, the most acceptable equivalent to a textbook is Walter H. Murphy and C. Herman Pritchett (eds), *Courts, Judges, and Politics* (2nd edn, 1974), with its model introductions to each sector and splendidly varied selection of readings. The next requirement is for a good history, not too detailed to obscure the broad surveys of constitutional development and yet not so general that the significant cases fail to be fully situated in their historical and intellectual context; Robert McCloskey's *The American Supreme Court* (1960) fills the bill ideally. Since the Court is very much part of the American political system, a book which relates it to the executive branch and the legislative branch would seem the fourth necessity; but here there are difficulties. I was tempted to include Henry Abraham's *Justices and Presidents* (1974) because it encompasses so much, or Richard Harris's somewhat unfair, but compulsive, *Decision* (1971), but Abraham seemed ultimately not to dig deep enough and the Harris case study of Richard Nixon's abortive attempt to nominate

Harrold Carswell was a little too narrowly drawn. In the end, therefore, I compromised with Walter H. Murphy's *Elements of Judicial Strategy* (1964) because it touches upon so many aspects of the Court's relationships, both external and internal. I chose that volume for a further reason; it treats decision-making within the Court in a fascinating manner and with much greater insight than the judicial biographies. My fifth choice would ideally be a study of a recent Justice, preferably Hugo Black, but none seems to me to focus enough on the questions which interest me or to analyse sufficiently the reasons for their subjects' behaviour. Nevertheless, I need one, and I would, with hesitation, settle for Thomas Alpheus Mason's *Harlan Fiske Stone: Pillar of the law* (1956) or, if a second-hand version of this out-of-print book were not available, Joseph P. Lash (ed.), *From the Diaries of Felix Frankfurter* (1975). My sixth choice is simple; to meet the need for a study of what happens after a decision has been announced, no book is as readable, as harrowing, or as moving as Jack Peltason's *Fifty-Eight Lonely Men* (1961), his story of the southern federal judges responsible for ensuring what fruit the *Brown* decision bore. Clearly my collection would be incomplete without some work on the proper role of the Court; there are too many books, and collections of papers, on the vexed and insoluble argument of self-restraint versus activism, but my favourite, perhaps because I came to it first, is Alexander Bickel's *The Least Dangerous Branch* (1962). This leaves me with one final choice. I was tempted at first by J. A. Garraty's *Quarrels That Have Shaped the Constitution* (1964), but plumped in the end for Henry Abraham's *Freedom and the Court* (1977), because it contains more food for thought and more complex questions to agonise about in the presumably ample spare time on the island. Assuming that a breast-pocket version of the Constitution survived the disaster which cast me upon the island, my luxury would have to be a set of Supreme Court decisions, and I think I would choose the Lawyers' Edition for the extra material it contains to supplement the decisions of the Court. With this battery of sources I, and I like to think many others, could gain a deep understanding of the United States Supreme Court while enjoying every moment of the experience.

Index

(References to cases mentioned only once in the text will be found under Appendix II)